The Cambodian Campaign

The Cambodian Campaign
The 1970 Offensive and America's Vietnam War

John M. Shaw

 University Press of Kansas

© 2005 by the University Press of Kansas
All rights reserved

Published by the University Press of Kansas (Lawrence, Kansas 66049), which was
organized by the Kansas Board of Regents and is operated and funded by Emporia State
University, Fort Hays State University, Kansas State University, Pittsburg State
University, the University of Kansas, and Wichita State University

ISBN 0-7006-1405-2

Printed in the United States of America

Amateurs study tactics. Professionals study logistics.
Anonymous

Contents

(Photo insert follows p. 79)

Illustrations

Preface and Acknowledgments

The Second Indochinese War, or the Vietnam War to most Americans, arguably ended with the fall of Saigon on 30 April 1975. The scholarly literature on the conflict has steadily improved in the years since, though within English-language works there appears to have been a tendency to focus on the politicians and policy makers, at one end of the spectrum, or else the soldiers themselves, at the other. Then, too, more historians have examined the military actions in Southeast Asia of the Kennedy and Johnson administrations than of Nixon's; only a handful have focused on the Cambodian incursion of 1970. Most studies mention it only briefly, describing it chiefly within the context of the resulting domestic uproar against Nixon's "widening" of the war. These accounts largely ignore the military aspects of the incursion, giving it a paragraph or two in their rush to discuss Kent State or congressional debates. For one of the biggest U.S.–South Vietnamese operations of the war, such dismissive treatment is inappropriate.

This account helps to redress the historical oversight, assessing the operation chiefly from the perspective of American commanders and staffs from the U.S. Military Assistance Command, Vietnam (MACV) down to brigade level. It is a detailed campaign-level examination of the operation itself, not an analysis of the politics of the war or the incursion's effects on that arena. Such politics present in this account are in the context of an overarching framework to military matters rather than as a central focus.

The work also briefly considers the Cambodian incursion as an initial test of "Vietnamization," the Nixon administration's strategy of improving the combat effectiveness of the Republic of Vietnam Armed Forces (RVNAF) to the point of their being able to defend South Vietnam without the continued involvement of American ground forces. Examining the major combat units that participated in the cross-border assault, an operation planned with little time and even less material preparation, it seeks to determine what factors made the incursion militarily successful. In doing so, the study relies heavily on U.S. military sources, both contemporary documents of the units involved and the memories of many of the officers participating in the events described in those papers.

One widespread assumption among opponents of the incursion, particularly for the first two decades after the war, was that the Cambodian Incursion was unnecessary because there was no *real* communist threat to South Vietnam or American forces emanating from Cambodia in 1969 or 1970. Such guerrillas as were still active inside South Vietnam were a nuisance, to be sure, but after Tet 1968, Hanoi was in no hurry to launch another major offensive while American ground forces were still present in South Vietnam.

This belief rests on either of two assumptions: the acceptance at face value of communist claims denying immediate hostile intentions for those forces or supplies in Cambodia, or else on the absence of serious North Vietnamese attacks out of Cambodia during 1970 and 1971 as proof somehow that there would have been no such attacks had the incursion not made them impossible first. Those who advance such arguments often point to the tremendous stress the incursion put upon domestic American politics, making even more acrimonious the heated debate between a polarized electorate. In this widely accepted view, the cost to domestic amity and the political process dwarfed the incursion's military successes.

Such concerns have some validity: the North Vietnamese did *not* attack out of Cambodia in 1970 or thereafter, and the damage to the American political process *was* severe. However, it is also worth considering the consequences had even a small part of Hanoi's 1972 twenty-division blitz come out of Cambodia instead of across the demilitarized zone and southern Laos: Saigon was only sixty-five miles from the biggest cross-border sanctuaries, and some lesser ones were far closer.

Responsible U.S. and South Vietnamese officers in Washington and Saigon in 1969 and 1970 could not base their plans for South Vietnam's defense on optimistic predictions or unwarranted trust in Hanoi's protestations of good faith. By training and experience, they were predisposed to expect the worse, and they acted accordingly. Given the heavy fighting of the 1968 Tet Offensive and Hanoi's extensive efforts during 1969 and 1970 to expand its stockpiles along the Cambodian–South Vietnamese border, for those leaders to have acted as they did was both prudent and appropriate.

I am solely responsible for any errors of fact or interpretation herein; others deserve the credit for what this study has done well. First among these was my doctoral adviser, George C. Herring, who somehow managed to bring order out of the chaos that was my first draft while never losing his patience or sense of humor. During my service in the Department of History at the United States Military Academy, Colonels Robert A. Doughty, James M. Johnson, and Cole C.

Kingseed and Lieutenant Colonel Conrad C. Crane gave constant encouragement toward the dissertation's completion. Likewise, my colleagues at the Department of History at the United States Air Force Academy, particularly Colonel Mark Wells and Lieutenant Colonels Vance Skarstedt and John Farquhar, helped me find some precious time to work on revising and updating the manuscript. Dr. Dennis Showalter of Colorado College was most generous with his expertise and steered me toward the University Press of Kansas and editor Mike Briggs, a bit of advice for which I am deeply grateful. Mike has been an absolute joy to work with, as have been production editor Larisa Martin and marketing manager Susan Schott. Heidi Perov Perry did a beautiful job of turning my rough sketches into legible maps. Finally, I owe a tremendous thanks to my copy editor, Susan Ecklund, who significantly improved the manuscript's clarity by her incredible attention to detail.

───────────

Dozens of active and retired officers and soldiers helped me in my inquiries. I have listed them in my bibliography, but three deserve special mention for their willingness to share their memories: retired U.S. Army Generals Michael S. Davison and Robert M. Shoemaker and Major General Edward Bautz.

I owe thanks to several people at various archives and collections. Dr. Dale Andradé, of the U.S. Army's Center of Military History (CMH), was particularly gracious in suggesting the topic to a new doctoral candidate in the summer of 1991, even though he would be working on it himself in the years to come. More than a decade later, his comments on this manuscript significantly improved my focus. Dr. John Carland, also of CMH, welcomed me to its collections and gave me valuable suggestions on avenues worth further pursuit. At the National Archives, Military Archivists Rich Boylan and Cary Conn made it possible for me to burrow through the greatest number of files within the limited time I had. The U.S. Army Military History Institute's Dr. Richard Sommers, David Keough, and Randy Rakers made my research there more fun than work. Charles Carroll, of what was then the Defense Mapping Agency, obtained copies of the military maps I needed to make sense of the hundreds of grid coordinates referred to in U.S. Army documents; without those maps, much of the material I found elsewhere would have been useless. At Texas Tech University's extraordinary Vietnam Center, Director Dr. Jim Reckner, Archivist Dr. Ron Frankum, and the dedicated staff were particularly valuable in aiding my latter researches. Finally, Dr. Jim Willbanks of the U.S. Army's Command and General Staff College at Fort Leavenworth gave wonderful advice on sources to look at and revisions to consider.

I wish to thank my wife and our two young sons for their patience and understanding over the past years as I tried to juggle a military career, family obligations, and this project. Wanting to spend more time with them has been a powerful spur toward getting this work finished.

Finally, I owe the greatest debt of all to the soldiers of that conflict—from both sides—and to their families. The former sweated, fought, and in many cases died for what they believed in; the latter supported them, waited for their return, and all too often mourned their loss. To those soldiers and families I respectfully dedicate this account.

1

The Johnson-Westmoreland Era, 1965–1969

For the first three years of the United States' open involvement in the Vietnam War, from early 1965 through late 1967, the American effort produced at best a bloody stalemate. President Lyndon B. Johnson had in part sent U.S. ground forces to South Vietnam in 1965 to protect it from North Vietnamese Army (NVA) regulars heading south to complete the work begun by the Viet Cong (VC).[1] By the end of 1965, the influx of American troops and firepower averted the imminent collapse of South Vietnam, ensuring Saigon's survival for the moment.

As 1966 turned into 1967, though, the conflict began appearing to many Americans to have become an interminable war of attrition. The American public's trust in and support for both civilian and military officials steadily waned despite upbeat assessments and predictions from Secretary of Defense Robert S. McNamara and General William C. Westmoreland, commander of the U.S. Military Assistance Command, Vietnam (MACV) and the senior American officer in Southeast Asia.

Through 1967 the Johnson administration's conduct of the war in Indochina rested upon a key assumption: that Hanoi's leaders had a breaking point, beyond which they would lose the will to keep fighting. Washington's "strategy of exhaustion" had the added benefit of appearing less costly in lives than either of the alternatives, strategies of annihilation and of attrition. An armed force executing a strategy of annihilation seeks to draw its opposite number into decisive battles, and thus win the war by quickly eliminating the other side's primary means of resistance. In a strategy of attrition, victory comes by bleeding the other force dry through cumulative losses. However, attrition takes longer than annihilation and incurs casualties on one's own forces as well; Germany's experience at Verdun in 1916 is a classic example. Further, while a government or general may wage a strategy of exhaustion, for the troops in combat it seems little different from attrition unless the commander is skillful indeed.

1

Overshadowing the U.S. war effort in Indochina was Johnson's domestic agenda. Seeking to build the Great Society and secure his own place in American history, he begrudged anything that diverted attention, energy, or resources from his programs. Johnson could not ignore Vietnam, but he was unwilling to pay the necessary price to win decisively there. He therefore opted to avoid military defeat, seeking options that offered at least a possibility of success. "Exhaustion" seemed to Johnson and his closest advisers the least bad of several unattractive choices, to be achieved by killing enough communist forces inside South Vietnam to persuade Hanoi it could not win. By late 1967, though, the strategy of exhaustion was largely discredited: Hanoi had shown no willingness to quit.

As the United States approached the election year of 1968, it was clear that the upcoming presidential contest would in large part be a referendum on Johnson's conduct of the war. The scale and intensity of Hanoi's 1968 Tet Offensive stunned the American public, whom top military and civilian officials had told shortly before that the situation was well in hand. As the communists' attacks failed to bring about the hoped-for general uprising across South Vietnam and Johnson decided to not seek reelection, circumstances were ripe for a reassessment of American strategy in the war.

The changed military and political environment in the aftermath of Tet 1968 gave General Creighton Abrams, Westmoreland's successor, new opportunities as well as further constraints. Abrams, who had been Westmoreland's deputy since May 1967, assumed command of MACV in early June 1968 upon the latter's reassignment to become U.S. Army chief of staff. Westmoreland had faced a two-pronged communist threat: NVA regulars operating conventionally, and VC guerrillas. After heavy fighting in the first half of 1968, though, the VC threat to South Vietnam's internal security was largely broken, permitting Abrams to concentrate on the NVA regulars. This in part allowed Abrams to fight a different war than had Westmoreland.

Political considerations were likewise noticeably different after Tet 1968. Sensitive to the new mood in Washington that sought (more so than previously) to minimize U.S. casualties, Abrams moved away from Westmoreland's greater reliance on attrition through firepower and mass in favor of small-unit actions and internal security for the population.[2]

Abrams's refocusing of the allied war effort, endorsed first by the lame-duck Johnson administration and then by the incoming Nixon administration, helped delay Hanoi's eventual conquest of South Vietnam. Appreciating the inherently political nature of the war inside South Vietnam and the critical importance of village security, and free of the significant VC threat that had plagued Westmoreland's commanders, Abrams targeted the NVA units' greatest vulnerability: their logistics system inside South Vietnam. However, his operations within South Vietnam would have been far less effective had not President Richard M. Nixon seized a fleeting opportunity provided by a drastically altered political and military situation within Cambodia. Although Nixon's decision unleashed a domestic firestorm over his "widening of the war," with unforeseen political consequences, the destruction of Hanoi's Cambodian border sanctuaries was a fully justified and reasonably well-executed campaign.

The Second Indochina War, 1954–1975, a civil war to determine Vietnam's future, was fought on both sides with extensive foreign support and participation. North Vietnam's goal was to unify the country under communist rule. Having to defeat and occupy the South to win, it assumed the strategic offensive. Possessing the initiative, Hanoi chose when, where, and how to attack, and controlled the duration and intensity of any fighting; it also adjusted the scope or the tempo of the conflict to suit its needs and resources. In requesting aid from the Soviet Union and China, it could play one off against the other; both Moscow and Beijing were aware of Hanoi's diplomatic intrigues but felt obligated to maintain their claims to leadership of the "anti-imperialist" struggle by giving Hanoi the help it sought.[3]

An additional advantage the North had was its broader view of the war's parameters. American recognition of Laotian and Cambodian "neutrality" was matched by Hanoi's disdain for its own diplomatic undertakings toward its two neighbors. As former secretary of state Henry Kissinger noted, "Washington had convinced itself that the four Indochinese states were separate entities, even though the communists had been treating them as a single theater for two decades and were conducting a coordinated strategy with respect to all of them."[4] In refusing to treat Indochina as one integrated struggle, as North Vietnam was doing, the United States severely handicapped itself.

Unlike the North, South Vietnam wanted to simply preserve its own existence. Although it was comparatively easier for Saigon to defend than it was for Hanoi to attack, South Vietnam suffered from several significant disadvantages. First, in war, at the strategic level offensives normally produce victory; Saigon's assumption of the strategic defensive forfeited the initiative to Hanoi. The North had a clear objective—victory—and highly competent leaders fanatically committed to achieving it. The South had leaders, to be sure, but they were neither as unified nor as zealous as their counterparts to the north. Further, being almost totally dependent on American military and economic assistance, Saigon was bound by Washington's diplomatic decisions respecting Laotian and Cambodian claims of neutrality, claims the North ignored.

Saigon's war-fighting doctrine, copied from the United States, was inferior to Hanoi's for the war then being waged in Indochina. Called *dau tranh,* Hanoi's approach emphasized a tightly coordinated political and military struggle.[5] Military considerations were important but were always supportive of political ones; in the Clausewitzian model, the North's government, military, and people were extraordinarily unified.

Such was not the case in the South, where such focus was more a dream than a reality. Westmoreland, as the senior field commander, concentrated chiefly on the conventional military threat, and, by Johnson's orders, only on that within the national boundaries of South Vietnam. His war of attrition, of killing more of the enemy than Hanoi could replace, was doomed to failure against enemy leaders willing to sacrifice as many men as it took to win. In emphasizing the "big battalion" war for the Americans and leaving the political and internal security struggle to the South Vietnamese, Washington and Saigon lacked the cohesive and coherent effort necessary to successfully withstand the North's integrated attacks. This allied division of responsibility made sense in the initial days of overt American involvement, when the newly arrived U.S. forces moved to the borders and fought NVA regulars in largely unpopulated areas. However, the lack of true allied unity of command, political as well as military, put the allies at a grave disadvantage.

Another superior aspect of the North's war-fighting doctrine was its emphasis on protracted conflict, of time as a weapon with which to wear down and defeat less patient and dedicated enemies. Hanoi had fought for its goal, of a unified Vietnam free of foreigners, since open conflict with the French began in 1946; by summer 1968, the North Vietnamese were starting their third decade of near-continuous war. In comparison, Washington's time scale was measured by the presidential election cycle, making it difficult if not impossible to think ahead more than a few years at a time. This stolid and unshakable endurance on the North's part, compared with Washington's constant need to show "progress" by whatever means, significantly affected the opposing strategies.

Where the North was fighting as a unified whole, the allies were fighting as a coalition, and one whose members were wildly disparate in strength and true aims. South Vietnam had the most at stake, but it was junior partner to Johnson and then Nixon; its success at war fighting varied considerably over the years, greatly complicated by three major factors. These were South Vietnam's senior leadership, an armed political alternative to the government based in Saigon, and the enemy's border sanctuaries.

Had South Vietnam not faced any external enemy, it would still have had a hard time establishing a viable country: it largely lacked a sense of national identity or individuals with countrywide appeal who put the nation's interests ahead of their own narrow bases of support. President Ngo Dinh Diem had valued personal loyalty over competence in selecting many senior officials and commanders in the late 1950s and early 1960s. These men's lackluster performances during his presidency had frequently given the VC grist for their propaganda mills, further weakening a nascent sense of national identity among the South Vietnamese population. The lack of governmental stability following Diem's November 1963 overthrow crippled the political structure and its legitimacy even more, while communist cadres could convincingly portray the Americans' arrival as yet another foreign occupying power come to oppress them.

For Hanoi, *dau tranh* provided the intellectual framework to coordinate these and other issues with effective military measures; Westmoreland and the other American and South Vietnamese leaders had no comparable response. Before the arrival of U.S. ground forces in 1965, the communists were well on their way to conquering the country from within. Stymied in achieving a clear military victory during the mid-1960s, the North and its southern adherents reemphasized political education and struggle: ultimate victory was assured, if delayed.

Yet another major problem for Saigon was the National Liberation Front (NLF), an umbrella organization for many of the factions within South Vietnam that sought the overthrow of the Saigon regime. The most aggressive members of the NLF were the southern communist guerrillas, the Viet Cong.[6] Hanoi depended on the VC to carry out its proselytizing and military operations, but it did not have as much control over the scattered VC as it would have liked. However, there was enough coordination and cooperation by the NLF and VC with Hanoi's overall goal of a northern victory to make them essential components of *dau tranh.*

The VC presented Saigon with a deadly internal threat; the NVA, an external one. Either could be fatal to South Vietnam, and together they put Saigon and Washington on the horns of a lethal dilemma that the latter never fully resolved.

Following Diem's crackdown on communists within South Vietnam in the middle to late 1950s, in early 1959 Hanoi made the critical decision to support armed struggle in the South. However, getting cadres and supplies to the southern fighters would be a major problem. Following Party Central Committee discussions in the first two months of 1959, the NVA created Military Transportation Group 559 on 19 May 1959 to start setting up the necessary routes.[7] The trail network, known in the North as the Truong Son Road after the mountain range it paralleled and called by Americans the Ho Chi Minh Trail, steadily expanded southward during the early 1960s through southern Laos and northeastern Cambodia. Rest areas along the way and base areas just inside the Laotian and Cambodian borders from South Vietnam provided numerous opportunities to reorganize units and stockpile and distribute supplies (see map 1).

Hanoi's ultimate target was the southern third of the country, where two-thirds of the population lived in Saigon and the densely populated rice-growing Mekong Delta southwest of the capital. From North Vietnam across South Vietnam to Saigon, the shortest distance was more than 400 miles, all vulnerable to ground and air attacks. Trails and roads through "neutral" Laos and Cambodia, though longer, let Hanoi's forces bypass allied units and arrive safely near Saigon: the greater safety was worth the extra miles and time.

The Cambodian bases gave Hanoi a tremendous military advantage.[8] From the border to Saigon was as little as thirty-five miles, although a distance of sixty to eighty miles was more typical. Most of the land between border and capital was fairly populated, making South Vietnamese and American commanders careful about indiscriminate use of the massive firepower at their call. If beaten, the NVA and VC could flee across the border, regroup, and attack again. The bases, or "sanctuaries," served as rest camps for communist troop movements along the

Map 1. Routes, Base Areas, and Major Cross-Border Operations, Spring 1970

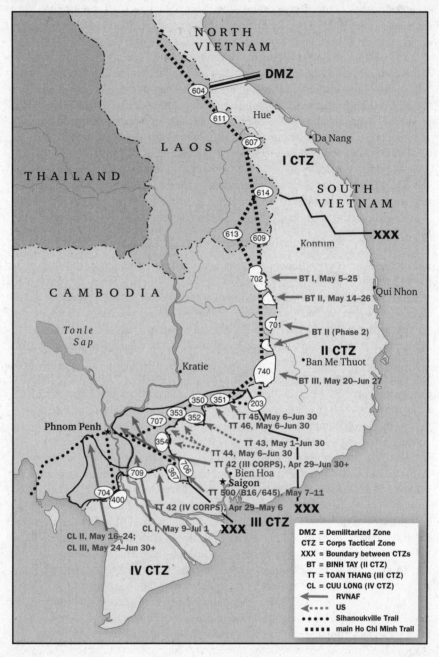

border and as supply dumps for forces inside South Vietnam. By the mid-1960s the Cambodian sanctuaries were indispensable to Hanoi's plans for the conquest of South Vietnam and, due to Washington's policy decisions concerning Cambodia's ostensible neutrality, were largely inviolable as well. MACV, unable to directly attack the sanctuaries, likewise did not devote undue resources to watching them intensely.

As Westmoreland's intelligence chief later said of the period around the 1968 Tet Offensive, MACV J-2, the command's intelligence office, never had even half a firm grasp on NVA logistics. It had much better order-of-battle information, in part because the NVA came out of the sanctuaries to fight and would lose men as prisoners of war or battle deaths. Regarding precise sanctuary locations, MACV J-2 had a fairly good idea of where the boundaries were, but the specifics of what was inside each was a question. Further, that detailed information was not really a high intelligence priority: MACV simply considered the NVA and VC had enough supplies for their purposes and let it go at that.[9] Thus, through the end of Johnson's administration, Hanoi's bases in eastern Cambodia were untouchable refuges.

As a springboard for offensive operations, Cambodia was extraordinarily valuable to Hanoi. Having the initiative, Hanoi could mass units to attack when and where it wanted. By the late 1960s, this included striking directly from Cambodia. South Vietnamese and U.S. forces thus had to watch more than 600 miles of the Cambodian–South Vietnamese border. Unable to be equally strong everywhere, the allies concentrating to shield populated areas like Saigon and the Mekong Delta put the less-inhabited rural regions like the Central Highlands at greater risk.

Westmoreland's decision to operate along the borders, though controversial then and now, made sense in light of the threat he faced in 1965. Believing the greater danger to be external aggression from Hanoi, particularly the regular NVA troops, he chose to stop the "bully boys with crowbars" first and worry about the "termites" inside the house (the VC) afterward. American military strengths were firepower and conventional operations, better suited for fighting the NVA than the hard-to-identify VC. However, the overarching parameters within which Westmoreland fought were shaped not in Southeast Asia but in Washington.

Johnson's limiting U.S. ground forces to the defense of South Vietnam and his acceptance of the strategic defensive in Indochina had disastrous consequences for the way the war evolved from 1965 on. Defining victory as "not losing or interfering with the Great Society," and trying to do it on the cheap without forcing the Congress to choose between guns or butter, Johnson set an impossible goal for his commanders.

This was not so clear at the time, however, and Westmoreland's emphasis on hitting NVA units over VC ones seemed a reasonable solution to Johnson's requirements and guidance. Although expensive in money, firepower was cheaper to Americans than paying in blood, and in any case American forces' ignorance of South Vietnamese customs and languages made the counterguerrilla mission inappropriate for most U.S. units (except the Army Special Forces). However, this heavy focus on conventional combat in the mid-1960s arguably also led the Americans to an overemphasis on the "big-battalion" component of the overall war effort.

The war would continue so long as Hanoi refused to quit; Hanoi also controlled the scope and intensity of any combat. Despite his massive superiority in firepower, a vast logistics system, and the flexibility provided by air force transports and army helicopters, Westmoreland could only respond to Hanoi's attacks. Limited to the strategic defensive, MACV relied on a military strategy of attrition from 1965 through 1968 within an overall American strategy of exhaustion.

Hanoi's substantial and sustained violation of Cambodian neutrality preceded the beginnings of major combat operations by the United States. Having regained its sovereignty following the breakup of French Indochina at Geneva in 1954, Cambodia found itself unwillingly caught up in the struggle of the neighboring Vietnamese, with tragic consequences. Vichy French colonial authorities had appointed the eighteen-year-old Prince Norodom Sihanouk to be reigning monarch in 1941, expecting him to be a figurehead. Sihanouk was fairly quiet until 12 March 1945, when he proclaimed Cambodia's independence. He was premature, though, and in October 1945 France reasserted its control. Sihanouk tried again on 9 November 1953, France and the international community recognizing this claim on 20 July 1954. Nine months later Sihanouk abdicated in favor of his father, to devote more time to politics as the country's prime minister; he was to remain head of the government until his deposition in 1970, and head of state from his father's death in April 1960 until the same 1970 coup.

As the leader of Cambodia, Sihanouk unsuccessfully sought to preserve his country's autonomy despite unrelenting pressure from both Hanoi and Saigon to more actively support their causes. In particular, Hanoi needed freedom of movement across eastern Cambodia, to give its forces access to the western border of northern and central South Vietnam. With its expanding presence within Cambodia, Hanoi was far better positioned to intimidate Phnom Penh than was Saigon, constrained by Washington from acting similarly had it been so inclined.

Sihanouk was aware that granting Hanoi such access violated Cambodia's neutrality, but he thought accommodating North Vietnam's "requests" was safer than risking open confrontation with its far more aggressive, better-armed, and battle-hardened troops. In the end, Sihanouk's agreement became a deal with the devil and helped bring about the very catastrophe he hoped to avoid.

While communist infiltration into northern and central South Vietnam took place through southern Laos and northeastern Cambodia, access into the lower part of South Vietnam was a different matter. Before 1966, communist forces in the southern half of South Vietnam had gotten their military supplies primarily by 100-ton trawlers unloading directly onto lonely southern beaches.[10] This was the result of inadequate land routes the full distance south, the South Vietnamese navy's inability to interdict coastal shipping, and the far greater speed and efficiency of moving bulk supplies by sea than land. However, in 1966 U.S. and South Vietnamese naval units began Operation MARKET TIME to secure South Vietnam's coast.

Stymied in one approach by the maritime patrols, Hanoi quickly developed other ways to sustain its forces in southern South Vietnam: the first shipload of weapons for them via Cambodia arrived in the port of Sihanoukville in October 1966. This occurred "with the tacit approval of the Cambodian government."[11] Sihanouk's relatives profited by letting Hanoi move its supplies through the country to the Vietnamese border, as did other Cambodian officials.[12] Many in the Cambodian government were concerned over the growing scale of North Vietnam's activities within Cambodia, as well as "the involvement of Sihanouk's fifth and then-recognized wife, Monique, her mother, and half-brother in selling protection, weapons, and land rights to the VC/NVA and in smuggling gold, jewels, and drugs."[13] Tensions mounted in time among Cambodia's political and military elites, which later led to the events of March 1970.

A special U.S.–South Vietnamese study in early 1969 traced these routes across Cambodia, which MACV collectively called the Sihanoukville Trail.[14] Between October 1966 and July 1969, an arms-bearing ship docked in Sihanoukville roughly every three months.[15] Trucks carried these supplies from the port to depots west of Phnom Penh; the Cambodian army operated one depot, and the NVA/VC operated the other.[16] From there weapons and materials went through regional facilities at Svay Rieng, Kratie, Kampong Cham, and Stung Treng before reaching one of eight communist base areas on the South Vietnamese border.[17]

Hanoi did not depend solely on the Cambodians' good faith and greed but also sent disguised troops to ensure its supply chain stayed secure. NVA historians admitted years later that K-20 (the unit designation of a particular NVA Logistics Group) "was a transportation unit of our army operating in Cambodia under the guise of a commercial company owned by local ethnic Vietnamese."[18] By 1969, Hanoi's logistics system across southern Cambodia had become both effective and capacious.

Although supplies sent via the Ho Chi Minh Trail sustained the fighting in northern South Vietnam, by 1969 MACV considered the Sihanoukville Trail the key to Hanoi's efforts in the southern half of the country. As one of the chief planners of the Joint General Staff (JGS, the South Vietnamese equivalent of the American Joint Staff in Washington) later wrote, "The tonnages moving through Sihanoukville were sufficient to meet 100 percent of the requirements of enemy units in the . . . III and IV Corps areas, and perhaps two-thirds of the requirements for enemy units in the II Corps area."[19]

It was about 175 miles from Sihanoukville to the border base areas, compared with nearly 700 miles from Haiphong, North Vietnam. Where the Ho Chi Minh Trail was subject to U.S. air strikes for much of its length through North Vietnam and Laos, the Sihanoukville Trail was off-limits to American attack. The Ho Chi Minh Trail's dirt routes and paths through Laos and northern Cambodia limited major resupply efforts to those few months when the roads were dry and streams passable. In contrast, Cambodia's asphalt roads from the port to the border regions let the NVA move supplies even during the monsoons.

There were thus clear advantages to using eastern Cambodia for communist logistic networks. As long as Sihanouk's government ignored the NVA's presence in Cambodia and Washington pretended that Cambodia was truly neutral, there was little MACV could do except fight those enemy forces inside South Vietnam.

Hanoi was well aware of the vulnerabilities of its supply lifelines. Operation MARKET TIME had interdicted its maritime routes to the South Vietnamese coastal areas, leading to the establishment of routes from Sihanoukville to complement those snaking south from Laos. However, Hanoi wanted greater certainties, possible only through direct control; its doubts about Sihanouk's commitment to the anti-imperialist struggle were well-founded.

Following the VC's near-annihilation during the 1968 Tet Offensive, Hanoi moved thousands of NVA regulars south on the Ho Chi Minh Trail to fight as guerrillas and maintain pressure on Saigon from within the country. These northern troops, however, lacked the same degree of popular support the local-born VC had enjoyed. With less local knowledge and different accents, they were easier for South Vietnamese authorities to identify and track down.[20] The changed composition of its forces in South Vietnam after mid-1968 also required Hanoi to provide a greater proportion of their logistical needs.

Ammunition and weapons were a primary concern. NVA assault rifles and machine guns used different bullets than did American arms; other NVA weapons, particularly mortars, 122mm artillery rockets, and rocket-propelled antitank grenades, were simply not available in the South. Where the VC had supplied itself in large part by ambushes and scavenging on southern battlefields, NVA troops inside South Vietnam were far more dependent on arms provided by Hanoi.

Feeding these men was another problem. The VC had gotten much of their food from relatives and neighbors. Lacking the same personal ties to the rural communities, northern troops in 1969 and 1970 had a harder time persuading southern peasants to give them food. When on full rations of a pound of rice per man per day, a thirty-man NVA platoon needed almost 1,000 pounds of rice each month. Poor southern villagers often did not have that much to spare, and taking it at gunpoint would alienate them and bring around South Vietnamese security forces. Farmers in eastern Cambodia were willing to sell the NVA/VC rice, but Hanoi still had to get it to its troops, along with weapons, ammunition, medicines, and other materials.

Moving and distributing supplies, their physical transport, was a major issue. Everything first had to reach base areas to then be stockpiled or sent on to field units. Allied air and naval supremacy over South Vietnam and off its coasts forced Hanoi to move its supplies by land. Although Cambodia was fairly safe, and Laos reasonably so less the occasional American air strikes, communist porters within South Vietnam died in increasing numbers as Abrams's logistics-focused strategy took hold after mid-1968.

Hanoi accepted such losses, if grudgingly, as a cost of the war: its units inside South Vietnam needed the external support to fight, and it could not allow Saigon to strengthen its grip on the southern countryside unchallenged. Trained and disciplined NVA regulars, with automatic weapons, mortars, and rockets, were a more serious military threat than the scantily supplied, partially trained, and less-disciplined VC. Their logistical reliance on Hanoi, however, made them far more vulnerable to supply interruptions.

There were several ways for MACV to block the communist supply lines across Indochina. Although the most effective means would have been by U.S. or Army of the Republic of Vietnam (ARVN) ground troops blocking Hanoi's land routes through Laos and Cambodia, domestic and international considerations made this impossible.[21] The Laotian and Cambodian governments had the right to refuse Hanoi the use of their lands, but neither government had the political stomach or the armed forces necessary to enforce such a demarche. Allied Special Operations units, such as Green Beret–led native tribes or small long-range patrols, harassed NVA forces and material moving south on the Ho Chi Minh Trail but lacked both the firepower and the numbers to totally halt the flow.

By default, airpower was MACV's only viable military option against the NVA inside Laos and Cambodia. The air force's interdiction campaign was a two-edged sword, however. The quantities of supplies and men Hanoi dispatched south down the Ho Chi Minh Trail in the early 1960s had been comparatively small because of the guerrillas' limited needs in South Vietnam and light losses suffered en route. As Hanoi's casualties and material losses mounted in the mid-1960s due to American bombing, increasing numbers of American troops and their firepower, and Westmoreland's strategy of attrition, Hanoi sent ever-larger numbers south to make sure the needed quantities made it out the other end of the pipeline, in South Vietnam.

Following Johnson's curtailment of bombing in North Vietnam, Hanoi shifted air defenses south, allowing more air defense weapons to cover less area; ultimately, some 60 percent of North Vietnam's air defense capability was committed to protecting its lines of communication. Further, with more trucks moving on steadily improving roads under a denser air defense shield, its material losses continuously dropped. In 1969 Hanoi lost to air attacks 13.5 percent of the tonnage it sent south; the figure was 3.4 percent in 1970 and 2.07 percent in 1971.[22] Hanoi's strategy was ultimately successful, defeating the American air interdiction campaign through increasing numbers and sheer endurance.

The massive effort Hanoi put into improving the trail's defenses and capacity showed in its steadily rising throughput. Group 559's tonnage in 1965 was about as much as it had sent in the previous five years. The year 1967 saw 66,000 tons dispatched south, with 132,000 tons the next year; by 1970 its total was about 170,000 tons.[23] Replacement troops headed out, with six times the number sent in 1966 as had gone in 1965. These helped raise the number of NVA combat battalions in South Vietnam from 103 in 1965 to 136 in 1966.[24]

Unfortunately for American strategists, though, once the communist throughput tonnage rose to a new, higher level, Hanoi did not scale it back whenever U.S. "peace initiatives" or bad weather stopped the bombing for a while. Repair crews quickly fixed any damage and steadily expanded the trail to increase its resiliency and capacity, while Moscow and Beijing made good most lost war materials.

Though the U.S. bombing of the Ho Chi Minh Trail was a valid short-term response to the North's dispatch of men and supplies south, in the long run it only delayed and made more costly Hanoi's conquest of the South. In June 1967 the Central Intelligence Agency (CIA) advised McNamara that the trail's capacity had become so great that U.S. interdiction efforts were essentially futile for affecting the war in the South so long as Hanoi was determined to win.[25] The steady trickle of men and material south in the early 1960s was now a fast-moving stream turning into a river, with the border base areas "ponds" becoming "lakes." Safe because of Johnson's decision to respect Laotian and Cambodian neutrality and prohibit ground attacks, the Laotian and Cambodian border sanctuaries became Hanoi's launching pads for new attacks and the forward stockpiles for supplies not immediately needed. This development continued throughout Johnson's administration, altered only slightly in 1968 by the U.S. bombing of Laos.[26]

2

The Nixon-Abrams Era, 1969–1970

Soon after becoming president in January 1969, Richard M. Nixon made a fateful decision: the United States would bomb North Vietnamese forces in Cambodia. Although Nixon had initially been undecided regarding whether to attack, a North Vietnamese offensive launched in late February, the day before he was to fly to Europe, struck him as a deliberate insult to his month-old presidency. Believing the resumption of air strikes against North Vietnam too costly domestically, he accepted military advice instead to hit North Vietnam's sanctuaries along the Cambodian–South Vietnamese border.[1] Opposition within his cabinet delayed any decision until mid-March, when Nixon finally ignored cabinet dissent and ordered a B-52 strike on a sanctuary in Cambodia just north of Tay Ninh Province, about sixty miles northwest of Saigon. This first attack, on 18 March 1969, was followed by another in April and marked the start of an aerial offensive that lasted until August.[2]

Operation MENU, the secret bombing of the Cambodian base areas, targeted those six of the sixteen key sanctuaries along the border that Washington considered the biggest threat.[3] From them the NVA could prepare attacks against Saigon, several major U.S. headquarters and supply dumps, and the critical air bases of Tan Son Nhut and Bien Hoa. The danger these sanctuaries posed, and Nixon's willingness to attack them, began the process that a year later culminated in the Cambodian incursion. Several key U.S. officials supported the start of the bombing, including Secretary of Defense Melvin Laird, U.S. ambassador to South Vietnam Ellsworth Bunker, and Abrams.

Abrams rightly "credited the Menu [*sic*] operations with disrupting enemy logistics, aborting several enemy offensives, and reducing the enemy threat to the whole Saigon region."[4] He also felt that MENU "played a significant, if not a decisive, part" in the Cambodian government's summer 1969 decision to lessen its acquiescence of NVA/VC activities within eastern Cambodia and, in conjunction with ground operations within South Vietnam, had "greatly reduced the VC/NVA flexibility."[5]

Bombing alone, whether against the Ho Chi Minh Trail in southern Laos or the Cambodian border sanctuaries, could not reverse the war's overall momentum in Southeast Asia. Even before his inauguration, Nixon recognized that Americans were becoming disenchanted with a war that seemed to have no end. Further, in its focusing on Southeast Asia for so long, the United States was neglecting its other global commitments and responsibilities. Accordingly, soon after entering office Nixon began a gradual disengagement of American forces from Southeast Asia and a reorientation toward matters he felt more appropriate for a superpower.[6] However, Nixon had been elected in part on the strength of his anticommunist reputation and could not be seen to "abandon" the South Vietnamese so soon after his inauguration. Accordingly, following guidance from the administration, for the first half of 1969 MACV kept extraordinarily tight wraps on anything hinting at a U.S. pullout.

As American troop withdrawals began in summer 1969, MACV's Operations staff spent proportionally more time reviewing preparations for units' departures and expanding the tactical zones of those that remained. The U.S. pullout and Vietnamization, the shift of responsibilities and equipment from American to South Vietnamese units, soon became MACV's two biggest concerns.[7]

The year 1970 was turbulent for those American units left in South Vietnam. As units departed for the United States, those remaining had to ensure those sectors' continued security. In many cases units were responsible for areas far larger than normal planning considerations warranted. For example, by April 1970 the U.S. Twenty-fifth Infantry Division's sector ran from the Cambodian border to the sea, a distance of more than 125 miles; such a spread was two to three times what a division might traditionally expect to control. This was not unduly dangerous, though, because VC activity at that stage was generally low and sporadic, NVA units were at or across the border, and ARVN units were steadily growing stronger and more numerous as they filled in for the departing Americans.

By the spring of 1970 the American pullout was well under way. Some 25,000 men had left in August 1969, 40,000 more departed in December 1969, and 50,000 went in spring 1970. In less than nine months, U.S. ground force strength in South Vietnam had dropped by about one-fourth, and another 90,000 were due to go by the end of 1970 (figure 1).[8]

Still confident in its ultimate victory but dismayed by the losses of 1968–1969, in spring 1970 Hanoi stepped up its political activities inside South Vietnam.[9] It sought first to undermine Nixon's policy of Vietnamization, which required a stable and peaceful South Vietnam and widespread popular support if Saigon was to establish its legitimacy. Continuing the rural pressure on the weak government of President Nguyen Thieu would keep Saigon from regaining control over disputed or once-communist areas.

Hanoi also sought to increase its own support within South Vietnam. The 1968 Tet Offensive had gutted the VC, and without local "muscle" to protect

Figure 1. The U.S. Withdrawal: American Troop Strength in South Vietnam, 1969–1972

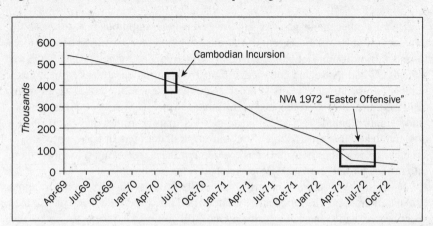

them by intimidating villagers into silence or support, communist political cadres had become much more vulnerable to identification and arrest. Programs such as Phung Hoang, or Phoenix, began to decimate the communist leadership's ranks within South Vietnam.[10]

Despite the catastrophic losses during 1968, the communists tried again in early 1969. An offensive from 23 February to 29 March failed, with the movements of the First and Fifth Divisions from Cambodia toward Saigon blocked. The primary force in their way was the First Cavalry (Airmobile) Division, which Abrams had ordered south on 26 October 1968. Redeploying some 570 miles in less than three weeks, from northern I Corps Tactical Zone (I CTZ, one of the four major military regions of South Vietnam) to between Saigon and the Cambodian border in III Corps Tactical Zone (III CTZ), the military region comprising the ten provinces around Saigon, the division achieved both strategic and tactical surprise by the speed and distance of the movement.[11] It quickly made its presence felt, inflicting about 2,500 battle casualties weekly from October 1968 to February 1969; total communist losses doubled, to about 5,000 per week, during the Tet 1969 attacks.[12] The First Cavalry Division's tremendous tactical mobility, speed, and firepower were far greater than its light-infantry opponents could match.

In July 1969, Resolution 9 of the Central Office for South Vietnam (COSVN, the Hanoi-directed political headquarters for operations in the South) acknowledged the grave difficulties the VC and southern-deployed NVA faced. Resolution 9 directed a return to protracted warfare and admitted the hoped-for early victory was not possible. Battlefield failures and doubts about their leaders began to affect many guerrillas; by early 1970 morale had declined sharply among the communist rank and file inside South Vietnam.[13]

As Saigon's strength grew, villagers became less fearful of the once-formidable VC; by late 1969 and early 1970, the allied pacification effort threatened Hanoi's long-term plans.[14] Without the help of South Vietnamese peasants the guerrillas could not survive, delaying Hanoi's planned reunification with the South that much longer.

Hanoi's other major goal for 1970 was far more ambitious but still possible, to be achieved by the B-2 Front in its role as Hanoi's forward field headquarters for the part of South Vietnam that roughly corresponded to the III CTZ. COSVN Directive 7 had instructed communist units to step up their attacks as U.S. troop numbers dropped, an unrealistic order given the deteriorating condition of many of those units. However, this and other indicators led U.S. Army officers to conclude Hanoi wanted "to create the impression that the Americans [were] being driven out, and that the actions [were] unrelated to the Vietnamization process."[15] Whether true or not, the Americans' perception that Hanoi sought to throw them into the sea partially led MACV to plan and act accordingly.

In spring 1970 there were still reasonable grounds for U.S. concern about Hanoi's intentions. The epic battle of Dien Bien Phu had taken place just sixteen years before, and General Vo Nguyen Giap still commanded the NVA and sat on the Politburo. Capturing or destroying a major American base or unit might indeed let the communists claim that they had driven the United States out of Indochina just as they had the French. After all, many Americans recalled, a major goal of the 1968 Tet Offensive had been to foment a general uprising that would overthrow Saigon and submerge U.S. forces in a sea of hostile Vietnamese. Further, MACV had not forgotten Dien Bien Phu, and during the 1968 Tet Offensive had produced a special staff study comparing that historic battle with the one then raging at Khe Sanh.[16]

Although Tet and the siege of Khe Sanh had brutally reminded the NVA of the folly of exposing its men to massed American firepower, as U.S. withdrawals continued and U.S. forces became more thinly spread across South Vietnam, the communists knew their opportunities might well increase.[17] Eventually, perhaps in late 1970 or 1971, the NVA might be able to destroy a major American base or seize it, however temporarily, from its fewer defenders. Such a victory, while not a triumph on the scale of Dien Bien Phu, would be invaluable to Hanoi's propaganda machine as evidence against the value of American security guarantees. Capturing or destroying such a base, though, would require thousands of regular NVA troops supplied with huge amounts of weapons, food, and ammunition (all present in eastern Cambodia). Even if, as Giap asserted after the war, he intended to wait until the Americans were gone before he struck, the NVA would still need forward supply depots to sustain its forces.[18] Logistics would largely determine what Hanoi could do, and when.

The physical constraints and limitations of logistics were but two of Hanoi's problems; it also had to deal with Abrams. Westmoreland's deputy commander at MACV since 1967, Abrams spent a year intimately involved in all aspects of the war at the highest levels before succeeding him on 15 June 1968. Changes began soon thereafter, in part due to the new commander and in part due to the changed strategic situation in the aftermath of Tet. Where Westmoreland's "search-and-destroy" operations had focused on such "hard" targets as enemy infantry units, the strategy of attrition also had the unfortunate consequence of a steady flow of American and ARVN casualties. It likewise resulted in accidentally killing and wounding many South Vietnamese civilians whose support Saigon ultimately needed. Believing "search and destroy" counterproductive, and not facing the same two-pronged threat of NVA and VC that Westmoreland had confronted from 1965 to mid-1968, Abrams refocused MACV's strategy upon taking command.[19] Without adequate and predictable flows of supplies, he knew, NVA soldiers would become a more manageable problem.

U.S. forces and the Republic of Vietnam Armed Forces (RVNAF) soon gave greater priority to targeting Hanoi's "softer" logistics units within South Vietnam. NVA and VC supply and transportation troops generally lacked the heavy weapons and aggressiveness of combat units like the infantry, commando-engineers ("sappers"), or artillerymen. Further, porters carrying heavy loads or pushing bicycles loaded with hundreds of pounds of cargo were watching where to step next, not looking for ambushes or mines. To help escape detection, supply columns crossing South Vietnam were usually small and had few guards. This was good for stealth but fatal should the column be spotted. Finally, if the porters survived by scattering and fleeing upon contact, the supplies they abandoned would not get through to the units needing them. Thus, attacking VNA and VC supply lines crippled enemy combat units inside South Vietnam while simultaneously reducing friendly military and civilian casualties.

MACV was not alone in wanting to seize opportunities arising from the communists' casualties during Tet 1968 and the drastic weakening of the VC position. One such tactical commander was U.S. Marine Corps Major General Raymond Davis, who took command of the Third Marine Division on 22 May 1968 and immediately sought a change in his mission. Unhappy with the division's more-static duties near the demilitarized zone (DMZ), Davis asked for and got more helicopter support.[20] The Third Marine Division's airmobile successes paralleled those of the First Cavalry Division far to the south. "By late October [1968] North Vietnamese prisoners reported that the 320th Division's scattered regiments, plagued by shortages of food and ammunition, were withdrawing back across the Ben Hai River."[21]

Initial indications early in the second half of 1968 were clearly positive from MACV's perspective. Vastly superior allied firepower and depleted communist numbers following the three failed offensives of 1968, coupled with airmobility and the higher priority accorded to attacking communist logistics, were driving back enemy forces despite continued high numbers of friendly casualties. As the fighting remained intense into 1969, the military initiative within South Vietnam was palpably shifting to the allies, and NVA/VC units were steadily falling back west to the border.

The new emphasis on pacification and on targeting logistics rapidly gained backers among American military and political leaders. Johnson accepted it in autumn 1968 as an alternative to "search and destroy," as did most senior officers and, following victory in the November 1968 election, Nixon's incoming administration. Nixon wanted to get the United States out of Vietnam and saw in pacification and attacking enemy logistics the means to do this; by then "search and destroy" had become a political liability, a bloody phrase from his predecessor's war. After almost six months in office, on 7 July 1969, Nixon formally changed MACV's mission from defeating the enemy and driving him out of South Vietnam to instead helping Saigon improve its forces, supporting pacification, and interdicting enemy supplies.[22] Abrams had already been doing this successfully for the past year, but by making it official Nixon gave him greater political support to wage the war in a manner more to his liking.

MACV immediately codified this approach in the Free World Forces' 1970 Combined Campaign Plan, issued jointly by MACV and South Vietnam's JGS on 31 October 1969. Of the plan's eight key military objectives for 1970, the first four dealt with supplies: attacking enemy units, bases, and logistics systems in Vietnam and "authorized contiguous areas" while cutting enemy supply lines to deny them rice and other materials.[23] South Vietnam's Regional Forces, Popular Forces, National Police, and local defense units would emphasize pacification, while the South Vietnamese, American, and allied troops would find and attack major enemy units, bases, and supply lines within South Vietnam, secure the borders and coasts, and help with pacification as required. MACV and the JGS believed that the Saigon region was Hanoi's ultimate target. In turn, those communist base areas that might support such attacks became MACV's chief targets.[24]

The Combined Campaign Plan's Intelligence Annex likewise clearly reflected MACV's overall emphasis on logistics. As of mid-1969 about half of the B-2 Front's total monthly supply tonnage into South Vietnam came through southern Laos, while the other half came from Sihanoukville; the final supply ship, unrecognized as such by MACV at the time, had unloaded its cargo of arms in July 1969. Unusually heavy monsoon rains in late 1969 and the allied bombing of the Ho Chi Minh Trail in southern North Vietnam and Laos had caused serious shortages for enemy forces in northern South Vietnam. (However, those units in the southern half of South Vietnam, supplied through Cambodia, were comparatively better off.) Constant pressure had made it hard for the logistics troops to conceal their caches' general locations from allied forces.

Losing ammunition stockpiles aborted several NVA and VC attacks in 1969. In the first half of that year, "tonnage of crew-served-weapons ammunition was three times the amount captured in all of 1968 and tonnage of small arms ammunition uncovered was twice that captured in all of 1968."[25] Without bullets, rockets, and mortar shells, NVA and VC units were far more vulnerable to attack and destruction, as well as to psychological warfare pressures and allied propaganda.

Some regiment-sized forces apparently moved their caches and themselves from the coastal regions west toward the Cambodian border, unable to sustain their activities across the width of South Vietnam.[26] Moving west increased the chances of getting their supplies, but it precluded their effective operations in their assigned areas.

Not only were communist forces within South Vietnam threatened by allied military action against them or their supply routes, but events within Cambodia itself further hampered their logistic efforts. By March 1970 it appeared to Abrams that Sihanouk's government had fulfilled its agreements with Hanoi to import and deliver munitions, had not assumed any more such obligations, and was increasingly pressuring NVA/VC supply and personnel infiltration routes across Cambodia in an attempt to lessen the NVA/VC presence in the eastern part of the country.[27]

Aware of the problems caused by Abrams and a "wobbly" Sihanouk, North Vietnam continued to improve the Ho Chi Minh Trail as a hedge against the possibility of worse logistics problems later. It imported "unusually large numbers of trucks," widened existing roads through North Vietnam and southern Laos to accommodate them, and built a pipeline through the Mu Gia Pass into southern Laos to transport fuel.[28] Between the beginning of October 1969 and the end of February 1970, Hanoi built 400 kilometers of new roads across southern Laos and added more surface-to-air missiles and antiaircraft artillery sites along the entire route.[29]

These measures supported Hanoi's plans for unifying Vietnam by force, supplied solely from the North via the Ho Chi Minh Trail alone.[30] By motorizing its transportation network, Hanoi increased exponentially its overall logistics capacity, a necessity given the greater material requirements of its forces inside South Vietnam and the losses caused by the U.S. bombing. One medium truck could carry 5,000 pounds of cargo 150 to 200 miles daily, compared with a porter using a bicycle to move about 400 pounds 10 to 15 miles. A single truck and driver could thus move in a day what would take twelve porters two weeks: 1 man-day versus 168. An added benefit was that Hanoi could reassign many porters to serve as infantrymen, helping to replace soldiers lost in previous battles.[31]

The North's logistics system was a matter of serious dispute during the late 1960s among American officials in Saigon and Washington. Analysts agreed that all northern troops heading south used the Ho Chi Minh Trail, but they differed on how supplies reached those troops inside South Vietnam. The CIA believed that nearly all supplies came down the Ho Chi Minh Trail, including those destined for the southern half of the country. MACV intelligence strongly dissented, arguing that while those supplies going into northern South Vietnam came via the Ho Chi Minh Trail, the material for the southern half passed through the port of Sihanoukville.

In hindsight, MACV's assessment was more accurate than was the CIA's. Troops north of Saigon near Cambodia had no doubts that the trucks they saw and heard across the border in the communist base areas came from the direction of Sihanoukville.[32] That U.S. troops patrolled the border in 1970 was testimony to the validity of Abrams's strategy: before 1969 the border region had largely "belonged" to the NVA and VC.

U.S. and RVNAF forces had driven enemy troops away from Saigon toward the Cambodian border by making it far more difficult for them to operate within South Vietnam. For those communist forces remaining within the III CTZ during 1969–1970, survival took precedence over fighting (see map 2). Between early February and late April, about 1,500 communist headquarters and supply troops died, hurting the fighting units' effectiveness.[33] An NVA officer captured east of Saigon on 14 April 1970 told questioners that his unit's last ammunition resupply had been twenty 122mm rockets about two months earlier, and no rice had come since January.[34] A unit thought to be from the Seventh Division noted on 30 April 1970 that "every member should be motivated to economize on food, especially beginning in May 70 when daily rations will be reduced. In addition, many soldiers should be motivated to volunteer not to draw clothing items for 1970."[35]

The guerrillas' situation was worse. One VC medic captured on 26 April 1970 said his unit had gotten no replacements since October 1969.[36] A midlevel VC officer captured on 1 May told his interrogators a similar story: no replacements had joined since September 1969, and "morale was at rock bottom." Of his regiment's 240 men, 180 were sick or wounded. "Should the Americans pull out immediately," he added, "South Vietnam would eventually fall to the communists; however, should ARVN have a chance to develop, the VC would have no chance for victory."[37]

Food was short everywhere, due to the increased allied attacks on the Ho Chi Minh Trail in mid-1969 and the arrival of the rainy season. Many units were reduced to eating about 80 to 120 grams of rice per day; one engineer unit on the trail ate only roots, berries, and weeds from June to September 1969 and used the ashes of burned straw in place of salt.[38]

Stress among communist headquarters personnel mirrored that of field troops. A political department staff briefing within the South Vietnamese National Liberation Army (the military headquarters for the VC) on 19 November 1969 assessed their fall 1969 performance in a grim tone. It read in part, "Combat capabilities of our spearhead battalions were poor. Our guerrilla warfare capabilities were poor, and our forces were driven to the border area." The briefing went on to berate the VC units' poor morale and fighting spirit.[39]

Things were no better the following spring. One VC logistics staff northwest of Saigon made a list of its units and the food each needed but inflated its troop numbers by 50 to 100 percent to compensate for the inadequate quantities expected from COSVN and the B-2 Front.[40] Although false reporting occurs in most armies, the extent to which these numbers were padded indicates significant problems. Supply shortages in late 1969 and early 1970 were clearly serious and affected the communists' combat effectiveness.

Map 2. NVA/VC Infantry Deployments in III CTZ, Early 1970

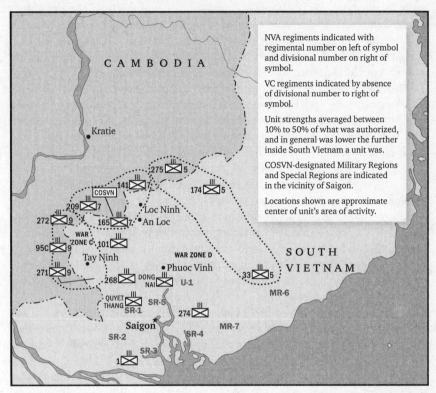

During early 1970 the communist cause was in trouble across South Vietnam, particularly throughout III CTZ. Despite intensive communist propaganda efforts west and south of Saigon, only thirty ARVN soldiers deserted and joined the VC in the first months of 1970; none were officers or sergeants.[41] Territorial Security Forces grew rapidly. A total of 416 Popular Force (PF) platoons were in training by 7 March 1970 and would later that spring deploy across the country; more Regional Force (RF) battalions were to be formed in several provinces, to give the province chiefs the sort of power previously provided by ARVN. Finally, in late February a six-week training course began for 7,785 platoon and squad leaders of the People's Self-Defense Forces (PSDF), the village militias. Saigon ultimately sought to train 60,000 of these leaders, the militias to be fully armed instead of sharing weapons among themselves.[42]

South Vietnamese peasants in 1969 and 1970 largely perceived the government as beating the guerrillas, and, if they did not support Saigon, at least most did not actively oppose it. Pacification made progress accordingly. In Binh

Duong Province, north of Saigon, sixteen of the forty-eight villages held local elections in March 1970 without VC interference, a marked contrast to earlier years. A total of 250 candidates ran for 158 seats, but only 47 incumbents were reelected in races with higher voter turnouts than in 1967. Villagers feeling safe enough to vote also felt safe enough to vote out unpopular officials.[43] These were positive, but indirect, benefits of the allies' military successes.

More apparent to field commanders than village security situations were the differences in their combat actions. The value of targeting communist supply units instead of infantrymen was obvious: fewer U.S. and ARVN soldiers died in combat, and the number of enemy attacks inside South Vietnam declined. Weekly averages of friendly killed in action (KIA) for February 1970 were 95 U.S. and 207 RVNAF; these numbers were 53 and 57 percent, respectively, of the 1969 weekly averages.[44] Hanoi's logistic units in South Vietnam had wilted under the sustained pressure.

There were consequences at the strategic level as well. Supplies, from autumn 1969 on arriving via the expanding Ho Chi Minh trail rather than coming up from Sihanoukville, reached base areas increasingly packed with undelivered material, further increasing their attractiveness as targets for allied strikes. The longer the bottleneck at the border persisted, the worse COSVN's logistic and thus military situation grew.

Fortunately for Hanoi, in 1969 and early 1970 the Cambodian border was still inviolable to U.S. and South Vietnamese ground forces, and Cambodia's armed forces were an insignificant threat. The only real danger to the base areas came from MENU, with the specific bombing targets located by aerial and secret ground reconnaissance units. Though bombs might toss around cases and crates or tear open rice bags, most supplies (other than fuel and high explosives) required direct hits to be destroyed. Dispersing supplies into dozens of smaller caches throughout each base area increased the chances of losing a fraction of the total but greatly reduced the likelihood of a single catastrophic explosion. Given the tonnage moving on the Ho Chi Minh Trail and that already secured in the base areas, the losses inflicted by the B-52 strikes were acceptable so long as the sanctuaries themselves remained safe from allied ground forces.

For pacification and Vietnamization to progress and succeed, the allies had to maintain the pressure on enemy supply lines within South Vietnam. This situation on the ground was comparable to that of the air campaign against the Ho Chi Minh Trail. Were the chokehold eased or ended, supplies stockpiled inside Cambodia could flow into South Vietnam in greater quantities than previously. The ammunition was the biggest threat, since the American way of fighting emphasized firepower in lieu of manpower, and there were one-third fewer U.S. troops in South Vietnam in late 1970 than had been there in 1968. With greater quantities of ammunition near at hand, increases in the communists' infantry firepower would negate much of the remaining American edge and make the United States' ongoing departure steadily riskier.

Hanoi's southern commanders thus would have greater freedom of action, and more options for bigger or more frequent attacks, than they would have without plentiful supplies readily available along the border. Finally, Thieu's government needed time and internal peace to establish its legitimacy throughout the country; any resumption of intense fighting would indicate pacification's likely failure and Saigon's eventual defeat.

The Cambodian base areas thus posed unacceptable dangers to American and South Vietnamese plans. Perhaps Hanoi intended to simply sit and watch the Americans depart before it resumed its actions against Saigon, a course of action strongly suggested by COSVN Resolution 9. This was, however, a chance that leaders in Washington were unwilling to take: after years of fighting, neither side trusted the other.

The best way American leaders saw to buy the time they needed for the United States to pull out safely and for Saigon to secure its position was to destroy those border sanctuaries that made possible any major communist assault against the southern, more populated half of South Vietnam. Doing this before the summer 1970 monsoon would prevent Hanoi from attacking in strength before mid-1971, and perhaps even 1972, since it would first have to rebuild its logistic bases along the borders. As it did so, the United States could accelerate its withdrawal, and Saigon would have a year or more of comparative calm in which to further reassert its control over the southern countryside.

The Cambodian sanctuaries were critical to both sides. Hanoi needed them to win before the United States left South Vietnam; Abrams had to destroy them to keep from indisputably losing. He and other senior officers had long wanted to attack the base areas, but President Johnson had rejected their advice. So long as the White House publicly accepted Cambodian claims of neutrality, MACV's hands were tied. Nixon, too, recognized the sanctuaries' significance, but given U.S. domestic opposition in 1969 he could not afford to "widen the war" with overt attacks on the base areas.

What changed Nixon's mind after a year in office was the radically altered situation inside Cambodia. With all else subordinated to its goal of Vietnamese unification, Hanoi ignored Cambodian assertions of neutrality. Sihanouk, making the best of a bad situation in the face of vastly superior North Vietnamese power, had yielded in the presence of Hanoi's forces operating in and from eastern Cambodia. This, however, had brought the U.S. bombing campaign, MENU, about which neither Phnom Penh nor Hanoi could publicly complain after their denials of any NVA or VC activity in Cambodia.[45]

In May 1969, following the initial MENU strikes in eastern Cambodia, Sihanouk had imposed a brief embargo against the North Vietnamese moving arms across his country. Four months later he released between 3,000 and 5,000 tons of supplies from the in-transit warehouses in exchange for Hanoi's agreement to limit its operations in Cambodia to the base areas, leave the sanctuaries when they were no longer needed, and stop supporting the Khmer Rouge.[46]

Hanoi's acquiescence to Sihanouk's demands was short-lived, Sihanouk having failed to pressure Hanoi into respecting Cambodian sovereignty. Instead, North Vietnam continued its operations from Cambodia against Saigon, leading to more U.S. bombings and further distorting the Cambodian economy by COSVN's widespread corruption of local officials and purchase or confiscation of large amounts of Cambodian rice.[47] This tense arrangement between the North Vietnamese and Cambodians continued through 1969 but collapsed following the March 1970 bloodless coup.[48]

Sihanouk's reign had been fraught with peril since the partition of French Indochina in 1954 had created an independent Cambodia. With his acquiescence, starting in 1962 Hanoi had begun moving into northeastern Cambodia and setting up early base camps along the South Vietnamese border. American protests had led Sihanouk to cancel further American military aid in 1963 and then break relations with Washington in 1965. These actions turned most of his officer corps against him; many educated, urban Cambodians became opponents as results of his one-man rule, his nepotism, and economic stagnation brought about by the loss of American funding.[49] For the next three years he openly proclaimed his neutrality and surreptitiously abetted Hanoi's activities in his country's hinterlands. The growing NVA presence disturbed him, but he was in no position to challenge it.

Things changed significantly, however, when Nixon started MENU; a month later Phnom Penh reestablished diplomatic relations with Washington. Hanoi was dismayed by this development and moved some 12,000 Khmer Rouge troops, armed and trained in North Vietnam, into Cambodia to pressure Sihanouk.[50] A civil war began thereafter in Cambodia, which further convinced Sihanouk of the need for Washington's backing. However, this was too little, too late; he had already alienated his prime minister, General Lon Nol, and enough of the national political leadership. All that remained was their need for an opportunity to act, a situation that arose when Sihanouk flew to the French Mediterranean in January 1970 for a vacation.[51]

Lon Nol, a former police officer and then army general, had been since August 1969 in his second tour as prime minister, the first having been from October 1966 to April 1967. The deputy prime minister was a rival cousin of Sihanouk's, Prince Sisowath Sirik Matak. Neither man was happy about the presence of the North Vietnamese inside Cambodia and thought they could act while Sihanouk was gone. Cambodian mobs attacked Hanoi's and the NLF's legations in Phnom Penh; random violence spread rapidly thereafter.

At this stage Sihanouk blundered. Rather than returning home and regaining control, he flew to Moscow to seek Soviet help in getting the North Vietnamese out of Cambodia. Failing, he decided to fly next to Beijing but learned on the way to the Moscow airport that Lon Nol and the Cambodian Parliament had voted him out of office and off the throne that morning.

Following his deposition of Prince Sihanouk on 18 March 1970, Lon Nol soon found himself in serious trouble. Alarmed at North Vietnam's de facto occupation of eastern Cambodia, soon after deposing Sihanouk, Lon Nol formally requested Hanoi to withdraw its troops. In so doing, he specified the unrealistic deadline of seventy-two hours. Not surprisingly, Hanoi refused, in part due to the abruptness of the demand but chiefly because its goal of uniting Vietnam would be immeasurably harder if it could attack only across the DMZ or through southern Laos.

Heavy fighting quickly broke out between Cambodian forces and the NVA across the eastern half of Cambodia in late March 1970. It began with North Vietnamese–directed pro-Sihanouk demonstrations by North Vietnamese laborers on large rubber plantations in eastern Cambodia near Snuol, Krek, Cup, and Kampong Cham. The Cambodian Armed Forces, known after the coup as FANK, moved to control the cities; these deployments away from the border eased their pressure on the sanctuaries.[52]

As FANK became distracted by riots and protests, NVA and VC units seized control of the areas they needed to sustain their war against Saigon. By 12 April Hanoi's forces openly controlled the Cambodian border from the Gulf of Siam to the Fishhook, a point on the border north-northwest of Saigon. In this zone, over 150 miles long and between 6 and 9 miles deep, "all Cambodian border posts and installations [more than twenty] between the Gulf of Siam and the Mekong River were eliminated and only Cambodian posts of company size [about 120–150 men] or larger existed north of the Mekong."[53] Subsequent fighting in May aimed at an NVA takeover of the northeastern quarter of Cambodia. Kratie fell on 5–6 May, followed by five other cities over the next several weeks. Kratie's loss was particularly significant because it was FANK's main weapons depot for most of central Cambodia. In taking it, the B-2 Front thus replaced many of the infantry weapons it lost in the border sanctuaries.[54]

Hanoi did not consider its actions in Cambodia wrong or illegal, since to the Politburo the fighting in Indochina was part of a larger, interrelated struggle. A VC document captured in April 1970 gave clear insight into the Vietnamese communists' attitudes toward the Khmer Rouge: "We should . . . make them realize that their existence depends on ours. Our helping them is one of our international obligations. On the other hand, Cambodia is our staging area."[55]

Another consequence of the outbreak of fighting was that the border regions were no longer safe for Hanoi's forward political and military headquarters, COSVN and the Provisional Revolutionary Government (PRG), on the one hand, and the B-2 Front, on the other. The day after Sihanouk's overthrow the elements of the different headquarters began evacuating from border regions about eighty miles northwest of Saigon, north to new sites near Kratie, some seventy miles closer to Laos. These moves were dangerous despite being widely dispersed and protected by troops of the Seventh and Ninth Divisions. A B-52 strike nearly hit the PRG's Ministry of Justice contingent on 27 March, while three days later an

ARVN helicopter-borne infantry raid almost captured the PRG's justice minister, Truong Nhu Tang. Fifteen years later Truong wondered "whether American and Saigon government military analysts realized how close they were to annihilating or capturing the core of the Southern resistance—elite units of [its] frontline fighters along with the civilian and much of the military leadership."[56]

South Vietnamese cross-border incursions on 20 and 27 March and on 5 and 12 April were mere raids of a day or so, taking temporary advantage of the confused and fluid situation inside Cambodia to hit fleeting targets of opportunity.[57] If not totally unexpected, they probably came as something of a surprise to COSVN and the B-2 Front's commanders: allied policy had prohibited ground combat forces from entering Cambodia. Perhaps after five years the NVA and VC had become a bit complacent; such a response would have been understandably human.

Nonetheless, conscious of the danger to its leadership cadres and headquarters from both the fighting within Cambodia and the possibility of more forays from South Vietnam, in late March COSVN began shifting its elements deeper into Cambodia, away from the no-longer sacrosanct border. Future allied attacks might achieve local surprise, but strategic surprise had been lost. By late April the key elements of COSVN had completed their moves to northeast Cambodia, near the Laotian-Cambodian border. The critical leadership cadres, both political and military, were safe from ground attack; the thousands of tons of supplies remained hidden in the base areas, to be moved as circumstances permitted.

With the immediate problem of the survival of its top southern cadres assured, Hanoi returned to the conquest of South Vietnam. Achieving it now included three goals in Cambodia: protecting the sanctuaries on the borders of South Vietnam and Laos, isolating Phnom Penh, and creating a communist Cambodian Liberation Army to establish a regime friendly to North Vietnam.[58] By late April 1970 Hanoi was succeeding in all its objectives in Cambodia, particularly the first. Cambodia east of the Mekong River belonged to North Vietnam in all but name. Of the country's seventeen provinces, by 17 April NVA forces controlled three in eastern Cambodia and were overrunning five others.[59]

As the NVA attacked in late March, FANK fell back upon Phnom Penh and frantically tried to expand. Virtually overnight its infantry strength jumped from some 20,000 men to around 120,000. However, these "soldiers" were untrained, lacked discipline and unit cohesion, and were equipped (if at all) with a random assortment of weapons and ammunition from the Soviet Union, China, France, and America. Of the 120,000 troops in late April, about 118,000 had no guns.[60] Such a mob was worthless, a liability more than an asset.

Opposing them were less numerous but better-trained, well-equipped, and far more disciplined NVA and VC veterans. In early April three NVA divisions threatened Phnom Penh from the east: the Ninth, Seventh, and Fifth, on a rough line from south to north.[61] A month earlier they had been menacing Saigon, but, having seen to the relocation of the key leaders of COSVN, the B-2 Front headquarters, and the PRG, they were now ready to conquer central Cambodia.

The B-2 Front, roughly comparable to a U.S. corps-level command, had even fewer fighters than unit designations implied. In April 1970 it controlled between 40,000 and 60,000 troops along the Cambodian–South Vietnamese border. "But only about 35 percent of these [were] believed to have been in combat units; 65 percent were in administrative units and charged with rear service missions."[62] Thus, B-2 could commit just 15,000 to 20,000 infantrymen in Cambodia, backed by roughly as many support troops. However, against their discipline, experience, and weapons, Lon Nol's 120,000 were essentially just targets waiting to be shot. Throughout April the North Vietnamese troops steadily and inexorably drove westward, overrunning one FANK outpost after another.

Confident of victory but wanting to explain why they were now fighting away from Vietnam, COSVN reminded its cadres that "the revolution in [South Vietnam], Cambodia, and Laos are one and the same. They are directly under the leadership of the Lao Dong Party [the Vietnamese Communist Party, led from Hanoi]."[63] Viewing Indochina and its war as a single entity, and having already lost Sihanoukville as a supply entry point, Hanoi was taking no chances that its last, and most important, Cambodian route into South Vietnam might be lost: its own needs took precedence over the interests of its neighbors.

Hanoi's primary motivation for going beyond merely securing the border region and its base areas, and instead attacking Lon Nol in March 1970, remains unclear. The North Vietnamese might have moved against Phnom Penh to face a future U.S./RVNAF invasion without the threat of FANK in their rear. Alternatively, overthrowing Lon Nol would give them a secure rear with which to continue their attacks on South Vietnam and perhaps regain the use of Sihanoukville and the road network of southern Cambodia.

Of the two possibilities, the latter was more likely. With the 1969 closure of Sihanoukville to Hanoi's logistics traffic and the pressure of the MENU bombing campaign, Hanoi continued to expand the Ho Chi Minh Trail across northeast Cambodia, as well as further securing that part of the country for itself. Following the March 1970 coup, for the B-2 Front to send its three divisions toward Phnom Penh, leaving only minor security forces between the base areas and the Cambodian–South Vietnamese border, suggests that communist leaders did not expect any significant forces to come across from South Vietnam. Further, FANK barely qualified as a nuisance in 1970, and it would be years before it might be able to face the NVA in open battle. Thus, its attack on Phnom Penh was more a prudent measure, to remove a declared enemy before it could become a genuine threat to Hanoi's goals.

By April 1970 the Ho Chi Minh Trail was the sole supply artery for all communist forces fighting inside South Vietnam. If Hanoi wanted to win, it *had* to keep the trail open. It would therefore deal first with Lon Nol, to secure the trail

and base areas, before turning its attention back toward Saigon. The communists'
assumption that the allies would sit by and respect the Cambodian-Vietnamese
border while it overthrew Lon Nol proved false, however, with painful consequences for COSVN, the B-2 Front, and Hanoi.

3

MACV's Initial Planning, Spring 1970

The heightened activity and outbreak of fighting in eastern Cambodia during spring 1970 did not unduly surprise Abrams. Having earlier considered such a development, or perhaps hoping Nixon might become receptive to seizing the Cambodian sanctuaries given his willingness to bomb them in MENU, in January or February 1970 Abrams started MACV's Intelligence and Operations staffs thinking seriously about such a possibility.[1] At his direction they drafted contingency plans for brief raids across the border by regiment-sized ARVN units supported by U.S. artillery and helicopters.

MACV's initial concept in early 1970 envisioned forces significantly different than those that actually crossed the border a few months later. The small size of the elements attacking (initially, ARVN regiments) meant they would be big enough to overrun the targeted base areas but would lack staying power if the NVA or VC chose to fight. ARVN's troops could not remain in Cambodia unless backed with significant amounts of firepower, aviation, replacements, reinforcements, and supplies. Generally speaking, an infantry battalion could manage about two or three days' sustained fighting before exhaustion and losses required its withdrawal and rebuilding; a regiment could last up to a week. Thus, early MACV planning saw cross-border attacks lasting at most ten or so days, generally less. Surprise would be essential: the small forces could not afford to meet an enemy waiting for them.

Since these "rough draft" plans were to serve simply as the basis for more detailed operational plans should such become necessary, MACV excluded Saigon's JGS from the initial studies. Operational security was paramount: the fewer people aware of the planners' subject, the less likely secrecy would fail. Reviewing the plans in late February, Abrams shifted their focus to enemy headquarters and told his staff to consider using forces bigger than regiments.[2] However, all this was still "just in case" contingency planning, with no certainty that anything would ever come of it.

Although Cambodia was officially off-limits to him, Abrams kept watch on events there during late 1969 and early 1970. When "Secretary of Defense Melvin Laird had visited Saigon in February 1970 . . . Abrams had made a strong case for invading not only sanctuaries in Cambodia, but Laos as well. . . . Laird was unconvinced."[3] Chief among Laird's concerns was his assessment that the American people would vociferously oppose anything they perceived as widening the war. However, the U.S. commander in chief–Pacific, Admiral John McCain, soon thereafter reminded the chairman of the Joint Chiefs of Staff, General Earle Wheeler, that the Cambodian border sanctuaries were critical to the communist conquest of South Vietnam, and that it appeared Hanoi was preparing to attack Cambodia in April or May.[4]

Less than a week before Lon Nol's coup, on 13 March Abrams sent a detailed appraisal to Wheeler in Washington and to McCain in Honolulu. Noting Hanoi's use of American bombing pauses to rush supplies south through Laos "to improve his [Hanoi's] capability for increased military activity throughout SVN during 1970," Abrams assessed developments within Cambodia. Indications were, he said, that the Cambodian government was trying to back away from its previous logistic support of the NVA/VC, was beginning to use the Cambodian army to interfere with the communists' supply routes, and was trying to "reduce the size of VC/NVA sanctuaries in Cambodia." Hanoi was aware of the threat to its operations and plans and was expanding the Ho Chi Minh Trail across Laos to give it greater capacity and reduced dependence on Cambodia.[5] These were accurate appraisals of what was happening across the border.

Abrams's closing observations in the cable centered on likely communist actions. Conceding to Hanoi the ability to make significant attacks in specific areas on short notice, he also felt it could not sustain such operations for long. Instead, he accurately described Hanoi's current strategy as "a blend of political and military activity calculated to achieve anti-war pressure in the US leading to a rapid redeployment of US forces, the collapse of the GVN, and the creating of a coalition government in South Vietnam."[6]

Though the direct military threat to South Vietnam in early 1970 was much less than in previous years, Abrams pointedly reminded Wheeler and McCain,

> Since 1 July 69, budget reductions have imposed a cut of about 22 percent in B-52 and [tactical air] sorties. This has reduced Allied capability to respond to multiple contingencies with massed firepower. Massed air strikes have in the past been the only real Allied reserve and will become increasingly important to the success of the Vietnamization process as US presence in SVN decreases.[7]

The warning was prescient; in 1972 massive American airpower broke the back of Hanoi's "Easter Offensive," while its absence in 1975 hastened the collapse of South Vietnam. However, the relative paucity of significant conventional targets

or an imminent threat within South Vietnam and growing domestic American opposition to the war in general made reduced airpower an acceptable risk to the
Nixon administration.

As the Cambodian situation deteriorated following Lon Nol's 18 March deposition of Sihanouk, the communications links between MACV and the Pentagon
heated up.[8] On the evening of 25 March, Wheeler directed Abrams to begin planning for overt ground attacks into Cambodia. According to Wheeler, the "urgent"
requirement originated with "higher authority" and was to be ready to execute
should the NVA/VC attack Phnom Penh. The plan was to be in outline form and
include "concept, forces involved, objective areas, and possible timing," as well
as addressing variations with all-ARVN, all-American, and combined ARVN-
U.S. operations. Wheeler gave Abrams less than ten hours to put his concept together and get it back to the Pentagon.[9] Abrams met the deadline, sending it to
Wheeler with about twenty minutes to spare.

This MACV response was the first within a brisk exchange of teletypes between the two generals. Nine hours after Abrams's transmission, Wheeler had
further instructions to him from the White House. Within a day of Nixon and his
staff giving Wheeler the initial guidance for Abrams, they wanted Abrams to develop more detailed plans for two different options: an attack on Base Area 352
(the COSVN headquarters area) and a near-simultaneous attack on Base Areas
704 and 367/706. Abrams was to plan on using combined ARVN-U.S. forces,
was to consider in his response ten specific questions asked by Nixon, and also
was to address how well the proposed operations might ease pressure on Phnom
Penh. He had less than four days to draft these plans and return them to Wheeler
for White House review.[10] A day later Wheeler added nine questions, generally
dealing with how much lead time MACV would need to position its forces and
then launch the attacks if Nixon gave the order.[11]

Obeying Wheeler's instruction to sharply limit the number of participants in
the planning process, Abrams had his operations officer, Major General Edward
Bautz, bring Lieutenant Generals Arthur Collins and Julian Ewell, the respective
commanders of the corps-sized U.S. I Field Force, Vietnam (IFFV) and II Field
Force, Vietnam (IIFFV), to Saigon. There, the four generals fleshed out MACV's
26 March concept with further details to meet Washington's requirements.

On 30 March, Abrams sent McCain (with an information copy direct to
Wheeler) his plan for ground operations in Cambodia. Consisting of twenty
highly classified teletype pages for McCain's and Wheeler's eyes only, it presented two alternatives for Nixon's consideration.

The first option, lasting up to four weeks, was an attack on Base Areas 352
and 353 in the Fishhook against COSVN, supply areas, and one divisional and six
regimental headquarters. Two major units, the U.S. First Cavalry Division and the
ARVN Airborne Division, would execute the plan under the First Cavalry's overall

direction. The second option involved simultaneous attacks, lasting about two weeks, against Base Areas 704 and 367/706 by combined ARVN and U.S. forces.

There was disagreement over which option was better. Abrams thought the first option, against the Fishhook, would hurt COSVN more and would probably cause fewer noncombatant casualties even though MACV would suffer more friendly military casualties. However, Saigon's JGS preferred the second option, in part because sanctuaries in the Parrot's Beak were closer to Saigon. In both cases Abrams felt the principal danger to MACV's plans was a major conventional NVA attack across I CTZ, in northern South Vietnam near the DMZ. Weather, a critical consideration, was best in March and April before the spring monsoons arrived: the rains and flooding would curtail major operations until the ground dried out.

In response to Wheeler's question on the proposed attack's effects on NVA operations against Lon Nol, Abrams believed it would be "significant" for both options. Further, disrupting the communists' command and control, logistics, and troop flexibility "could severely degrade the momentum of the enemy attack." Abrams also pointed out that the depth of any incursion would generally need to be only ten to fifteen kilometers; this became a major point in Nixon's address to the nation on 30 April. Finally, Abrams noted that he would need seventy-two hours to execute *after* receiving the final implementation order, the last twenty-four to pre-position units and make final coordination.[12] Although Abrams sent the plan to Wheeler on 30 March, MACV's operations chief Major General Bautz heard nothing more of it before leaving on 2 April to take command of the Twenty-fifth Infantry Division.[13]

The next day Wheeler sent a message to McCain in Honolulu and to Abrams in Saigon indicating that "higher authority" (i.e., Nixon) was considering shifting the MENU strikes to those areas that would "make best contribution to [the] current situation in Cambodia." The message then asked McCain and Abrams for their views on "substantially increasing MENU program, both as part of ground operations into Cambodia, or in lieu of ground operations."[14] Nixon would soon change the focus of his questions from air strikes to major ground actions.

Early April was the calm before the storm. Nixon's subsequent guidance on cross-border planning directed any incursion to be a combined operation with both U.S. and ARVN troops, so Abrams included Saigon's JGS in MACV's planning process.[15] Wheeler was well aware of the danger of leaks: in Saigon they could lead to battlefield defeat, while in Washington the information could ignite a political firestorm over perceptions of widening the war. Accordingly, he told Abrams to restrict to American eyes any plans involving U.S. units.[16] Since other allied involvement was unnecessary militarily and would increase both political complications and the chances of leaks, MACV plans considered only American and ARVN participation in Cambodian operations.

As the situation continued to deteriorate in Cambodia and the White House reviewed his 30 March plan for ground attacks into Cambodia, Abrams called a meeting in his office. Present were MACV's chief of staff, operations officer, and head logistician. Smoking his cigar, Abrams told the three major generals,

"We have from time to time engaged in operations around here, and sometimes they leaked. Now," he said, "we're going to have an operation, and if there's a leakage, it's gonna be one of the four of us. You people sitting in the room with me, that's gonna be it. We're going to maintain surprise in this."[17]

He later included Lieutenant General Michael Davison, Ewell's successor as IIFFV commander, who would command the major American effort in attacks on the base areas across from III CTZ. Augmenting the earlier work done by Abrams, Bautz, and the two Field Force commanders, at least eight American generals in South Vietnam were now aware of the proposed incursion. With the addition of a mere handful of MACV planners and communications officers, and even fewer JGS generals and planners, the knowledge remained extremely closely held in both Saigon and Washington for an operation of this magnitude.

Like Abrams, Wheeler was obsessed with operational security. Near the beginning of MACV's detailed planning process for an incursion, on 26 March Wheeler told Abrams that the State Department was not being informed of MACV's planning but would be once it was closer to actual execution. He authorized Abrams to inform Ambassador Bunker if he felt it necessary (to continue good U.S. in-country working relations), but only on the condition that Bunker agree to not let the secretary of state know.[18] Secretary Rogers was opposed to any cross-border operations, even by the South Vietnamese, although he supported unrestricted bombing in Cambodia following Lon Nol's overthrow of Sihanouk. The White House, particularly Nixon and the National Security Council staff under Henry Kissinger, was taking no chances of leaks that would ignite domestic controversy and thereby preclude possible options.[19]

As MACV continued to plan and await decisions from Washington, South Vietnam acted unilaterally. Its two quick raids in late March had been fairly successful, and ARVN III Corps commander Lieutenant General Do Cao Tri became increasingly eager to take advantage of fleeting opportunities across the border. On 8 April he proposed to Ewell, his American counterpart and the IIFFV commander, that they insert three disguised ARVN radio teams via U.S. helicopters to help Cambodian troops reestablish communication with isolated headquarters. Ewell wired Abrams he intended to support Tri's request unless Abrams said otherwise.[20]

Tri continued to push for action. On Monday, 13 April, he talked with Ewell and Lieutenant General Michael Davison (who was to succeed Ewell on 15

April) about a cut-off Cambodian army outpost on Highway 1 that had several troops desert; its commander thought his entire unit might leave to rejoin other Cambodian forces to the west toward Phnom Penh. If they abandoned the post, Tri wanted to either occupy it with Vietnamese troops of Cambodian ancestry armed with AK-47s and wearing FANK uniforms or else destroy it. Ewell told him he had to hold the post if the Cambodians left. Tri then asked Ewell for his opinion of Tri's proposal to go deeper into Cambodia. Ewell said that it was too ambitious and that he needed to first clear it with President Thieu; further, it might well cause problems for Lon Nol.[21] Nothing else came of this particular idea, but it was indicative of how senior allied commanders were thinking in mid-April.

His position deteriorating steadily in the face of the NVA's advance, on 14 April Lon Nol asked for military help from anyone willing to give it. Saigon struck in force that same day. It had long wanted to attack the sanctuaries just inside the Cambodian border. Reports of widespread massacres of Vietnamese nationals by various Cambodian groups were an additional incentive to act, Saigon feeling compelled to rescue ethnic Vietnamese in danger inside Cambodia. The speed and size of Saigon's response to Lon Nol's plea were evidence that Saigon had only been waiting for a justification to move openly.

III Corps's TOAN THANG 41 (Total Victory 41) took place from 14 to 17 April in the border region known to the allies as the Angel's Wing, a base area in Cambodia about fifty kilometers west-northwest of Saigon (see map 3). As headquarters personnel evacuated their camps and headed north toward Kratie, B-2 Front commanders moved in the Ninth VC Division's 271st Infantry Regiment to provide security to the remaining personnel and supplies. However, the 271st's

Map 3. Mid-April: TOAN THANG 41 and CUU LONG/SD9/06

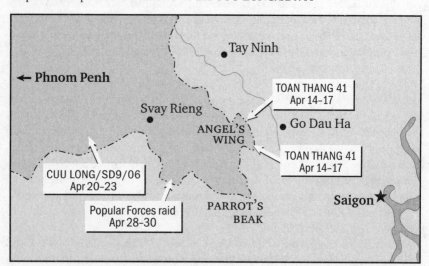

resistance was futile, failing to stop Tri's three regiment-sized task forces of tanks and mechanized infantry which swept west across the border into Base Area 706.[22]

Such a result was almost inevitable, given the maldeployment of the NVA divisions and VC Main Force units. Base Area 706 and the other major border sites were almost totally exposed to Saigon's raid from the east, since communist support troops were moving supplies west to sustain NVA divisions then fighting Lon Nol near Phnom Penh.[23] Only fragmentary guard detachments remained scattered across the sanctuaries Tri was starting to overrun.

TOAN THANG 41 was predominantly an RVNAF operation, the U.S. participation consisting chiefly of four battalions from the Twenty-fifth Infantry Division taking positions inside South Vietnam east and south of the Angel's Wing; their job was to prevent communist troops from fleeing into South Vietnam to escape ARVN units.[24] Taking advantage of surprise and the general absence of NVA/VC infantrymen, Tri's men killed or captured 415 enemy troops and seized 118 weapons, several tons of ammunition, and ninety-nine tons of rice against the loss of 8 RVNAF dead, 67 wounded, and one helicopter destroyed.[25]

Nearly as valuable to allied intelligence were several captured documents that disclosed Hanoi's new policies concerning supply routes from southern Laos to the border base areas. According to the papers, one drawback of the Sihanoukville Trail had been the constant bribes in money and weapons demanded by Cambodian bureaucrats and military officers.[26] Lon Nol's coup and the fighting with FANK had made southern Cambodia unsafe as a supply conduit. On the other hand, the Ho Chi Minh Trail passed across northeast Cambodia through areas firmly under NVA control. Although distances were greater than from Sihanoukville, these would become less important as the quality of the Ho Chi Minh Trail's road network improved and NVA supply units continued to receive more trucks from Moscow and Beijing. This confirmed Abrams's message of 13 March to Wheeler and McCain, which had asserted Hanoi's shift to relying solely on the trail and curtailing the use of Sihanoukville.

Abrams and Wheeler watched developments inside Cambodia with interest. On 22 April Abrams wired McCain and Army Chief of Staff Westmoreland that three battalions of Khmer Serai troops, totaling about 1,500 men, were available immediately to help Lon Nol, and another battalion of 600 could be ready in five days. These troops were organized, somewhat trained, and "equipped with US M-16s which they must retain." Abrams added that "we could now divert up to 10,000 M1 carbines and appropriate quantities of ammunition presently in ARVN logistics channels and destined for the [People's Self-Defense Forces]."[27] However, the U.S. arms lift had only limited effect in the long run: the problem was less a shortage of weapons than the absence of trained and disciplined Cambodian soldiers able and willing to use them.

MACV's planning grew in scope and complexity through April, even as ARVN made its own cross-border raids. TOAN THANG 41 had dashed across the Angel's Wing; TOAN THANG 42 would overrun the Parrot's Beak, as well as return to the Angel's Wing. Meanwhile, MACV concentrated on the area around the Fishhook, where it was sure bigger prizes were hidden. In January, MACV planners had expected incursions to last seven to ten days, but by April they expected such operations to run for two to four weeks, and longer if needed. Attacks would involve U.S. and ARVN forces, operating in two separate zones to minimize mutual interference.

The intelligence available to MACV shaped the detailed planning and, to a degree, the success of the subsequent attacks. Several assets were available in theater, including human sources and reconnaissance, electronic means, and aerial overflights and photography. All collected and analyzed information based on targeting guidance from the MACV commander, concentrating on what first Westmoreland, and then Abrams, felt most important. For most of the 1960s, though, this meant the "big war" and communist units already in South Vietnam, not activities in the Cambodian base areas.

MACV had not ignored Cambodia during Westmoreland's years, even if it could do little against the base areas. Arriving in theater in 1965, American radio monitoring stations and airborne radio direction finders across Southeast Asia triangulated communist transmitters in the Cambodian border area and recorded the broadcasts. From these and other reports, MACV Intelligence determined the general locations and major functions of each of the base areas.

However, by administration policy Cambodia was off-limits for all but covert U.S. reconnaissance efforts for most of the 1960s. Prohibited from extensive intelligence gathering inside Cambodia, Major General Philip Davidson, MACV's top intelligence officer from 1967 to 1969, later stated that MACV J-2 had simply assumed enemy forces in South Vietnam had enough supplies to support their current levels of operation.[28] This focus on NVA/VC combat units to the comparative exclusion of enemy logistics was a flaw in Westmoreland's strategy of attrition that in part explains MACV's difficulties between 1965 and 1968.

Abrams's tactical change in focus, away from enemy combat units to instead targeting their logistical support, altered MACV intelligence's focus as well. Although MACV had run agents and deployed reconnaissance teams inside Cambodia for years, these efforts had been limited at best.

Most of Abrams's intelligence on communist operations across the border came from MACV's Studies and Observation Group (MACV-SOG), a top secret special operations unit that directed covert actions throughout Indochina. SOG had been active in Laos since 1966. There, its teams watched heavily laden NVA trucks head south on Laotian highways and cross into Cambodia. Additionally, SOG knew, NVA agents bought rice in Cambodia: 55,000 tons annually from Sihanouk, and another 100,000 tons directly from Cambodian farmers. This food was moved to the Vietnamese border without U.S. interference; its purchase inside Cambodia freed up the equivalent of more than 60,000 truckloads of cargo each year that Hanoi could use for other purposes.

SOG could only watch and report, and that from outside Cambodia until 1967. Sihanouk had closed the U.S. embassy in Phnom Penh in May 1965 to hobble the CIA and other U.S. intelligence efforts; Johnson and McNamara refused to permit covert American intelligence operations inside Cambodia until summer 1967.[29]

Once authorized, SOG teams operated within Cambodia under a program first named DANIEL BOONE and then SALEM HOUSE. Twelve-man teams crossed the border and gathered information inside NVA-controlled areas. Most SOG missions within Cambodia took place in the northeast part of the country, watching the Ho Chi Minh Trail. This was prudent, since the greater density of Cambodian civilians made operations near the NVA/VC border base areas across from III CTZ and IV CTZ (the Mekong Delta, just south of III CTZ) very risky.[30] Further, Hanoi's troops were infiltrating from the north, and not via Sihanoukville. Counting them required human observation by SOG.

The SOG units were a mixed bag. Most Americans came from veterans of the Army Special Forces and were trained to operate alone or in small units far behind enemy lines. Many Vietnamese were either Chieu Hois, ex-communists who had surrendered and now worked against their former comrades, or ARVN troops dressed in NVA uniforms. Other SOG teams included Cambodians disguised as Khmer Rouge. SOG could field about twenty ARVN-led teams for SALEM HOUSE inside Cambodia itself and almost thirty U.S.-led teams for missions inside South Vietnam along the Cambodian border.[31]

SOG's efforts meant there were often friendly eyes reporting from within or near Cambodia, trained scouts who could see what was happening under the triple-canopy vegetation that so hindered air reconnaissance. However, each report was a single snapshot of one place at one time; it took many such reports, collated with and cross-checked against other material, to make sense of what was happening along the border. By the end of 1968, though, there were enough reports and records to provide adequate and accurate understanding.

Abrams thought very highly of the intelligence he received from SALEM HOUSE. As he told McCain and Wheeler in a message on 1 September 1969, the program was "the only surface reconnaissance capability in Cambodia available to [MACV]. . . . I consider the continuation of SALEM HOUSE operations essential to support the operations of this command as long as VC/NVA forces are present in Cambodia." Abrams credited MENU's success to intelligence provided by the teams on the ground, adding that 70 percent of MENU poststrike assessments came from SALEM HOUSE pilots flying low and taking pictures with handheld cameras.[32] Many of the bombers' targets had come from SOG as well: all the major Cambodian sanctuaries had been located, MACV concealing the origins of this information by calling the source a "friendly guerilla unit."[33]

SOG's teams, though in Cambodia on reconnaissance missions, had a combat effect disproportionate to their tiny numbers. By preference, SOG teams would remain undetected throughout their cross-border missions. However, when spotted and pursued, they would try to break contact by calling in air strikes to permit their safe extraction. SOG's estimated kill ratio was 108:1 in 1968, 93:1 for the first two months of 1969, and 153:1 for 1970. In comparison, conventional U.S. infantry units in Vietnam averaged around 15:1.[34] Such communist losses were an added, if unintended, benefit to the intelligence the teams collected.

Complementing SOG's "black" efforts were more conventional programs. A U.S. Army Vietnam unit, the 525th Military Intelligence Group, ran Cambodian and Vietnamese agents and spies inside Cambodia; one program, BLACK-BEARD, had been watching the sanctuaries since 1966.[35] The U.S. Air Force's FRENCH LEAVE consisted of covert air force photographic reconnaissance overflights of Cambodia from 1967 through 1970. Both programs supplemented the picture provided by SOG.

Merging all the available intelligence, MACV J-2 estimated NVA stockpiles along the border as large as 20–30 thousand weapons, 10–15 million rounds of ammunition, 5–10 thousand tons of rice, thousands of gallons of [petroleum, oil, and lubricants], 5–10 hospitals and assorted medical supplies."[36] Such quantities were tempting targets for MACV planners, particularly after the logistics strategy had begun crippling communist supply lines within South Vietnam. As the populated interior grew safer for civilians from mid-1968 on, ARVN and allied troops steadily shifted operations westward toward the Cambodian and Laotian borders.

In late 1969 COSVN and B-2 Front leaders grew concerned about increased allied activities along the Vietnamese-Cambodian border, worries compounded by their heavy losses when NVA or VC troops fought SOG teams. A communist document captured in early February 1970 near Katum warned of U.S. Special Forces infiltrating into the border area and of allied aircraft dropping sound detection devices.[37] Compiling sensor and SOG/Special Forces reports over several days could indicate patterns of communist activity and the size of units in given areas; U.S. troops could then use this information to ambush enemy supply columns. Such attacks might be with mines or gunfire but could also involve calling in air strikes by jets or helicopter gunships.

By spring 1970, MACV's analysts had a fairly good idea of what was in the sanctuaries, if not the precise cache locations. At the end of April, a few days before the U.S. incursion, MACV's intelligence staff gave the Field Force and division headquarters the base areas' general boundaries and the major units and types of supplies within each. However, this was long before the days of satellite-provided capabilities like the Global Positioning System (GPS) and tactical satellite communications links, when reconnaissance teams were doing well if they could locate themselves in the forests and jungles within half a mile of their true position. They generally did not have the detailed information infantry units would want for their own tactical planning, such as photographs or stockpile locations within a hundred meters: to get such information would require the teams to actually prowl through the base areas themselves, an invitation for disaster. In the actual event the ground troops had to occupy the sanctuaries and find individual stockpiles and caches by searches on foot through the forests.

———————

MACV planners also had to consider the weather. Southeast Asia experiences two monsoons each year, one from the southwest beginning in April or May, the other from the northeast around the end of November. Afternoon thunderstorms were increasing in April as the spring monsoon approached. MACV felt that by early June the weather would make military operations far more difficult, especially for aviation, motorized, and armored U.S. and ARVN units.

Rainfall in particular would cause major problems. In III CTZ during a monsoon week it ranged between three and twelve inches, with six to eight inches being typical along the border and in Cambodia. However, one spot got more than five inches in a single thunderstorm.[38] Such downpours made flying nearly impossible and quickly turned small creeks into unfordable torrents. The ground became too soft to support trucks and tracked vehicles moving across country, thus limiting them to main roads. Without the firepower carried by the jets, helicopters, tanks, and armored personnel carriers, allied infantrymen would face NVA and VC troops more on the latter's terms, at much higher risk to friendly lives.

MACV realized the weather limited Hanoi's options as well. Should the U.S. and ARVN forces destroy the sanctuaries before the spring monsoon began, Hanoi would have to wait several months before starting to rebuild its forward stockpiles. The fall monsoon would impose another delay, cumulatively leading to perhaps six to nine months for Vietnamization to proceed unhindered; it might well be as late as 1972 before the B-2 Front was again a threat to III CTZ, some thought. Thus, the success of any incursion depended on acting promptly: such a confluence of base area vulnerability, comparative allied strength, weather, and U.S. administration predisposition would almost certainly never again appear.

———————

In Washington the debate over what to do about Cambodia had deeply divided Nixon's cabinet.[39] Discussions following the 18 March coup had been inconclusive, but a meeting on 22 April finally brought matters to a head. Lon Nol faced disaster as three NVA/VC divisions moved on Phnom Penh from the east; from Saigon, Abrams and Ambassador Bunker recommended shallow incursions into Cambodia to overrun the base areas. A decision at last seemed unavoidable. Some secretaries favored taking no action; others, attacking either the Fishhook or the Parrot's Beak but not both; there was also support for using ARVN troops but not Americans.

After a long and inconclusive debate, Vice President Spiro Agnew framed the issue in blunt terms. As Kissinger later noted, "Either the sanctuaries were a danger or they were not. If it was worth cleaning them out, [Agnew] did not understand all the pussyfooting about the American role or what we accomplished by attacking only one. Our task was to make Vietnamization succeed."[40] Despite Agnew's pithy summation and his recommendation to attack both base areas and use U.S. forces, Nixon did not make a clear-cut decision, and the meeting broke up.

Late on Sunday, 26 April, though, Nixon finally chose to "go for broke" by destroying the sanctuaries in the Parrot's Beak and the Fishhook.[41] On Monday morning, 27 April (late Monday night in Saigon), he ordered Abrams to do so.[42] Diplomacy and MENU's bombs had not stopped Hanoi's use of the Cambodian border zone, so America would remove by ground action the threat posed by the base areas.

4

ARVN's Opening Attack and Final U.S. Planning

As MACV stepped up planning during the first months of 1970, the units that would eventually execute its orders were busy with pacification efforts and compensating for the ongoing U.S. troop departures. Years earlier Saigon had for military purposes divided the country into four Corps Tactical Zones (CTZs), numbered from I in the northern provinces to IV in the Mekong Delta; an ARVN lieutenant general commanded all RVNAF units in each zone. A corps-sized U.S. force was colocated with the first three ARVN corps: the First Marine Expeditionary Force (IMEF) in the north, IFFV with II Corps, IIFFV alongside III Corps, and the division-sized Delta Military Assistance Command (DMAC) in the Mekong Delta with IV Corps. Each American headquarters concurrently directed U.S. combat operations in its CTZ and advised its South Vietnamese counterpart.

Of the four CTZs, arguably the most sensitive in 1970 was III CTZ, comprising the ten provinces around Saigon (but excluding the capital itself; see map 4). Also stationed in III CTZ was the U.S. Army's IIFFV, which directed the main American effort in the Cambodian incursion. Although from 1965 to 1969 IIFFV had concentrated on the combat operations of its subordinate American units, by 1970 the policy of Vietnamization meant that helping III Corps' development was at least as important as its own tactical actions.

The two corps had different sectors within III CTZ in early 1970, IIFFV generally guarding the borders against forays from Cambodia, and III Corps securing the less threatened interior. With U.S. troop withdrawals starting in 1969, senior American leaders knew that the RVNAF needed to significantly improve its combat performance before the United States left, and quickly. Communist forces had lost heavily in the 1968 Tet and subsequent offensives, and during 1969 they lacked the power to launch major attacks of that scale. No one doubted, though, that Hanoi would resume its attacks as soon as it was capable of doing so. RVNAF and U.S. units thus had a window of strategic opportunity in 1970 to emphasize

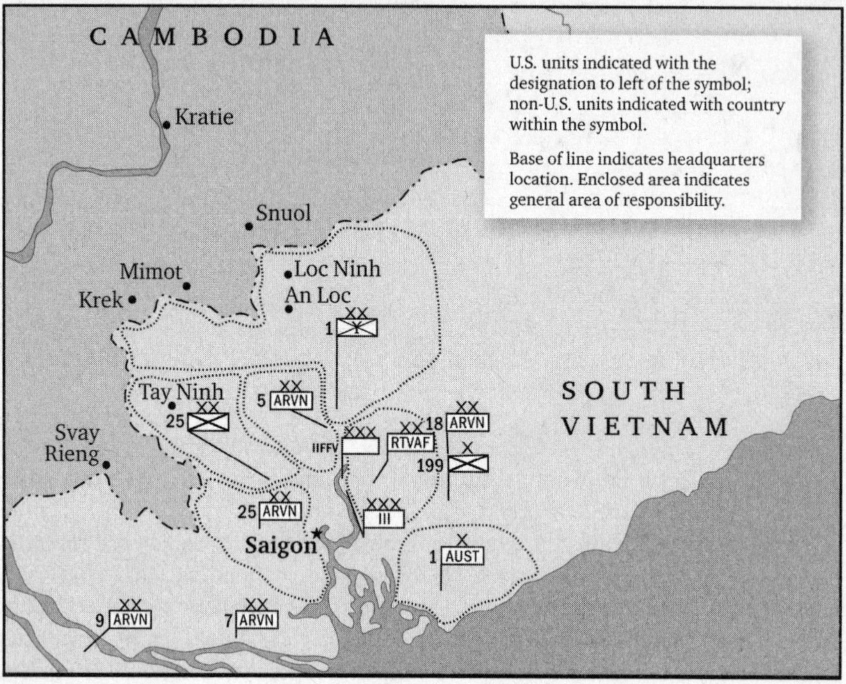

Map 4. ARVN and IIFFV Deployments in III CTZ and Northeast IV CTZ as of 31 May 1970

pacification and small-unit operations. However, Lon Nol's March coup, III Corps' mid-April cross-border raids, and Abrams's order to begin planning an attack on the Fishhook led to developments few would have predicted at the end of 1969.

IIFFV was MACV's most powerful ground unit in early 1970, but its strength was waning from the ongoing troop withdrawals. Headquartered about twenty-five kilometers northeast of Saigon, near Long Binh and the headquarters of III Corps, it was just seven kilometers northwest of Bien Hoa, the sprawling headquarters of the U.S. Army, Vietnam, and the U.S. Air Force's primary tactical air base in the southern half of the country. These short distances helped commanders and staffs from the various units meet regularly to coordinate their plans and operations.

Besides ongoing troop withdrawals, a second factor affecting IIFFV's preparations for the Cambodian incursion was its changing commanders on 15 April. Lieutenant General Julian Ewell, an aggressive infantryman who had previously commanded the Ninth Infantry Division in the Mekong Delta, had begun implementing Abrams's logistic strategy during late 1969 and early 1970. His successor, Lieutenant General Michael S. Davison, was a career armor officer who years before had commanded a tank brigade in Abrams's division and knew him well from their service together in Europe during World War II. Davison arrived at IIFFV from the Pacific Command staff in Honolulu; just two weeks after he assumed command of IIFFV, Abrams ordered him to attack into Cambodia. As Davison later recalled, "I had absolutely no idea how damn busy I was going to be after I got here."[1]

IIFFV had several major units spread across the III CTZ. The best known was the First Cavalry Division, which guarded the northern part of III CTZ with nine light infantry, five artillery, and three helicopter battalions. The Twenty-fifth Infantry Division was responsible for the western and southern parts of III CTZ. Centered in Cu Chi, it had eleven light and mechanized infantry, the latter in armored personnel carriers (APCs), one tank, and four artillery battalions. Each division had several additional battalions and separate companies, for signal, maintenance, supply, and other specialized functions. IIFFV Artillery, its headquarters adjacent to Davison's, had its seven battalions of medium and heavy guns spread across III CTZ to support various tank and infantry units. It also had a battalion of self-propelled air defense weapons (twin 40mm rapid-firing cannon and quadruple-mount .50-caliber heavy machine guns), which it most often used in escorting convoys to help the truckers fight their way out of ambushes.

IIFFV also commanded several independent brigade-sized combat units. The Eleventh Armored Cavalry Regiment (11ACR) was the most powerful tank force in Indochina. It had three squadrons of M48-series tanks and Armored Cavalry Assault Vehicles (ACAVs)[2] and in early 1970 operated most often in northern War Zone C with the First Cavalry Division. The Ninth Infantry Division's Third Brigade remained after the rest of the division had returned to the United States. Centered in Long An Province in the southwest corner of III CTZ, it consisted of one artillery and three infantry battalions and normally received its missions from the Twenty-fifth Infantry Division's commanding general. The Twelfth Combat Aviation Group at Long Binh, which included eighteen helicopter companies and two air cavalry troops, worked closely with the First Cavalry Division. Its mobility and lift capability were vital to the incursion's success. Finally, the 199th Light Infantry Brigade had four infantry battalions in Long Khanh Province, about fifty kilometers east of Saigon, but it played no direct role in the incursion. Davison had at his disposal within IIFFV tremendous combat power: twenty-eight U.S. infantry battalions, seventeen of cannon, four of armor, about nine of helicopters, and thousands of support soldiers.

Three unique assets helped IIFFV secure its rear areas in III CTZ when it crossed into Cambodia. Company A, Fifth Special Forces Group, advised and trained South Vietnamese Regional Forces and Popular Forces (RF/PF) across III CTZ. A defensively minded Royal Thai Army division was about twenty kilometers east of Saigon with seven infantry and three artillery battalions; its presence in a relatively quiet area permitted ARVN and U.S. forces to be used elsewhere, in more threatened sectors. Finally, a brigade-sized task force from Australia and New Zealand worked in and around Phuoc Tuy Province in south-central III CTZ, along the coast east of Saigon. A dependable unit that had quickly earned the Americans' respect upon its arrival in 1965, its six infantry battalions had the fire support of one of artillery,[3] boosting to about seventy-five the total number of non-ARVN combat battalions Davison commanded.

ARVN's III Corps was less powerful but nonetheless possessed significant combat elements. Its units included most of the ARVN Airborne Division, as well as the ARVN Fifth, Eighteenth, and Twenty-fifth Infantry Divisions. IV Corps, in the Mekong Delta, controlled the ARVN Seventh, Ninth, and Twenty-first Divisions. Although ARVN's divisions were not as heavily armed or armored as comparable American units, both corps routinely received American support, particularly in regard to firepower and helicopter lift. Leadership at the division and regimental levels varied considerably across units but generally improved during 1969 and 1970. These gains were more apparent at the regimental than the divisional level, though: political connections and personal loyalty to the president of South Vietnam had long been a prerequisite for divisional command, to the detriment of ARVN's combat effectiveness. However, surprisingly respectable performances against the VC during and after TET 1968 had begun to build ARVN's confidence in its own fighting abilities. Operations during 1969 had further improved morale and effectiveness.

There were, nonetheless, some serious shortcomings that raised doubts about the likely success of Vietnamization. The Seventh Division was marginal at best, its potential hindered by its lack of control over its own units: in summer 1969, five of its twelve infantry battalions took their orders from provincial chiefs rather than the division commander.[4] Things were little better with the ARVN Twenty-fifth Infantry Division, which improved under its new commanding general "but was still a mediocre division even by South Vietnamese standards."[5]

Probably the worst of the lot during the late 1960s was the ARVN Fifth Division. In 1968 South Vietnamese intelligence had assessed ARVN combat action records. Its evaluation of the Fifth's performance was brutal:

> Out of almost 2,000 combat operations supposedly conducted by one of the 5th Division's regiments that year, only 36 had led to engagements with enemy forces, and these resulted in only 17 enemy reportedly killed and 5 captured, at a cost of 14 killed and 3 weapons lost.[6]

President Thieu finally took action, appointing Major General Nguyen Van Hieu as the Fifth's commanding general in August 1969. Developing a closer working relationship with his new counterpart at the U.S. First Infantry Division, Major General Albert Milloy, Hieu rapidly set about improving his division, emphasizing offensive actions over defensive postures.[7] This was clearly a step in the right direction as far as the Fifth Division was concerned, but it was not matched by comparable decisiveness in other low-performing divisions. The time squandered was irreplaceable; further, Vietnamization's long-term prospects rested heavily on assumptions that ARVN would be able to defend South Vietnam before Hanoi could successfully attack once more.

In comparison to its ARVN and U.S. opponents, the B-2 Front had fewer and much less well-equipped forces (figure 2). Its major regular units in III CTZ and the Cambodian border area included the Fifth Viet Cong, Seventh NVA, and Ninth Viet Cong Divisions, the Sixteenth Armor Office (despite its misleading name, commanding three battalions of sappers), the Sixty-sixth Base Section (a regiment of two battalions to guard the sanctuaries), and the Sixty-ninth Artillery Division (two rocket regiments and an antiaircraft machine gun battalion). However, B-2's units were at far lower strengths than authorized, ranging from 50 down to about 10 percent.[8] In early 1970, B-2 deployed the Ninth VC Division against Tay Ninh Province and War Zone C, the Seventh NVA Division in the Fishhook and along the Cambodian–Binh Long Province border, and the Fifth VC Division on the boundary inside South Vietnam between the II and III CTZs.

COSVN's hopes for 1970 centered on Campaign X, which sought to undermine pacification and cause "increased political pressures for a US withdrawal from the war . . . hopefully with violent and uninterrupted attacks as extensive and intense as those of the 1968 Tet Offensive."[9] To do this, following a series of local attacks across III CTZ the B-2 Front would move its Fifth VC Division to the northeast and the Ninth VC Division to the northwest of Saigon; the two division would then launch a coordinated attack on the capital.

Given the vast disparity in power between the opposing forces in spring 1970, this concept was unrealistic. The allied capture around 1 February of a large communist munitions cache in War Zone D, about thirty kilometers north-northeast of Saigon, cost the B-2 Front about 1,000 weapons and 200 tons of ammunition.[10] This loss derailed Campaign X before it ever seriously started, the outbreak of fighting in eastern Cambodia and III Corps' fleeting mid-April incursion making the plan even more impossible to execute.[11] It was probably fortunate for Hanoi that its two divisions never tried to attack Saigon: they would have lost thousands of troops, and the open defeat would have incurred additional political costs.

Lon Nol's coup led the B-2 Front to shift its forces to better secure the border base areas and then reverse directions to attack west toward Phnom Penh. Most of the Ninth VC Division moved west and south, while the Seventh NVA Division spread itself thinner to cover the area the Ninth VC had left. MACV's radio monitoring units followed these major redeployments along and west away from the border. At the same time the B-2 Front's divisions attacked Lon Nol, it also tried to continue low-level guerrilla operations inside South Vietnam.[12]

Communist attacks against military targets in South Vietnam increased during the week of 21 March 1970 in Campaign X's opening phase, in large part to

Figure 2. Main Force Units against III CTZ, Spring 1970

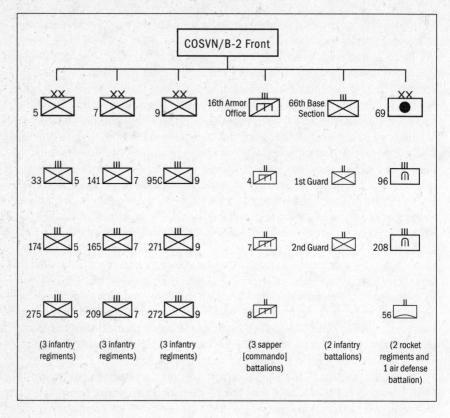

reopen COSVN's supply routes toward Saigon across Tay Ninh, Binh Long, and Phuoc Long Provinces.[13] To achieve this goal, NVA and VC forces made fifty-six attacks throughout III CTZ during the night of 31 March–1 April, including ground assaults against U.S. and ARVN positions and heavy attacks by fire.[14] At the same time, terrorist incidents declined significantly, with weekly totals between 12 April and 9 May falling steadily from ninety-eight to forty.[15] This pattern of activity continued throughout April.

Campaign X's pressure was supposed to steadily increase, peaking during the first half of May.[16] However, in the various III CTZ sectors around Saigon, particularly those along the border, attacks by fire rose from eighteen during the week of 13–19 April to thirty-one the following week, then fell to fifteen the next.[17] Davison's intelligence analysts had predicted these bursts of activity but correctly doubted they would last more than a few days.[18]

In the event, COSVN and its military leaders paid a high price in blood. To attack "harder" military targets with NVA and VC companies, battalions, and regiments rather than "softer" civilian targets with squads and platoons, the communists massed their forces to form far fewer, but much stronger, units. This helped pacification in two main ways. First, it reduced terrorist activity in many areas; second, the bigger groups were easier to spot, target, and kill with massed U.S. and ARVN firepower.

Communist forces suffered heavily in III CTZ during Campaign X. In the six days ending 25 April they lost 567 killed, 46 captured, and 73 defectors to the Hoi Chanh program. Material losses included 249 individual weapons, eighteen machine guns, mortars, and rocket launchers, and almost four tons of rice.[19] On the eve of the allied attack into Cambodia, the B-2 Front's main forces were in no condition to resist effectively, even had the COSVN and B-2 Front senior leadership wanted to fight instead of preserve their soldiers' lives for future battles.

The departure of forces during 1969 and early 1970 was increasingly affecting subordinate commands throughout MACV. IIFFV had gained significantly in late 1968 when Abrams shifted the First Cavalry Division from I CTZ south to III CTZ, to reinforce the western approaches to Saigon against the growing threat from the Cambodian border region. While other divisions had a few dozen helicopters each, the First Cavalry Division's hundreds let it shift its forces to achieve numerical superiority wherever and whenever the commanding general wished. The division quickly made its presence felt, its airmobility combining with frequent attacks on the infiltration routes entering South Vietnam from the sanctuaries.

Working with the "anvil" provided by other units that would establish blocking positions, the First Cavalry Division's airmobility let it rapidly deploy infantrymen, cannon, and helicopter gunships to become the "hammers" that smashed infiltrating communist forces. However, the drawdown of MACV's forces put a premium on any unique capabilities of those remaining units. Helicopter companies and battalions in particular were retained as long as possible, to compensate with mobility for fewer forces on the ground. This applied to the First Cavalry Division, as well as to other divisions' aviation units.

Although IIFFV's troop strength dropped with the loss of the First Infantry Division and various support units, its mission requirements did not. As the First Cavalry Division and the 11ACR continued to attack communist supply routes running south from Cambodia toward Saigon, IIFFV enlarged Major General Harris W. Hollis' Twenty-fifth Infantry Division's zone of responsibility. In response, Hollis shifted units to cover his new sectors. The Twenty-fifth's First Brigade continued operations in Tay Ninh, particularly in the center and western parts of the province. Its Third Brigade focused on the Michelin plantation and the region known to American forces as the Trapezoid, about thirty kilometers east of Tay Ninh City; the fourth brigade, known by its previous name of the Third Brigade, Ninth Infantry Division (Third/Ninth), stayed in Long An. IIFFV took operational control of the Twenty-fifth's Second Brigade and moved it far to the southeast corner of Bien Hoa Province and the western part of Phuoc Tuy Province, near the Australians. Although Second Brigade now worked for IIFFV some thirty kilometers outside of the division's sector, the division still had to support it logistically.[20] The Twenty-fifth Infantry Division thus covered about 150 kilometers from northwest to southeast. Such dispersion was possible only in the absence of any major NVA or VC threat and because of the RVNAF's slow but steady improvement.

It was fortunate that the enemy threat was less than in previous years: not only were total U.S. numbers starting to decrease, but the overall quality of individual U.S. soldiers had declined since 1965. By 1970 the U.S. Army was showing the effects of President Johnson's refusal to activate the reserves and mobilize the country for war. Dismay at having to serve repeated tours in Vietnam had led many career soldiers to leave the army, reducing small-unit performance. In infantry units, especially, disabling casualties suffered during multiple combat tours had steadily reduced the number of experienced officers and veteran senior noncommissioned officers (NCOs) available for service in Vietnam.

In average U.S. infantry companies in Vietnam in 1970, only 3 men of an authorized strength of about 160 had more than two years' total service. These were generally the company commander, the first sergeant, and either a platoon sergeant or the lieutenant serving as executive officer (if the company was fortunate enough to have its four authorized lieutenants).[21] The platoon sergeants and squad leaders in 1965 were career NCOs, who largely taught their new second lieutenant platoon leaders. By 1970 these men were dead, crippled, or otherwise gone, their places filled by the best of the privates who had gone to an "instant NCO" school to meet the insatiable need for sergeants in Vietnam. However motivated they might be, these new NCOs were as green as their platoon leaders.

Because of this lack of experience, the overall skill and ability of most rifle companies in 1970 were lower than before 1965. For example, on 2 March 1970 Major General Hollis told his division that it was getting sloppy. Its 18:1 kill ratio for February, of enemy to friendly combat deaths, was much lower than its monthly average of 45:1 from September through January. Hollis attributed this drop-off to units ignoring the basics of small-unit infantry tactics. They were becoming predictable, sleeping on ambushes, and bunching up during movements; too few company commanders went on night patrols and ambushes. As Hollis reminded his men, they needed to deal with the current enemy remnants "before he [the enemy] has the opportunity to lay out the carpet for the spring class of NVA infiltrators due to arrive about April."[22]

Troops did their duty, but their doubts that the war would end soon and the knowledge that they would leave Vietnam within a year made some soldiers less willing to risk themselves by aggressive action. Fortunately, firefights during the Cambodian incursion generally did not escalate to heavy combat, and U.S. troops instantly realized that the more enemy stockpiles they captured, the harder it would be for the NVA or VC to attack them later in Vietnam. Commanders thus had few problems motivating their men to seize sanctuaries, even though it was a different scale of operation than most units had been involved with over the previous years.

From 1965 on, the chief form of U.S. activity in III CTZ had been short-range company and platoon patrols against small VC or NVA forces, with bigger U.S. units held in reserve to "pile on" when someone made contact. Combat units became accustomed to such routines, and support units tailored their operations accordingly. However, in the last days of April and the opening days of May the scope of action shifted abruptly to brigade- and division-level attacks into Cambodia with little planning and even less logistical preparation. Light enemy resistance, units' ability to improvise at short notice, a huge and flexible logistics system behind them, and solid leadership got the allied efforts off to a good start. All things considered, IIFFV and III Corps did a good job of throwing together the incursions into the most dangerous border sanctuaries.

As part of the Vietnamization program and the concurrent U.S. withdrawal, ARVN became increasingly responsible for the security of III CTZ. During the first years of America's overt involvement, U.S. combat units felt it necessary to safeguard their ARVN counterparts' zones as well as their own. Partly as a result of the U.S. pullout, and partly a demonstration of American confidence in its developing competence, when MACV relieved the departing U.S. First Infantry Division of its tactical duties on 19 March 1970, Hieu's Fifth Division assumed most of its sector,[23] as well as part of the First Cavalry Division's.

Hieu was pessimistic to a senior ARVN general regarding the likely success of Vietnamization, though, noting that his three regiments would now have to cover the same area previously guarded by three divisions.[24] A squadron of the 11ACR was on call to provide it extra combat power, but no American unit stood behind the Fifth Division to shield Saigon. As Bunker observed to Nixon in late March, "How well the 5th Division handles this will be an important test of Vietnamization."[25] Two regiments of the ARVN Twenty-fifth Division and two brigades of the ARVN Airborne Division likewise expanded their own zones to cover the remainder of the First Infantry Division's former area.[26]

Despite years of the U.S. advisory effort and receiving millions of dollars' worth of equipment, ARVN had serious problems that weakened its overall combat effectiveness. One such was economic. As Ambassador Bunker noted to Nixon in late March 1970, "Low pay, poor housing and care for dependents, and corruption in many parts of the officer corps and widespread pilfering by ARVN forces were already part of the picture before the cost of living increases" which started in October 1969.[27] Soldiers whose families were in need found it hard to concentrate on their military duties, a problem the RVNAF never completely solved before Hanoi's 1975 victory.

A second factor behind ARVN's shakiness was the relative inexperience of many commanders and staffs. On 2 May 1970, Major General Nguyen Viet Thanh, the IV Corps commanding general, died in a midair collision with an American helicopter above Cambodia; he was thirty-nine and had been in the job since August 1968. Before that, Thanh had been the Seventh Infantry Division's commanding general. His successor, Major General Ngo Quaong Truong, and his III Corps counterpart, Lieutenant General Do Cao Tri, had roughly comparable careers to Thanh's. Though all three were dynamic and tactically aggressive, their promotions had come so quickly that they had been shortchanged in their formal professional military education and staff time at higher levels. In consequence, ARVN generals were on average administratively weaker than their American counterparts, who usually had ten to fifteen more years of experience before taking command of comparably sized formations. Mobile large-scale combat operations such as those in Cambodia thus offered valuable training opportunities for senior commanders and staffs at brigade and higher levels.

Similar inexperience was present in the field grade and senior NCO ranks. In 1969, almost half of ARVN's infantry battalion commanders (normally a job for lieutenant colonels) were captains. Major efforts to fill the vacant slots by promotion raised the fill rate to only 63 percent, due to force expansion creating additional spaces in brand-new battalions. The immediate demands of war meant many of ARVN's officers and NCOs were rarely fully trained in their new duties before assuming them, further hurting unit effectiveness as they learned by trial and error.[28]

To help get Vietnamization off to a good start, Lieutenant Generals Ewell of IIFFV and Tri of III Corps established in III CTZ the Dong Tien program, pairing an American unit with an ARVN counterpart. This mentoring initiative, which supplemented the existing U.S. advisory effort, soon began delivering solid returns, particularly with ARVN infantry, artillery, and RF/PF battalions. However, progress was less impressive at higher levels, where all too often too many division and regimental commanders paid too little attention to the key functions of command and control, intelligence, logistics, and fire support because they accurately assumed that the Americans would "take care" of those matters.[29]

––––––––––

MACV and IIFFV hoped greater responsibilities would encourage ARVN to improve its skills at conducting military operations. IIFFV's Lieutenant General Mike Davison later observed, "Over the years, the ARVN forces had developed into a sound organization. What was needed was confidence in their own ability to operate independently of US forces."[30] Most units were slowly getting better, but by 1970 only the ARVN Airborne Division, paired with the First Cavalry Division and respected by U.S. officers for its fighting skills, had "border" duties adjacent to Cambodia.[31] Elsewhere in III CTZ, U.S. units guarded those provinces nearest Cambodia, leaving the interior for ARVN, the RF/PF, and the National Police.

   This deployment resulted from two key considerations. First, Saigon and the surrounding region were too important to take chances with, or let infiltrators get close to; the Cambodian sanctuaries were too near. Second, senior U.S. commanders felt the safety of U.S. troops and bases was more certain if they could block the NVA and VC at the borders. Still, ARVN's morale and competence were steadily improving, and ARVN's officers and men knew they were a better fighting force relative to their enemy than they had been a year earlier.[32]

As senior adviser to ARVN's III Corps and the IIFFV commanding general, Davison worked closely with Tri. Even as Davison assumed command, Tri was raiding the Angel's Wing on 14–17 April in Operation TOAN THANG 41 on the orders of President Thieu and was planning a bigger attack, TOAN THANG 42, for late April.

   Fighting spread steadily along the border as ARVN seized opportunities presented by the NVA being engaged in attacking FANK. IV Corps launched Operation CUU LONG/SD9/06, a raid by the Ninth Division against Base Area 709, just west of the Crow's Nest from 20 to 23 April. It netted 187 enemy dead against 24 ARVN plus 111 wounded and captured more than 1,000 weapons and large stocks of ammunition. Thirty sorties by U.S. CH-47 medium-lift helicopters were not enough to evacuate the material, so ARVN blew up the remaining ammunition in place. Five days later, from 28 to 30 April, territorial forces under the command of the Kien Tuong Province chief crossed three kilometers into Cambodia and hit the Crow's Nest, killing 43 enemy troops while losing 2.[33] These actions were of limited tactical value, pinpricks more than serious threats to COSVN's long-term plans.

Although precluded by U.S. policy from crossing the border themselves, the Americans were very interested in ARVN's activities in Cambodia, both for what ARVN discovered and as a test of Vietnamization's progress to date. IIFFV tracked III Corps' progress in a special room in its operations center set up specifically for the purpose; duty officers passed III Corps' reports and messages on to MACV.[34]

   Davison was pleased with Tri's achievements and hoped his late-April attack would make South Vietnam safer. He generally provided Tri with what the latter requested, such as spare parts or support in areas where ARVN was weak (such as fire support or helicopters), but such aid increased the strain on those same units once IIFFV launched its own incursions into Cambodia. That those supporting units were able to work for both corps simultaneously was only because of the vast capability of the U.S. Army's logistics system within Vietnam by 1970 and because the NVA did not seriously resist the initial assaults.

   Where ARVN's March and April cross-border operations in Cambodia had been brief raids, III Corps' attack at the end of April, TOAN THANG 42, was a

Map 5. TOAN THANG 42's Initial Phase, 29 April–5 May

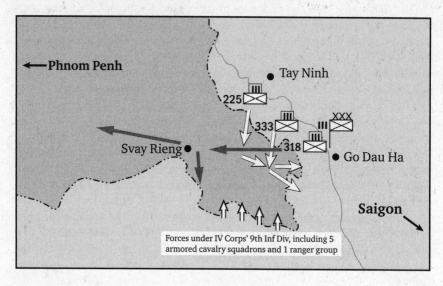

Forces under IV Corps' 9th Inf Div, including 5
armored cavalry squadrons and 1 ranger group

major undertaking (see map 5). Saigon felt it needed to act soon, before the B-2
Front could evacuate more supplies and documents from the sanctuaries. III Corps
would overrun the Parrot's Beak and Angel's Wing to destroy Base Areas 367 and
706 (the latter damaged two weeks earlier in TOAN THANG 41), then drive west
toward Phnom Penh to rescue Vietnamese refugees trapped by the Cambodian-
NVA fighting and help the FANK units fighting the NVA/VC forces in eastern
Cambodia. Success would enhance ARVN's morale and self-confidence in its
ability to fight on its own, demonstrating the progress of Vietnamization. Further,
capturing the two sanctuaries would remove a major communist presence just
fifty kilometers west of Saigon.[35]

Since contact with the NVA was likely, and the previous operation had forfeited strategic surprise, participating III Corps units would be more numerous and
stronger than those in TOAN THANG 41. Tri informed Brigadier General Dennis
McAuliffe, the U.S. deputy senior adviser to III Corps, of the pending attack and
requested a brigade-sized U.S. blocking force move to the border to block any
communist forces seeking to escape into South Vietnam.[36] McAuliffe passed up
Tri's request to Davison, who obliged; Abrams forwarded details to McCain and
Wheeler a day later.[37] McAuliffe respected the III Corps staff's competence, noting that their operational plan was a "thorough and professional document."[38]

Mobility was a key to launching a successful attack, but III Corps first had to
cross the Vam Co Dong River, located inside South Vietnam about thirteen kilometers west of Tay Ninh City and a bit less than that east of the border. On the
evening of 22 April, McAuliffe's engineer adviser learned of the planned attack

and of Tri's urgent requirement for a floating bridge across the river at Ben Soi. The two northernmost task forces needed it to get in position to attack on the twenty-ninth. Although Ben Soi had a ferry, it was too small to carry ARVN armor or the heavy logistical traffic following the tanks and APCs. Accordingly, the Twentieth Engineer Brigade loaned III Corps' engineers bridging equipment to span the river, the various components reaching Ben Soi between the morning of 24 April and midafternoon the next day.[39] This gave III Corps engineers enough time to build the bridge, their task forces crossing stealthily and achieving surprise when they finally struck into Cambodia.

Luck was with Davison and Tri regarding bridge availability. When Tri had asked for bridging gear on 22 April, Davison's staff concurred, expecting no U.S. need for it. By late on 24 April, Davison had a warning order from Abrams to start planning an attack of his own, but he envisioned only the First Cavalry Division and the 11ACR entering northward into Cambodia. IIFFV had enough mobile and floating bridge sets for its own needs, but not for III Corps' as well. Major problems could have arisen had the NVA/VC blown bridges and other U.S. forces such as the Twenty-fifth Infantry Division and the numerous IIFFV support units been moving at the same time. This did not occur until early May, so IIFFV was able to provide for itself and Tri.

III Corps commanders wanted every tank and armored personnel carrier running for the attack on 29 April. A U.S.-ARVN maintenance team spent 27 April visiting five ARVN armored cavalry regiments to identify broken vehicles and necessary repairs. Supply teams at Long Binh Depot worked through the night to have the needed parts ready for pickup at daybreak on the twenty-eighth. ARVN mechanics and twenty-two men from the U.S. 185th Maintenance Battalion worked on 27 and 28 April to fix broken combat vehicles, getting seven of the ten light tanks and eight of the eleven armored personnel carriers working in time.[40]

One problem Tri caused Davison was alien to most Americans' experience. He was supposed to attack on 29 April but delayed for a day because his astrologer told him the heavens were not auspicious. "He and the Twenty-fifth ARVN Division [commanding general] dug themselves in and didn't do a damn thing because the stars told them they'd have an exorbitant number of casualties" if they began as planned, McAuliffe explained. Davison "went through the roof," but he could not budge Tri.[41]

The stars, however, smiled on the undertaking. A few hours after Tri's announcement and Davison' explosion, officials in Washington called Abrams, wanting him to hold the attack for twenty-four hours while they attended to last-minute details.[42] Such an eleventh-hour delay would normally have caused problems for military operations by disrupting coordinated schedules, but Tri's obstinacy let Abrams successfully "postpone" the assault. This satisfied both Tri and Washington, neither realizing what Abrams had managed by playing each off against the other. III Corps crossed into Cambodia on 30 April, finding caches but few enemy troops.

III Corps' organization of TOAN THANG 42's attacking units reflected the imperatives of speed and shock. Two of the corps' own armored cavalry regiments, with two ACRs from the Fifth and Twenty-fifth Divisions, an infantry regiment from the Twenty-fifth Division, and four ranger battalions from III Corps' Second Ranger Group, were the "teeth," arranged into three provisional task forces: the 318th, 225th, and 333rd,[43] each led by a handpicked and experienced colonel. Dissatisfied with his divisions' commanders and staffs, Tri commanded the assault personally, bypassing the division headquarters entirely.

Tri's plan called for the three task forces to attack south and west to overrun the Angel's Wing (Base Area 706); subsequent actions would seize the Parrot's Beak (Base Area 367), supported by IV Corps' attack from the south. Meanwhile, Task Force 318 would drive west along Highway 1 toward Svay Rieng to help FANK forces and fleeing Vietnamese refugees.[44] After overrunning the base areas, attention would turn to searching for caches and stockpiles; additional ARVN units would then join the hunt.

Following their seizure of the Angel's Wing and Parrot's Beak, III Corps units pushed west along Highway 1 and spread out across the Cambodian side of the border. Initial fights on 29 and 30 April were intense but short: ARVN suffered 16 killed and 157 wounded while killing 84 NVA/VC.

Problems soon became apparent. Many of the communist troops fought from bunkers, which ARVN's tanks and ACAVs should have quickly destroyed with their heavy weapons. However, the armor frequently lacked aggressiveness, instead holding back while the ranger and infantry battalions charged forward into unbroken defenses. This led on several occasions to the tanks and ACAVs being unable to safely shoot, due to the danger of hitting friendly forces in their backs, and contributed to higher casualties than might otherwise have been the case. ARVN commanders immediately began work on fixing these and similar issues.[45]

Phase II of TOAN THANG 42 brought the participation of IV Corps' Ninth Infantry Division. Attacking into the Parrot's Beak from the south with four tank-infantry task forces, it hit those still-resisting NVA/VC units from the rear; after three days the total count was 1,010 enemy dead and 204 prisoners for 66 ARVN dead and 330 wounded. NVA material losses included more than 1,000 individual and 60 crew-served weapons, plus more than 100 tons of ammunition.[46]

On 7 May, III Corps began Phase III of the operation, Task Force 225 crossing the border west of Tay Ninh and driving north toward Base Area 354 alongside Task Force 318. Their goal was to find enemy supplies in the border sanctuaries, but Thieu's and Vice President Nguyen Ky's visit to Tri's headquarters on 11 May changed things considerably. Ethnic tensions had erupted inside Cambodia, and reports reaching Saigon of ethnic Vietnamese being assaulted or massacred in Phnom Penh had inflamed South Vietnamese attitudes. Sensitive to the public mood, Thieu ordered Tri to redirect his forces to clear Highway 1 west toward Phnom Penh to help the ethnic Vietnamese escape.[47] This attack, Phase IV, opened two days later, on 14 May; three task forces headed west and reached

Kampong Trabeck, where they met a IV Corps force heading up the Mekong. By mid-May the ostensibly "friendly" Cambodian media in Phnom Penh were alleging RVNAF mistreatment of Cambodian civilians and ARVN's stealing their property.[48] As May progressed, the situation slowly but steadily deteriorated throughout eastern Cambodia.

Beginning 23 May, III Corps was active around Kampong Cham, Cambodia's third-largest city. There, the Ninth VC Division threatened 1,000 FANK troops supported by four 105mm light howitzers with only 1,000 shells. Heavy fighting ensued, but by 1 June the Ninth VC had withdrawn as III Corps task forces had approached the city. Over the next ten days ARVN forces pulled back from around Kampong Cham; as they did so, the Ninth Division returned. To drive it away once again, III Corps made a second assault to relieve the city, from 21 to 27 June.[49] Though the second assault was successful in forcing back the NVA, III Corps' eventual departure meant the city ultimately fell into communist hands. Limited numbers of RVNAF forces remained in Cambodia after June, the result of Thieu's 19 June decision to continue cross-border operations unilaterally after U.S. forces had withdrawn to Vietnam.[50]

TOAN THANG 42 supported both the objectives of the South Vietnamese government and Abrams's broad concept of fighting the NVA. During May, III Corps encircled and mauled the 88th NVA Regiment, killing more than 200 enemy soldiers; it also inflicted heavy losses on the 271st NVA Regiment in several engagements. The 272nd NVA Regiment was so weakened it avoided further contact.[51] An NVA lieutenant colonel who surrendered in summer 1970 said that TOAN THANG 42 had spoiled Campaign X as well as COSVN's plans to overthrow Lon Nol and install a communist government in Phnom Penh. Between 30 April and 9 July, III Corps captured an estimated 90 percent of the stored NVA rice in the Angel's Wing and Parrot's Beak and 350 tons of ammunition, and destroyed about half of the NVA's medical supplies and facilities in the region. It also killed or captured some 40 percent of all enemy personnel in those areas (including up to 75 percent of Tay Ninh Province's VC cadre at the headquarters and district levels, political entities roughly analogous to a U.S. state and its counties).[52]

The casualties inflicted on communist political leadership were more significant than COSVN and the B-2 Front's material losses. "The replacement of trained cadres will be more difficult for the enemy than replacement of his loss of supplies," McAuliffe correctly concluded.[53] Hanoi could readily build and fill stockpiles and caches, but the new political cadres it sent south would first have to learn local and regional peculiarities while avoiding detection and capture before they became fully effective. The cadres' problems unintentionally helped Saigon's pacification programs during 1970–1971.

Another result of TOAN THANG 42 was a boost in confidence among the RVNAF. The VNAF flew 166 sorties above ARVN during its first day in the

Parrot's Beak–Angel's Wing area; by the operation's end it had flown more than 1,600 sorties, supported by 310 USAF sorties.[54] ARVN troops performed fairly well during the incursion, their cache discoveries and engagements with fleeing enemies making them more willing to conduct future operations with less American participation or presence.

The various South Vietnamese militia and security elements also won some small victories against the communists within III CTZ. On 14 May northeast of Saigon they captured the VC assassination section chief for Phuoc Long village. Four days later, RF and PF troops found a cache containing mostly small arms and machine gun ammunition just north of the Twenty-fifth Infantry Division's base camp at Cu Chi.[55] Although Viet Cong attacks and ambushes continued at a lower level, for the most part the South Vietnamese kept the region under control. Having reduced threats in their rear areas allowed both American and RVNAF commanders to focus on events to their fronts.

III Corps' senior leadership was painfully aware of the many shortcomings in the overall operation. Most significantly, Tri felt that FANK was of questionable effectiveness, lacking as it did competent and aggressive leadership, combat experience, and almost every type and amount of needed equipment. Further, Tri told a visiting delegation from the National Security Council led by Brigadier General Al Haig, most FANK commanders were unwilling to cooperate or coordinate actions with ARVN. Tri then identified for Haig his key needs: U.S. helicopter support (particularly medical evacuation, gunship, and CH-47 Chinook cargo lift), USAF tactical air support, and the replacement of his old M41-series tanks with more recent M48s.[56] Without these, he said, ARVN would have more difficulty continuing operations in Cambodia.

————————

When the JGS and III Corps had begun planning TOAN THANG 42 in mid-April, American forces did not expect to participate, or if they did, they did not intend to cross the border. This changed following Nixon's decisions of late April. As a result, IIFFV helped III Corps with three assets that it lacked in sufficient quantities: helicopters, artillery fires, and communications.

U.S. helicopters were important to III Corps' successful attacks. Although ARVN moved more than 90 percent of III Corps' supplies, Tri's forces needed Davison's helicopters for short-notice deliveries of fuel and ammunition.[57] ARVN trucks could have driven the cargoes to the requesting units but would have done so through unsecured territory at night. Further, the units needing resupply would be vulnerable to enemy attack until they got more bullets. It was faster and safer to get the ammunition and fuel there by air, and Davison usually had enough lift capacity to oblige.

American artillery continuously supported III Corps by rapidly responding to targets and by coordinating fires with maneuver, both skills being major weaknesses of ARVN's own gunners. To reduce the problems of the latter in the assault on Base Area 706 in the Angel's Wing, a cell from IIFFV Artillery's Twenty-third Artillery Group operated in Tri's forward command post and approved fires supporting III Corps units. Four platoons of U.S. heavy artillery fired in support of the opening attack. As III Corps pushed deeper into Cambodia, two medium (155mm) self-propelled and two heavy (8-inch/175mm) batteries went along as far west as Svay Rieng. When two of the three ARVN task forces turned north along the border near the Dog's Head, a medium and a heavy battery followed, the other two staying with the third task force in the Parrot's Beak.[58] The Twenty-third's liaison cell ensured that U.S. guns were where they were needed and firing where they were wanted, and additionally handled III Corps' calls for U.S. air strikes. Though the cell's help improved the effectiveness of artillery and close air support for Tri's units,[59] ARVN's reliance on U.S. fire support coordination meant it appeared better at such essential skills than it actually was. Unfortunately, this deficiency was a fatal flaw brutally exposed during the RVNAF's failed 1971 incursion into Laos.

III Corps' attack also relied heavily on American communication assets. Tri set up a forward operations center on 28 April at the Go Dau Ha district compound, ten kilometers east of the Angel's Wing.[60] IIFFV's Fifty-third Signal Battalion had less than a day to extend the U.S. communication system from the Twenty-fifth Infantry Division headquarters at Cu Chi twenty-five kilometers northwest along Highway 1 to Go Dau Ha so that Tri and his staff were linked to IIFFV and Saigon.[61] As with most such operations, there were never enough circuits to meet the demand: of the initial twenty-four channels to Cu Chi, III Corps got fifteen and McAuliffe's advisers got nine. However, continuing southeast between Cu Chi and IIFFV headquarters at Long Binh, the U.S. total dropped to seven, hindering their ability to get help for III Corps.[62] Further, Tri and his staff, finding their own fifteen dedicated links insufficient, conducted much of their business on McAuliffe's channels by demanding their U.S. advisers pass their ARVN messages on before their own. Getting information through in the opening days of the attacks was a frustrating business for everyone involved.

The problem worsened when IIFFV launched its own attack on 1 May, causing a large increase in demands for telephone, microwave, and teletype lines. Critical messages from units in combat often bumped or got bumped by reports or requests from U.S. advisers with ARVN units, exacerbating already confused situations. To reduce such problems IIFFV Signal augmented the III Corps advisers' regular equipment with eight small AM radios, light enough to backpack. These radios had much greater range than the standard tactical FM radios, used different frequencies, and were not limited to line-of-sight transmission or reception. They enabled the advisers to keep in contact with IIFFV during the incursion.[63] Like their engineer, helicopter pilot, and artillery brethren, Davison's signal troops ended up supporting Tri and IIFFV simultaneously.

Besides helping his counterpart's operations, Davison had his own corps to run. In the two weeks after becoming IIFFV's commanding general, he toured his major units to meet his subordinate commanders, provided Tri the support necessary for III Corps' success, and launched his own short-notice incursion into the border sanctuaries. It was a hectic but satisfying start to a new job.

Assuming command on 15 April, Davison was stunned when Abrams told him on 24 April to begin planning to attack the Fishhook; he was so new, he later claimed, that he had to peek at a wall map to see where he was to go. Abrams wanted him to be ready to attack with just seventy-two hours' notice and forbade him to tell anyone lower than his division commanders. Davison insisted that he could not move so soon if he could not warn as well his brigade commanders and key division staff officers. Abrams relented, but reduced the response time to forty-eight hours.[64]

Unknown to Davison, secret planning for just such a contingency had begun a month earlier within IIFFV headquarters. Nothing came directly of these plans, but discussions at the time alerted the commanding generals of the First Cavalry and Twenty-fifth Infantry Divisions to their likely directions of advance and got them thinking how they would attack if ordered.

Within IIFFV's headquarters, planning for Cambodia was an extremely sensitive subject, initially involving just two men: Lieutenant General Ewell, the commander, and Major Earl W. Leech, in the Operations staff's Plans section. Leech was IIFFV's contact with MACV and the U.S. Army, Vietnam (USARV), MACV's army component headquarters, for all planning related to the withdrawal of U.S. Army units from Vietnam, an explosive topic during the politically charged days of late 1969 and early 1970. Further, within Vietnam most commanders wanted to retain their own troops as long as possible, preferring the cuts to occur in someone else's unit. A MACV counterpart told Leech that Abrams had directed MACV to appoint and deal only with one officer at each of its major subordinate headquarters because Abrams "didn't want to get in a pissing contest with the corps commanders" over which units were leaving when.[65] Leech thus worked closely with MACV and USARV to determine IIFFV units' departure dates, a matter of great interest to Ewell.

Accordingly, when Abrams told Ewell in March 1970 to draft secret contingency plans for an attack into Cambodia, Leech was Ewell's secure channel to pass his ideas to MACV; given his knowledge of scheduled unit withdrawals, he was more familiar than anyone else in IIFFV with which units would be available to conduct future operations. Ewell told no one else in IIFFV about his Cambodian planning, including Leech's superiors on the Operations staff; instead, to maintain secrecy, he and Leech worked in Ewell's quarters late at night.[66] As the workload became too great for one man to do as an extra duty, Ewell included Lieutenant Colonel Thomas Smith. The three officers determined the IIFFV attacking forces' organization and tentative objectives and came up with a general concept of how the major units would maneuver. Each division would do its own detailed planning, to include logistics.

U.S. withdrawals forced constant adjustments in IIFFV's Cambodian plans to reflect changes in unit availability and departure dates: MACV did not always send units home in the sequence or numbers that IIFFV had expected. Ewell was particularly concerned about losing any of his aviation units, since their mobility and firepower partly compensated for declining U.S. infantry strength.[67] The chaotic situation inside eastern and northern Cambodia caused further problems, particularly knowing where FANK's units were at any time.[68]

Abrams monitored Ewell's progress. Stopping by Long Binh one day in late March or early April, he told Ewell he didn't "'want a damn briefing!'" but got one anyway. At Ewell's command Leech and Smith spread their maps on his office floor and spent a half hour explaining the IIFFV plan; Abrams declared it fine. A few days later Smith and Leech briefed Major Generals Elvy Roberts of the First Cavalry Division and Harris Hollis of the Twenty-fifth Infantry Division, whose units would make the attacks.[69]

The two planners' efforts were largely for naught: Roberts and Hollis so modified Ewell's plan that only its concept of having each division attack the base areas nearest its sector within III CTZ remained intact. Further, Ewell's excluding his own chief of staff and operations officer from knowledge of the planning meant that Davison knew nothing of the work to date when he took command; he did not even know to ask, since Smith and Leech were too comparatively junior to have the chance to approach him unbidden.

———————

Getting his mission from Abrams on 24 April, Davison considered Cambodia a "unique situation." Unaware of Ewell's groundwork, Davison developed what he regarded as his "own" plan. It was essentially the same as his predecessor's, largely due to its similar parameters: Abrams's insistence on surprise, the major units available and their locations, and common staff officer training in solving military problems. While III Corps attacked west into the Angel's Wing and Parrot's Beak and then on westward toward Phnom Penh, the First Cavalry Division and the 11ACR, supported by the Eleventh Aviation Group and IIFFV Artillery, would go north into the Fishhook; the Twenty-fifth Infantry Division would cover the border areas vacated by the 11ACR. Davison briefed Abrams on 26 April.[70] Abrams approved the plan, since it resembled what he had previously discussed with Ewell, and because he trusted Davison from their previous years of service together. Believing in decentralization, Davison gave the job of attacking Fishhook to the First Cavalry Division and let Roberts do it.[71]

Davison sought to disguise IIFFV's intentions. Rather than creating a complicated deception plan for his attack, he would instead use units already near the border, moving as few others as possible, and those only at the last minute. Since building forward stockpiles would be a key indicator of upcoming advances, those units attacking into Cambodia would initially use only the supplies they already had with them.[72] Davison also limited advance knowledge to protect operational security and hopefully catch COSVN by surprise. Brigade commanders

found out less than a week before the incursion, while many battalion commanders had only two or three days' notice: one cannot inadvertently reveal what one
does not know. However, any surprise gained would be of only tactical value,
since ARVN's March and April raids had already shown COSVN the border was
no longer inviolable to the allies.

Surprise can cut both ways, and to avoid it one needs to know one's enemy.
Like Abrams, Davison wanted intelligence about the base areas and what was in
them; unlike Abrams, he had no reconnaissance troops and aircraft of his own
crossing the border, and no authority to send anything over. Because III Corps
had been more interested in Cambodia than had IIFFV, Davison asked Tri for
help; the latter shared what III Corps had collected during 1969 and early 1970,
as well as during TOAN THANG 41.[73]

The American pullout also affected the intelligence available to Davison. At
the height of the Vietnam War, each field force and U.S. division had its own
Ranger unit serving as the commander's "personal" scouts. However, Company
D, Seventy-fifth Infantry (Ranger) was deactivated on 10 April 1970, as part of
the U.S. withdrawal and its soldiers reassigned or sent home to the States. Thus,
just before the incursion Davison lost his own Rangers and had to borrow teams
from his divisions' Ranger companies to work in areas unfamiliar to them.[74]

The IIFFV intelligence units remaining had to operate from within South
Vietnam, such as aerial reconnaissance flights along the border. These included
normal photographic missions with cameras aimed into Cambodia, RED HAZE
infrared detectors, and airborne ground radars. In the RED HAZE program, U.S.
military aircraft flew along the border and above those areas of III CTZ where the
enemy had revealed his presence by attacks. However, RED HAZE had a very
limited lateral sensing ability and had to overfly targets to detect them; this made
missions against Cambodian base areas impractical before 1 May. Once RED
HAZE missions began over Cambodia, though, their flight patterns changed, permitting analysts to target strips along the border one hundred kilometers long by
ten wide to examine more area faster with less wasted fuel and film.[75]

Another special aircraft carried the Side-Looking Airborne Radar (SLAR).
SLARs could spot moving vehicles at ranges of more than 100 kilometers, useful
for monitoring truck traffic on enemy supply routes. Between mid-April and
early May, IIFFV SLAR missions looked across the Cambodian border three to
five times each night.[76] They detected a consistent pattern of nighttime truck activity along Highway 7 from areas north of the Dog's Head to northwest of the
Fishhook, through the region including Base Areas 707, 353, and 352. These
were NVA forces, evacuating troops and supplies from the potential paths of invading forces.

Davison's aerial reconnaissance effort was substantial, averaging some ten
RED HAZE, four SLAR, and thirteen photographic missions daily.[77] The nature
of the flights changed as the incursion approached and began. In late April RED
HAZE flights dropped off noticeably, while SLAR missions held steady and pho-

toreconnaissance increased. As U.S. and ARVN tanks and vehicles entered Cambodia, the few tiny NVA/VC cooking fires became much harder for RED HAZE to find. SLAR missions, mostly at night, remained valuable because the radar could spot movements deep in enemy territory. Photographic missions peaked just before the incursion and in its early days because tactical commanders could understand and immediately use the pictures to help attack their objectives along the border. Further, recent pictures of an area often showed details not included on maps made years earlier.

Monitoring enemy radio transmissions was the job of the 303rd Radio Research Battalion augmented by the 101st Radio Research Company, both based at Long Binh. These two units sent out electronic warfare and radio monitoring teams to IIFFV's divisions and separate brigades or regiments, giving them immediately usable tactical intelligence about units they were fighting.[78] The teams used radio direction finding to locate headquarters, jammed enemy transmissions, and monitored their broadcasts to try to learn their plans.

The various assets available to IIFFV thus gave Davison worthwhile intelligence, but he was not privy to some of Abrams's most sensitive material. Unaware when he arrived at IIFFV that MENU's B-52s had been bombing Cambodia for more than a year, Davison learned of their strikes only on 1 May when he saw hundreds of craters as he flew over Cambodia.[79] Abrams had withheld from Davison all preincursion cross-border aerial photographs because they would have revealed the secret bombing.

Besides exclusion from certain matters, Davison felt some of the intelligence he got from MACV was questionable. Other reports MACV J-2 had given him were later disproved, and Davison believed his wariness subsequently justified by his findings in Cambodia. Abrams's analysts had depicted the base areas as "sort of straddling the border"; IIFFV discovered that most caches and camps "were at least five [kilometers] back from the border."[80] Though MACV-SOG units sometimes told of concrete pillboxes inside the Cambodian border, protecting the sanctuaries, Davison "never found any. I often wondered about the accuracy of the reports made by these patrols."[81]

Despite problems, the intelligence available to Davison and his subordinates was in general sufficient. It told them where major enemy units were and, equally important, where they were not. It pointed IIFFV in the correct directions and gave fair ideas of where to look for enemy camps. The lack of detailed intelligence most affected units by not providing detailed locations for the NVA's stockpiles and caches: time spent looking for caches was unavailable for evacuating captured supplies and hunting more sites. Better intelligence might have resulted in more caches found sooner, and even greater damage to Hanoi's ability to threaten the southern half of South Vietnam, but it would not have significantly affected the incursion's overall outcome.

Both 25 and 26 April were particularly hectic in IIFFV's headquarters. On 24 April, Abrams had given Davison the mission to attack the base areas; the IIFFV staff had to coordinate a myriad of issues among the different units and staffs over the next two days. On the evening of 26 April, most matters were in hand, Davison had satisfactorily briefed Abrams, and the orders had been issued to the subordinate headquarters. He spent the next four days visiting IIFFV units as their new commander and attending to routine business at Long Binh. The focus turned to the American units preparing to destroy the NVA sanctuaries: the First Cavalry and Twenty-fifth Infantry Divisions.[82]

5

TOAN THANG 43,
1 May to 30 June

During the last week of April things were as busy for the First Cavalry Division as they were for IIFFV and III Corps. Major General Elvy Roberts, the division commander, gave the job of leading the attack to one of his two assistant division commanders, Brigadier General Robert Shoemaker. Shoemaker, who later retired as a four-star general, had four days to form a task force headquarters, plan an operation by three brigades and supporting units, and launch the incursion on time.

The First Cavalry Division had been active to the north and northwest of Saigon in Tay Ninh, Binh Long, and Phuoc Long Provinces since its move south from I CTZ in 1968. Following Abrams's change of MACV's focus that summer, the division shifted its emphasis from hunting NVA and VC units to instead stopping the flow of enemy supplies from Cambodia toward Saigon. To do this Roberts had nine infantry battalions, one helicopter rocket and four cannon artillery battalions, a divisional cavalry squadron, two battalions of UH-1 utility helicopters, a battalion of CH-47 medium helicopters, assorted support battalions, and the regular help of a company of IIFFV's CH-54 heavy-lift helicopters. Other U.S. divisions in Vietnam had at most 80 helicopters of all types; with 435, Roberts could move his units farther and faster than anyone else. He also routinely directed the operations of Colonel Donn Starry's Eleventh Armored Cavalry Regiment (11ACR), three squadrons of tanks and ACAVs. Finally, the First Cavalry Division worked in close cooperation with the ARVN Airborne Division, frequently directing combined operations of the two divisions' units. With his helicopters' mobility and aggressive soldiers, the firepower of Starry's armor, and the complete cooperation of ARVN's best division, Roberts had by far the single most powerful division of any army in Southeast Asia.

During 1969 and early 1970, the First Cavalry Division and the 11ACR had steadily driven enemy forces in its sector back toward the Cambodian border.[1] Action in early 1970 had been intense: in thirty-one days of fighting between 1

February and 16 April during Campaign X, the NVA and VC suffered more than 1,600 dead and several thousand wounded compared with 86 U.S. dead and 313 wounded.[2] The division was inflicting unacceptable losses on its opponents, forcing them out of III CTZ for the safety of the Cambodian sanctuaries.

By April 1970 American troops had reached the border and could chase the NVA no farther. The military situation was nonetheless grim for COSVN and its subordinate military commands despite the political success for Hanoi of the continued polarization of the U.S. body politic. Supplies were piling up in the border base areas for lack of porters to move them into and across South Vietnam. Units had little freedom of movement within South Vietnam, and replacements from the North went into action with little training. Prisoners of war told interrogators they "were forced-marched straight off the infiltration trail and into combat."[3] NVA morale suffered accordingly, and casualties among its officers and NCOs mounted as they exposed themselves more often while seeking to motivate their troops by personal example.

Roberts credited this turn of events to Abrams's strategy emphasizing pacification and attacking enemy logistics, calling it "the most important decision that was made and carried through in the past year."[4] Conducting operations during the monsoons had helped American forces destroy the communist logistics system across northern III CTZ and keep it inactive. However, Roberts stressed the need to continue attacking the supply routes to prevent the NVA from restoring them and rebuilding its capabilities. "The enemy was more restricted to the trails and at a greater disadvantage than we. He had to have the trails to conduct his business. We didn't."[5] Roberts exaggerated somewhat (his own bulk supplies normally moved by road, too), but his basic point was valid.

Although the B-2 Front could not get its troops and supplies where it wanted within South Vietnam, it could still move them laterally along the Cambodian border. The high-quality roads (for Southeast Asia) in and north of the Fishhook were particularly important to these shifts. Highway 7, running southwest-northeast between Krek, Memot, and Snuol, and Route 13, from Snuol south to Binh Long Province (and ultimately to Saigon), were two lanes wide and made of gravel. There were several dirt roads, but only Highway 7 and Route 13 could carry B-2's steady truck traffic to the border sanctuaries during monsoons.[6] Highway 7 in particular was critical to the communist logistics system, linking the Sihanoukville Trail and the Ho Chi Minh Trail.

COSVN's actions in early 1970 inadvertently increased its vulnerability to attack from South Vietnam. By moving units, the Ninth Division in particular, south and west along the border, it reduced units' distance from and thereby increased the danger they posed to the Saigon area. However, these moves also increased those units' dependence on the steady flow of supplies. The March 1970 deposition of Sihanouk and the closing (and renaming, to Kampong Speu) of Sihanoukville to communist freighters put the three NVA divisions opposite III CTZ at greater risk than when they had been closer to Laos. On the other hand, they were better positioned to attack Phnom Penh, defeat Lon Nol, and reopen their supply routes. The possible presence of three NVA divisions and their experienced commanders along the border made any allied incursion an undertaking with greater risk. Most important for the First Cavalry Division's attack was the Seventh Division's deployment of its 165th and 209th Infantry Regiments out of the Fishhook and border regions.[7] These units, which could have inflicted heavy casualties on U.S. and ARVN troops had they defended the sanctuaries, were by late April deeper in Cambodia fighting Lon Nol's forces and securing the southern end of the Ho Chi Minh Trail.

Fortunately for the First Cavalry Division, despite ARVN's mid-April raids neither COSVN nor the B-2 Front apparently realized U.S. forces were preparing to cross the border in strength. Enemy papers dated 28 April and captured in the Fishhook revealed that COSVN believed U.S. and ARVN attention would remain on the western side of Tay Ninh Province rather than the northern. ARVN's raids had suggested the possibility of other minor incursions, but three days before Roberts's men went into the Fishhook, the NVA had no inkling of a major U.S. attack.[8]

The First Cavalry Division's direct involvement with Cambodia began on Sunday, 26 April, when Davison called Roberts and Shoemaker to his headquarters at Long Binh. The three generals discussed the changed Cambodian situation and Abrams's order to begin planning an attack on the Fishhook sanctuaries. Closer to the Fishhook than the Twenty-fifth Infantry Division, and with better tactical mobility due to its helicopters, the First Cavalry Division was the logical choice for the mission. The generals agreed on a concept for seizing the Fishhook, using the First Cavalry Division's Third Brigade, the 11ACR, and the Third ARVN Airborne Brigade. Once the area was secure, they would seek out and destroy enemy base camps and supplies.[9]

Returning to the division's headquarters at Phuoc Vinh, Roberts and Shoemaker discounted the likelihood of an incursion. They "agreed that [it] *really* looked serious, . . . [but they] really didn't believe it would happen."[10] Nonetheless, the next day Roberts told Shoemaker to form a task force headquarters and start planning an attack.[11] Colonel Edward C. Meyers, the division chief of staff (and future U.S. Army chief of staff), assigned five officers to help Shoemaker: the Division Artillery's Lieutenant Colonel Vincent Falter to head the team; a lieutenant colonel and a major from Division Operations; the assistant division signal officer; and an artillery liaison.

Ordinarily, this would have been too small a staff to coordinate the actions of more than 12,000 troops on just four days' notice. It worked here because the headquarters had no administrative responsibilities and could focus exclusively on tactical matters. Davison and Roberts had agreed to send detachments forward to the Quan Loi base camp to monitor the task force's radio traffic and prepare all necessary reports and supply requests on its behalf.[12] Thus relieved of those requirements, Shoemaker and his planners went to Quan Loi, base of the Third

Brigade. At midmorning on 29 April the task force became operational. Shoemaker evicted Colonel Robert Kingston and his Third Brigade staff from their command bunker without explanation and limited entrance to his five officers. The bunker already had the proper border maps on the walls and communications links to several other headquarters; it was the logical spot to work from.[13] Assuming that the raid would last perhaps a week and be limited to the Fishhook, Shoemaker's team got busy.[14]

Success with the fewest possible casualties required surprise, and Shoemaker made several early decisions to increase the odds of achieving it. Because moving new units up to the border or concentrating units already there might suggest imminent activity, he would use forces already in the area. Kingston's Third Brigade was along the southern edge of the Fishhook, just west of two of the 11ACR's three squadrons. Starry, the 11ACR commander (who, like Kingston, would retire as a four-star general), would bring the third squadron up from its base about thirty kilometers to the south as though he was replacing one squadron with another, such reliefs in place being routine. Once it was in position, the full regiment would attack into the Fishhook beside the Third Brigade. The Third ARVN Airborne Brigade would precede it with a helicopter-borne assault on the morning of 1 May (30 April in Washington), launched from assembly areas at Loc Ninh to the east of the Fishhook. The First ARVN Armored Cavalry Regiment (ARC) was already screening the Fishhook's eastern edge and would continue to do so in support of Shoemaker's task force. The First Cavalry Division and IIFFV Artillery batteries would have to move forward to range deeper into the Fishhook, but Shoemaker could do little about this except delay their shifts as long as possible. Finally, the movements of the artillery, the 11ACR, and the attached Second Battalion Forty-seventh Mechanized Infantry and Second Battalion Thirty-fourth Armor into attack positions near the border would be under radio silence to hide the massing of armored forces.[15]

Changing logistics patterns, such as creating, moving, or enlarging supply dumps near the future area of action and improving or building roads, are obvious signs of a pending operation. Shoemaker therefore decided to launch the incursion with only the supplies units already had, then bring more forward after he crossed the border. However, should the NVA choose to stand and fight, his soldiers might quickly need more ammunition and fuel than they had on hand. Without forward stockpiles near the border, the troops would be in greater danger until the supplies could be rushed up from Long Binh, Saigon, and other depots. Not establishing advanced supply dumps was a calculated risk against the more important need for surprise.

Finally, Shoemaker sought to increase his odds of gaining surprise by keeping his own units in the dark until the last minute. He did not tell Kingston what was going on until the evening of 29 April, when he called Kingston and his battalion commanders into the bunker.[16] After giving them their orders, he had each repeat them to ensure they understood exactly what they were to do. Watching all this were Davison, Roberts, Major General Du Quoc Dong of the ARVN Airborne Division, and Dong's top U.S. advisers.[17] Concealing the details of his plans until thirty-six hours before the attack helped Shoemaker preserve some secrecy and surprise. However, his own presence and the takeover of Kingston's bunker had been an indicator of something unusual going on, which the arrival of the three senior generals for his briefing had confirmed.

In the event, Shoemaker's efforts were so good the media only learned of the U.S. incursion several hours after it began. Davison visited Tri's command post at Go Dau Ha on the morning of 1 May while U.S. troops were attacking the Fishhook. The fifteen or so reporters there covering III Corps' TOAN THANG 42 all recognized Davison but ignored him in their focus on III Corps' activities. Later that day, when word got out about Shoemaker's attack, one reporter complained that he had not alerted them to it. Davison's answer to him was, "'Well, nobody asked me.'"[18]

When Shoemaker gave his commanders their missions, he could provide only general information about their objectives inside the Fishhook. Having previously been off-limits to most U.S. forces, and with their attention focused on combat operations within South Vietnam as allied forces pushed the NVA back to the border, there had been little reason to collect detailed information about what was in Cambodia.

The land was generally rolling, averaging around 100 meters elevation above sea level, but the multicanopied forests covering roughly 80 percent of the area made aerial observation nearly impossible. Cross-border helicopter flights were prohibited as forfeiting surprise, and aerial photographs were unavailable from MACV because (as Davison and Shoemaker later found out) they clearly showed MENU B-52 craters across the Cambodian border region.[19] Maps were therefore essential, although less detailed than those in South Vietnam. As in Vietnam, ground visibility ranged from about fifty meters in former rubber plantations to as little as five meters elsewhere. While there were occasional radio intercepts, prisoner interrogations, and captured documents from MACV or IIFFV, most of Shoemaker's tactical information came from firefights in Vietnam.[20] This included unit identifications and the locations where certain communist units normally operated.

This lack of detailed information did not unduly disturb Shoemaker, who expected to find the enemy simply by bumping into him. "I thought I *knew* what they wanted done," he later said, ". . . to enter Cambodia, and, using any clue that came up, to root around and destroy and make unusable that base area."[21] The division intelligence analysts were more cautious. They predicted about 7,000 enemy troops in the Fishhook, mostly in logistics, headquarters, or administrative units.[22]

The task force staff knew, however, that should COSVN choose to defend the Fishhook, it could commit up to 2,000 infantrymen within two days and as many as 9,000 within a week.[23] These could draw freely upon the stocks of ammunition and food in the area. With hundreds of tons of bullets immediately at hand, NVA soldiers could fire their weapons on automatic with little fear of running short of ammunition; this would permit their commanders to make far more intense counterattacks than American troops had generally experienced before.[24] The division's preincursion intelligence estimate was somber, recommending "a deliberate and careful employment of the troops. Rapid encirclement and exploitation by armor is not possible. The enemy will probably defend and reinforce."[25]

This prediction turned out to be wrong. However, Shoemaker's staff planned for the worst case—running into prepared defenses—and based its work on four assumptions. First, they were to expect heavy demands on allied ammunition resupply. Second, given the poor road network in the area, they would use forward airfields and fixed-wing aircraft whenever possible. Third, to preclude NVA propaganda photos and claims of victory, they would leave no U.S. equipment in Cambodia once the last U.S. soldier left. Finally, the task force would support ARVN logistically if required.[26]

These guidelines served them well. Although infantry units in general did not face heavy combat until later in the operation and thus used fewer bullets and grenades than expected, liberal artillery fire consumed and exceeded those savings in tonnage. Air force cargo aircraft, especially those flying supply missions, freed the less-capacious army helicopters for tactical emergencies and unforeseen developments. Planners expected to use five airfields near the Fishhook to support the task force's operations: Katum, Tonle Chom, Quan Loi, An Loc, and Loc Ninh. These first needed engineering work to handle the increased traffic, but the staff could begin moving the necessary assets immediately to ensure the airfields were ready in time. All U.S. equipment was removed, no matter how badly damaged, avoiding anything that might be misrepresented as a communist "kill." Finally, ARVN's Third Airborne Brigade and First ARVN ACR needed less logistic aid than expected, reducing Shoemaker's concerns and easing the burden on IIFFV's logistic units.

Shoemaker's plan for attacking the Fishhook was simple, largely a result of the limited preparation time and his reliance on commanders' initiative and flexibility; as General George Patton had said years earlier, "A 70 percent plan on time is better than a 100 percent plan a day late." Recognizing the fluid nature of the forthcoming incursion, particularly after the opening moves, the plan concentrated on the first day's operations. After that, Shoemaker would exploit opportunities as they presented themselves.

This approach, of almost "winging it," would be dangerous with weak commanders, with bad communications, or against a ready enemy. In Shoemaker's case it was acceptable. He had aggressive and experienced officers and good communications, and he caught his enemy largely by surprise. The plan's biggest weakness was in its bare-bones logistical support, a matter that did not become an issue until units used the supplies at their camps along the border.

TOAN THANG 43 was to start on 1 May with a very big bang indeed. Between 0400 and 0600 hours, thirty-six B-52s would hit the area just across the border along the southern edge of the Fishhook with 774 tons of bombs. Shoemaker neither controlled the bombers nor knew exactly where they would strike; his main concern was that they be finished by 0600.[27] For the next hour, massed artillery would fire at known or suspected enemy positions, followed by an hour of fighter-bombers attacking. From 0800 to 1000, two air troops of the First Squadron Ninth Cavalry (the division's veteran and storied reconnaissance unit) would look for and fire at any enemy movements. Meanwhile, the three ARVN airborne battalion commanders would overfly the area in helicopters and pick their landing zones, then return to brief their company commanders. At around 1000 the first ARVN troops would land between the Fishhook's southern border and Cambodian Highway 7.

Upon the ARVN battalions' lifting off, Shoemaker's ground forces would attack north across the border at 1000 on two routes, the crossing time set at Washington's directive to coincide with President Nixon's evening telecast informing the American people of the incursion.[28]

Moving forward in two main thrusts, with the 11ACR on the right and the Third Brigade on the left, the units would link up with the ARVN battalions inserted a few hours earlier, then push farther north to secure the area against any counterattack. The Second Battalion Forty-seventh Mechanized Infantry and the Second Battalion Thirty-fourth Armor would advance to Highway 7 to keep the NVA from using it. Finally, the 11ACR would attack farther north along Highway 7 to exploit any initial successes and keep COSVN off balance, uncertain of how far or in which direction the Americans might go. Once the movement phase was complete, the emphasis would turn to searching for supply caches and base areas.

Shoemaker's plan was sufficient for the opening assault of TOAN THANG 43. However, the day before he crossed the border, he still had two unanswered questions indicative of the operation's ad hoc nature: "Were there any Cambodian civilians in my operating area, and . . . what [was] the operating area?"[29] Leading some 10,000 troops into Cambodia within twenty-four hours, he did not know his boundaries. He also had no idea how long he would be there, assuming it was simply a raid a week or so long.[30]

This uncertainty affected how Shoemaker planned and started the attack. To reduce the danger to any civilians who might still remain in the Fishhook, his staff drafted and issued rules of engagement (ROE) hours after U.S. forces entered Cambodia.[31] The ROE defined the area of operations as running from the Fishhook's eastern border west about twenty-five kilometers and from the southern border north about fourteen kilometers. Within this zone those rules pertaining to civilians and populated areas in Vietnam would apply. The Fishhook's southeastern corner was a "free-strike" area where commanders could conduct "reconnaissance by fire" subject to certain restrictions. However, all unobserved fires had to land at least 500 meters from known Cambodian villages and hamlets; eight such places were identified by name and map coordinates.[32]

Adherence to the spirit, if not the letter, of the ROE ultimately depended on the leaders on the spot. Many soldiers regarded the border as "just a line on the ground," and the assault as merely a continuation of their current fight against the same enemy on the other side of a border the NVA and VC had never respected.[33] When the rules were published, the attack was already under way. It was a day or so before commanders in the field could get copies and pass them down to the troops; until then, the needs of the moment took precedence.

Realizing that Cambodian civilians would inevitably be affected by military operations, Shoemaker and Roberts tried to minimize the risks to them. The division's Civil-Military Liaison staff prepared to evacuate refugees to centers at Tay Ninh, An Loc/Hon Quan, and Song Be;[34] the division made a major effort to evacuate captured rice from the Fishhook to these centers. The Civil-Military staff also produced five leaflets and two tapes in late April, made by a Cambodian Kit Carson Scout who spoke and wrote Vietnamese and Cambodian. The propaganda sought to calm Cambodians' fears by explaining what was happening and persuading enemy troops to surrender. Although crude, it was the best available at the time, and was used until 3 May.[35]

While Shoemaker and his tiny staff prepared for the attack, Roberts and the rest of the division headquarters continued during late April with their normal operations. Although forming a small task force headquarters to direct three brigade-sized units plus supporting troops was within Roberts's authority, in hindsight it was a mistake. Davison later commented, "There [were] so many growing pains that it [was] just not worth the effort," adding that Roberts's staff was "fully capable of running not only the initial operation into the Fishhook but also all the other activities of the division."[36]

Had the division headquarters controlled TOAN THANG 43 (also known within U.S. circles as Operation ROCKCRUSHER), it would have avoided the turmoil caused by a new and minuscule command post establishing routines and its links with other units while planning the incursion. Fortunately, Shoemaker did a good job getting things ready in time.

Dependable communications were critical, since talking "on the fly" would largely compensate for hurried planning. The short notice between Shoemaker's receipt of the mission and the incursion's start was not a problem for the Thirteenth Signal Battalion: due to the First Cavalry Division's frequent moves, it routinely set up large communications networks. An initial signal plan on 27 April by the division's signal battalion commander and one of his officers became the basis for Shoemaker's signal support. Two days later a small detachment arrived at Quan Loi to add more communications links between the task force and its brigade-level headquarters.[37]

Although Kingston's bunker contained several radios and telephones, these were intended only to control his own units as they operated within range of the base. The incursion's expanded scale made better radio coverage imperative. Jeeps carrying four-channel radios augmented the bunker's, and more went west to Kingston's new Third Brigade forward command post at Katum.[38] Finally, a courier shuttled between Quan Loi and Phuoc Vinh for such documents as map overlays that could not be sent by radio or telephone.[39]

The fluid situation in late April and early May made FM radios the chief means of communication. Unlike AM signals, which could bounce for great distances off the ionosphere and linked brigade headquarters back to Phuoc Vinh, tactical FM radios had maximum ranges of only about forty kilometers. Dense vegetation lessened this in practice, and the FM radios' requirement for electronic line of sight between transmitter and receiver reduced it further. At Quan Loi in late April there were more than a hundred FM radios used by or supporting the task force. Since raising an FM antenna above ground level greatly extends the range of its signal, the base's one tower, 200 feet tall, rapidly became overloaded with antennae. By early May it carried at least nine VHF, one UHF, seven HF (AM), and thirty-six FM antennae. Most were multiplexed, with several transmitters sharing the same antenna.[40] However, so many antennae so close together and using the same frequency bands produced mutual interference. The self-inflicted jamming lasted until signal officers could identify vacant frequencies whose harmonics would not create new problems, as well as remove nonessential antennae.

Another problem was the tower's vulnerability to attack. Its height above the surrounding trees meant an aircraft warning light had to illuminate its top at night, to preclude helicopters hitting the tower or its supporting guy wires. However, this light, and the tower itself in daylight, served as aiming points for communist gunners to shoot at the Quan Loi base. A lucky mortar or rocket shot that hit the base or cut a wire could drop the tower and silence the hundred stations, temporarily decapitating the task force.[41] In the event, the task force was fortunate, as no attack damaged the tower during the incursion.

As planning jelled in late April, units started to move into their attack positions. Lieutenant Colonel Scott Smith, Roberts's engineer battalion commander and the division engineer, was given a third job when Shoemaker made him the liaison to the First ARVN ACR on or about 27 April. Smith was to ensure that the regiment (about the strength of a U.S. cavalry squadron) moved up to and across the Saigon River by 30 April to establish screening positions along the eastern side of the Fishhook.[42] Leaving his battalion in the hands of his "young stud company commanders and a good array of staff officers,"[43] Smith spent most of the last days of April with the First ARVN ACR.

The Saigon River formed part of the border between Vietnam and Cambodia. Getting the First ARVN ACR across its ten- to fifteen-meter width on schedule was critical for the start of the attack, as the regiment had to link up with ARVN paratroopers inserted earlier that day following the B-52 strikes. On 30 April Smith and the 11ACR's intelligence officer scouted the river and its banks for six hours, looking for fording sites and checking the conditions of the banks. They did so without any escort, opting to be inconspicuous instead of safe: they thought a lone jeep would attract less attention near the border than a column of armored vehicles or hovering helicopters. Years later, Smith admitted to having been "scared out of [his] wits while they were alone in 'Indian Country.'"[44] This was risky, from mines as well as for the operation's security if they were captured and tortured to reveal secrets. That same day 11ACR units hit mines south of the Fishhook in four separate incidents; two tanks were lightly damaged and a water trailer almost destroyed. Smith was lucky, as a jeep and its occupants would not have survived a mine blast.[45]

From his personal reconnaissance and study of the maps, Smith knew that the two ACRs would need his bridges to keep moving through the Fishhook over streams or damaged bridges. Though the 11ACR's regiment's mobile, sixty-foot long bridges could handle most of these, maps suggested there was one wide gully where they would probably be too short. For this spot Smith had his men assemble an M4T6 Bailey bridge in late April at the Second Brigade's base camp at Phuoc Long. It sat on the Vietnamese side of the border until needed, when a CH-54 heavy-lift helicopter flew the pieces into Cambodia for its final assembly and emplacement across the gully.[46]

Like the Thirteenth Signal Battalion, the Division Artillery units were accustomed to short-notice and frequent moves.[47] However, TOAN THANG 43's preparations entailed some problems demanding quick solutions. One difficulty was coordinating the volume of fire: ninety-four cannon would shoot for hours into an area about twenty kilometers wide and ten deep, along with rockets from thirty-six Cobra gunships.[48] With dozens of planes and helicopters plus cannon shells traversing the same airspace, keeping the artillery from shooting down aircraft was a major headache.

Shoemaker's five-man staff had neither the resources nor the time, so Division Artillery made a detailed fire plan of who would fire what, at which target, and when.[49] It took the air liaison officer (ALO) and the fire support coordinator fifteen hours to check each of the 600 targets for possible conflicts, comparing aircraft flight paths and times with artillery trajectories. Upon finding possible conflicts, air strikes took precedence over artillery fires, which were rescheduled as necessary to preclude fratricide.[50] Computers make this easy today, but the two officers had only pencils and paper. This sufficed, and no aircraft fell to friendly cannon fire on 1 May.

The fire plan also included suppressing enemy air defenses. The skies above the Fishhook would be full of helicopters after the attack began, and artillery commander Colonel Morris Brady wanted to make sure that no NVA heavy machine guns would fire at them. He, operations officer Major Anthony Pokorny, and two officers in Shoemaker's headquarters included as targets all likely sites for heavy weapons, such as hilltops or clearings. Cannon fired on them before the helicopters arrived; no helicopter pilots reported machine gun attacks afterward, though whether there would have been any fire absent such artillery fires will remain unknown.[51]

Brady's biggest problem was integrating ARVN artillery units into the operation. Although the ARVN Airborne Brigade's infantrymen were very good, comparable to Shoemaker's own soldiers, ARVN artillery batteries were not. In particular, ARVN gunners were bad at ensuring their shells would not endanger friendly troops. To reduce the odds of ARVN-originated fratricide, U.S. and ARVN artillerymen set up combined fire support coordination centers. These checked and approved fire missions before guns shot and gave the U.S. artillerymen a subtle way to verify ARVN's targets. Brady loaned forward observers to ARVN infantry and armor battalions to help them properly call for artillery and air strikes. "The result [of all these measures] was a thoroughly integrated fire support effort."[52]

Artillery batteries and platoons spent the last days in April shifting to new locations. Eight moved on the twenty-ninth, and fourteen more on 30 April.[53] Shoemaker included the fire plan in his briefing to the commanders on 29 April. The next day his staff gave each firing unit lists of specific targets, times to fire, and the numbers and types of shells to shoot. To improve coordination, they gave copies of the target lists to the forward air controllers and helicopter units, allowing pilots to call for fires by referring to targets the guns were ready to engage.[54]

While artillery provided sustained firepower to the assaulting troops, airpower contributed massive if sporadic deluges of high explosives, particularly in the attack's opening hours. Told on 27 April to start detailed planning, the Seventh Air Force headquarters was also to limit such knowledge to the fewest possible officers.[55] Like the ground commanders finding out at the eleventh hour, the air staffers met the requirements. Shoemaker's ALO wanted to make sure he would have sufficient airpower to deal with any emergencies. TOAN THANG 43 being the biggest show in Southeast Asia that morning, he got what he wanted.

Waves of B-52s, six strikes of six planes each, started the attack; an hour later COSVN made its last radio broadcast and went silent.[56] Task Force Shoemaker received fighter-bombers in flights of four arriving every fifteen to thirty minutes from 0700 to 1900, a total of 148 tactical aircraft sorties for the first day alone.[57] The ALO's initial plan had called for half that number, but because intelligence feared up to 7,000 enemy troops might be in the Fishhook, Seventh Air Force headquarters doubled the ALO's figure to make certain Shoemaker had enough.[58] The Seventh Air Force provided some special assets, too: two flareships from the air base at Cam Ranh Bay, four AC-119K gunships from Phan Rang, ten extra alert sorties, aerial tanker support, and nighttime forward air controllers (FACs).[59] As with other major operations, aerial resources were plentiful.

Following the B-52 strikes came smaller aircraft. Two 15,000-pound bombs rolled out the back of C-130 cargo planes, creating Landing Zone (LZ) East at

0630 and LZ Center at 0645 by blasting flat two areas hundreds of feet across.[60] Starting at 0700 the FACs directed their fighter-bombers onto the areas where the Third ARVN Airborne Brigade's three battalions would land in a few hours. Fuses on most of the bombs were set to blow up just above the ground, to knock down trees without excavating craters.[61]

At 0730 helicopter scouts of the First Squadron Ninth Cavalry crossed the border. As they began looking for any enemy forces still moving, the ARVN Airborne Brigade, then at Quan Loi, was loading onto helicopters for the short ride to the landing zones in the Fishhook. At 0810 the Third ARVN Airborne Battalion's Fourth Company, along with six light and three medium cannon, occupied LZ East; it promptly became "Fire Support Base East" and harassed retreating NVA forces with artillery fires and infantry patrols.[62]

While the Third Battalion dug in at LZ East, other battalion commanders were flying over the central part of the Fishhook. By 0930 they had decided where their units were to go. As they returned to their staging areas along the border to brief their company commanders, the artillery and air force attacked these future landing areas. Five minutes after the last shells fell, the Fifth ARVN Airborne Battalion landed at LZ Center, having moved its four infantry companies in one massive flight of forty-two Huey helicopters escorted by twenty-two Cobra gunships. The Ninth ARVN Airborne Infantry Battalion landed just west of LZ Center shortly after noon in the morning's final air assault.[63]

Heavy thunderstorms across III CTZ the previous afternoon and evening had soaked the ground,[64] but not enough to stop the 11ACR and Third Brigade from moving toward the border by 0730. C Company, Second Battalion Forty-seventh Mechanized Infantry, was the first U.S. unit officially in Cambodia, at about 0945, minutes ahead of the 11ACR and the rest of the Third Brigade. The 11ACR might have beaten it across had not one of its lead vehicles hit a mine at 0930 at the border.[65] This slowed the regiment, but Colonel Starry moved it on.

TOAN THANG 43 picked up speed as U.S. forces pushed deeper into Cambodia. The Second Battalion Thirty-fourth Armor and Second Battalion Forty-seventh Mechanized Infantry drove north through the western edge of the Fishhook to block any enemy counterattack from the direction of Memot while the 11ACR passed through the Fishhook's center. The Second Battalion Forty-seventh Mechanized commander later recalled that his orders for 1 May "consisted basically of objectives, routes, and fire support planning. We had no decent maps, little intelligence, and lousy communications from my command and control helicopter."[66] Enemy contact was fortunately sporadic, most of it in the form of helicopters shooting small groups of fleeing troops.

Although each such engagement was small, the cumulative effect was to inflict several hundred losses on COSVN's units. The day's moves ended with the landing of two infantry companies from the Second Battalion Seventh Cavalry about five kilometers north of Highway 7. They were to serve as an early-warning outpost and delay any counterattack from the north. Shoemaker's staff had planned this mission as a contingency to launch on very short notice if resistance was light. Because there had been no major fights that day, he ordered the Second Battalion Seventh Cavalry forward; it occupied its position without incident.[67]

Of the many groups involved in TOAN THANG 43, it was probably the First Cavalry Division's aviators who pushed themselves the hardest on the first day; their 1,303 hours of flying time were far more than normal.[68] Further, every hour of flight meant two to three hours' maintenance afterward; mechanics had to work throughout each night to make the helicopters ready to fly the next morning. They would finish with the first helicopters at around midnight and the last around dawn, then do the same thing each subsequent night. Helicopter mechanics were the unsung heroes of the attack.

The air force was creative in adapting to the unique circumstances it found above Cambodia. Normally, a single FAC controlled air strikes within a specific area for a ground unit. This worked well for the pair or so of planes that might respond to a particular call for aid. However, with so many planes above the Fishhook supporting three different brigade-sized units, Seventh Air Force headquarters created a "super-FAC" to direct the other FACs. This officer, called "Head Beagle" to distinguish him from the regular FACs ("Beagles"), orbited above northern Tay Ninh Province and received all requests for air support.[69] Comparing priority and needs with the bombs and rockets carried by inbound planes, he passed off the fighter-bombers to the appropriate FAC for each strike. This system, first used at Khe Sanh in early 1968, worked well on 1 May.

During operations in the Fishhook, under directions of Head Beagles the USAF flew 3,047 sorties and the VNAF 332.[70] Excluding the B-52s, 196 air strikes killed several hundred enemy soldiers while wounding only twelve friendly troops, a very good rate given the number of aircraft in the area, the amount of ordnance they dropped or shot, the numbers of ground troops moving in limited areas, and the primitive avionics then extant for determining locations.[71] To better use its aircraft in the face of light and scattered enemy resistance, on 5 May the air force cut the number of planes in each strike package from four down to two; this doubled the requests for immediate support it could respond to.[72]

Shoemaker's area of operations changed substantially on 2 May as his ground units continued to move forward. At 1125 an airborne radar indicated that an NVA convoy was trying to escape the Fishhook northward to reach Highway 7; Shoemaker ordered an AC-119 gunship to look for the convoy and destroy it if spotted.[73] To better attack these routes, Roberts tripled the area of eastern Cambodia over which the pilots could fly. This reduced the problem of crowded airspace, which had become increasingly dangerous. For example, on 2 May an AH-1 Cobra helicopter and an OV-2 observation aircraft collided above the Fishhook; both helicopter pilots died in the crash, while the legs of two air force officers were severed by the rotor blades (they both quickly bled to death).[74] However, the expanded area of operations also made it harder to spot targets on

the ground: fewer eyes were watching any given spot. Further, the limited preat-
tack intelligence meant that the target lists for planned air strikes for 2 and 3 May
were simply restrikes of those hit on 1 May; only with combat-developed intelligence did new targets appear on the lists, for 4 and 6 May and thereafter.[75]

Davison also got involved, interceding with Shoemaker's otherwise excellent
handling of matters to order the 11ACR north to Snuol to cut off as many NVA
troops and supplies as possible.[76] Smith and Leech, the IIFFV planners, had recommended Snuol because it was easy for Americans to pronounce and find on
their maps, and because Highway 7 ran directly to it.[77] Accordingly, the 11ACR
headed north up Highway 7, passing through an infantry force air assaulted south
of Snuol on 3 May and reaching Snuol on the fifth.

Snuol would pass for a small hamlet in most American counties, but for eastern Cambodia in 1970 its two-story cinderblock main street was exceptional. An
important distribution point for NVA supplies coming down the Ho Chi Minh
Trail and up the Sihanoukville Trail, Snuol was likely to be defended, but no one
at IIFFV headquarters knew for sure.[78] Starry did not know either; he found out
when he reached the town and got into a brisk firefight with NVA troops.

Snuol's airstrip, though dirt and grass, was one of the few in the area. Having
fought the First Cavalry Division in Vietnam, NVA defenders knew it would be a
very attractive objective for the heliborne American attackers. Accordingly, they
dug in their 12.7mm heavy machine guns around it, sited so as to cut troop-filled
helicopters to shreds. Unfortunately for them, the attack instead came on the
ground from two squadrons' worth of tanks and ACAVs from the 11ACR, which
quickly overran the ill-positioned machine guns and seized the airfield and city.[79]
This one clash alone justified the 11ACR's inclusion, since many more American
lives would likely have been lost had the U.S. force been helicopter-borne light
infantry instead of an ACR with its firepower and armor.

In racing to and through Snuol, though, Starry unintentionally violated one of
Nixon's guidelines. Seeking to dampen the rapidly growing domestic outcry
shortly after the incursion had begun, Nixon announced that it was limited in
both time and scope: U.S. troops would be out by the end of June and would go
no deeper into Cambodia than thirty kilometers. However, commanders in Southeast Asia never got that word in time. Securing the far side of Snoul, the 11ACR
exceeded Nixon's thirty-kilometer limit by about five kilometers. Out of touch
with the news, Starry first learned of the limit from communist radio broadcasts
complaining about his disobeying Nixon's orders. Confirming the limit with
Shoemaker, he pulled his forces back,[80] having so surprised the NVA by the
speed of his advance that fleeing enemy engineers left their surveying instruments on the Snuol bridge.[81]

Davison likewise was surprised, first hearing of COSVN being an objective
and there being a thirty-kilometer limit on the U.S. advance by listening to
Nixon's speech on a U.S. Armed Forces Network news broadcast the day after
Nixon gave it. Neither fact greatly affected what he was going to do.[82]

Once the zone of operations was secure against any organized NVA/VC resistance, the heavier forces became less immediately relevant to the hunt for
caches. Although the 11ACR's tanks and ACAVs could flatten vegetation to
make paths through the jungle, it lacked the foot soldiers to spot the paths and indicators that led to the hidden supplies. Accordingly, the 11ACR was soon back
in South Vietnam escorting convoys, guarding land-clearing operations in the
Fishhook and War Zone C by Rome Plows, giant armored bulldozers that flat-
tened forests, and patrolling routes across northern Tay Ninh and Binh Long
Provinces.

It was back in Vietnam, however, without much of the regimental command
group. Outside Snuol an NVA soldier had refused to climb out of an underground
bunker and surrender to Colonel Starry and his staff. Instead, he tossed out a
grenade, which killed the regimental command sergeant major, blew off most of
Major Frederick Franks's foot (Franks was the regimental operations officer, and
another future four-star general), and seriously wounded Colonel Starry with a
grenade fragment in the stomach. The NVA soldier immediately died in his turn,
and the wounded Americans were evacuated back to South Vietnam.

Just as the 11ACR's time soon passed, so also it did for the U.S. jets that had provided heavy firepower in the opening attack. On 4 May they had tried to destroy a
bridge near Snuol to help Starry isolate the Fishhook, but five passes left it "still
usable for jeep traffic," with a hole in the center span and some damaged abut-
ments.[83] By week's end the priority shifted from sealing off the Fishhook to looking for caches. Helicopters and the low- and slow-flying USAF spotter aircraft
could more readily find such sites due to their longer loiter time above a given
area and thus became more valuable to the searchers than the fast-moving fighter-
bombers.

As the task force pushed into and beyond the Fishhook in the first days of
May, like the aircraft its emphasis shifted from movement to looking for caches.
Given the lack of specific information on where they might be, the First
Squadron Ninth Cavalry's aviators played a critical role in finding them. As the
division's reconnaissance unit, it was normally first in an area and had an edge
over UH-1H pilots whose primary task was to get their passengers safely to the
landing zones. Although the First Squadron Ninth Cavalry's helicopter-borne rifle platoons, or "blues," could land and investigate, most often the platoons simply reported their finds and let the division's infantry battalions move to and
capture the stockpiles. This kept the "blues" free for emergencies such as securing helicopter or airplane crash locations for rescue and recovery.

The First Squadron Ninth Cavalry's aggressive pilots and its aerial vantage
point made the squadron particularly good at finding caches in and around the
Fishhook. On 4 May, an average day, its pilots spotted five different bases and
sites.[84] These varied in size and contents, the most significant being open-sided

sheds filled with 460 tons of rice, which upon capture went to feed refugees in South Vietnam instead of NVA infantrymen.[85]

One of the biggest finds, early in the incursion, occurred on 3 May south of Snuol. On 2 May a First Squadron Ninth Cavalry scout was flying at treetop level just across the border from the northwest corner of Binh Long Province when his rotors' downdraft blew aside some branches of the jungle canopy and revealed a large encampment below. Because Third Brigade's forces were committed, Kingston asked Shoemaker to give him Lieutenant Colonel James Anderson's First Battalion Fifth Cavalry to investigate.

Shoemaker agreed and around midnight told Anderson to follow up the pilot's spotting. Anderson and his staff quickly changed gears from working with ARVN in Binh Long Province to preparing for an air assault and sent out the necessary orders to his companies. At daybreak Anderson assembled his scattered units; by 1330 on 3 May he moved the battalion by helicopter to an area about ten kilometers south of Snuol.[86] Leaving one company to build and man a fire support base, he pushed south toward the reported location.[87]

That afternoon C Company discovered a huge NVA complex with paths and roads made of bamboo laid crosswise. The roads were about five to six feet wide and rested on the ground, while the "sidewalks" were raised off the ground. The vast size of the base, about three kilometers long by almost two wide, quickly led troops to name it "The City." More significant than its dimensions was the material captured: its 182 bunkers contained 171 tons of ammunition, plus clothing, food, and weapons.

The munitions included artillery shells of perhaps 130mm caliber. These, along with the 1,200 75mm shells found in a cache in War Zone C on the afternoon of 29 April by Second Battalion Fifth Cavalry, should have attracted more attention than they did.[88] While NVA divisions had used tube artillery in I CTZ, in the northern quarter of South Vietnam just below the DMZ, in 1968 communist artillery units had previously fired only rockets and mortars in III CTZ, and shot a captured cannon but rarely in IV CTZ. This was because cannon could move neither fast enough nor far enough immediately after firing to long survive within South Vietnam under the allies' air supremacy. Only those lightweight and expendable systems permitting quick departures by the crews upon firing, such as mortars and rockets, were practical for continued use.

Shells, especially those used by the long-range 130mm gun, were an unambiguous indicator that Hanoi was preparing to escalate the war by using large conventional forces within the next year or so. Had anyone remembered, Giap had prepared for Dien Bien Phu months before the battle started by secretly stockpiling tens of thousands of artillery shells in the hills around the French positions prior to moving in his cannon to open fire.

Giap had been open about his intentions, telling a journalist in a spring 1969 interview, "Dienbienphu, madame, Dienbienphu . . . history doesn't always repeat itself. But this time it will. We won a military victory over the French, and we'll win it over the Americans, too. . . . We'll beat them at the moment when they have the most men, the most arms, and the greatest hope of winning."[89]

The founder and commander of the NVA may well have been speaking figuratively, with no intention of launching a combined infantry-artillery assault against a major U.S. or ARVN base. On the other hand, his greatest victory resulted from an artillery siege followed by infantry assaults overrunning isolated garrisons. Further, it is doubtful that a "logistical genius" like Giap, or a staff as smart and committed as that in Hanoi, would have been so foolish as to have sent numbers of artillery shells south if they had had no intention of using them reasonably soon.

In any case, despite Giap's admission and the evidence of the shells, media attention focused instead on The City's size and contents. There were hundreds of open-sided huts, grouped according to function: classrooms for training, a hospital and recovery area, and huts of varying quality (the best promptly said to be for NVA officers). The base was big enough to handle a regiment of up to 2,000 troops at a time. Because of the size of the complex and the impossibility of one infantry company of about 150 men adequately searching and securing it, Anderson assigned a second company to help him.[90] A few days later, the First Cavalry Division found an even bigger complex; by then Task Force Shoemaker's time had passed.

Task Force Shoemaker's attack succeeded for two key reasons. First, its leaders successfully improvised amid rapidly changing circumstances. More important, though, there was no serious NVA opposition. Had the NVA chosen to stand and fight atop its ammunition stockpiles, the assault would have been much bloodier. Further, U.S. preparations had deliberately downplayed logistics as a consequence of the limited time and the desire to preserve secrecy. However, had the NVA fought, Shoemaker's units would probably have run short on supplies. Further, the lack of forward depots would have hindered the units' remaining in Cambodia had the monsoons come on time (instead of weeks late), crippling the aerial resupply effort on which the division depended. Luck, opportunity, and aggressive commanders thus played major roles in Shoemaker's success.

Go Dau Ha in northwestern Tay Ninh Province was the site of ARVN III Corps' forward headquarters for its operations in Cambodia during the incursion. (Photo taken on 19 May 1970 by 1LT Norman C. Royce, 221st Signal Co. National Archives, no. CC66535)

Runway and southwestern portion of Thien Ngon, a forward base in northwest Tay Ninh Province. (Photo by Sp4 D. S. Denges. National Archives, no. SC655849)

Elements of the Eleventh Armored Cavalry Regiment enter Snuol, Cambodia. (Photo taken on 5 May 1970 by SSG W. Bryant, 221st Signal Co. National Archives, no. SC655522)

Tanks and ACAVs of 2-47 Armor return fire while entering Cambodia. (Photo taken by SP5 Hank Smith, 1st Cavalry Division. National Archives, no. SC655881)

E Troop, 2-11 ACR, advance on 10 May 1970 through a wooded area ten miles inside Cambodia and thirty miles north of Loc Ninh, South Vietnam. (Photo taken by SP5 Lindee, 221st Signal Co. National Archives, no. SC655565)

A UH-1D helicopter of the 16th Air Cavalry carries soldiers of ARVN's 21st Infantry Division into Cambodia. (Photo taken on 25 May 1970 by SP5 Willie E. Waters, 221st Signal Co. National Archives, no. SC655721)

Armored vehicles of A Troop, 3-4 Cavalry, 25th Infantry Division, move through the Cambodian jungle on 18 May 1970. (Photo taken by SP4 Hinton, 221st Signal Co. National Archives, no. SC655585)

A typical hut containing ammunition crates in The City, Cambodia. The corrugated roof protects the ammunition from rains. (Photo taken on 7 May 1970 by SSG W. Bryant, 221st Signal Co. National Archives, no. SC655506)

SP4 Russell D. Battley of Ventress, LA, a door gunner for C Troop, 16th Air Cavalry, above Tay Ninh Province on a flight into Tuk Meas, Cambodia. (Photo taken on 25 May 1970 by SP5 Willie E. Waters, 221st Signal Co. National Archives, no. SC655722)

Troops at the Quan Loi landing zone examine captured enemy weapons from the Fishhook area of Cambodia. (Photo taken on 5 May 1970 by SSG W. Bryant, 221st Signal Co. National Archives, no. CC66327)

Ammunition storage hut in The City, Cambodia. (Photo taken on 7 May 1970 by SSG W. Bryant, 221st Signal Co. National Archives, no. SC655503)

Stored ammunition cache eighty miles northwest of Saigon. (Photo taken on 11 May 1970 by SP4 S. McFarland, 221st Signal Co. National Archives, no. SC656178)

ABOVE: Ammunition crates under a black plastic covering in The City, Cambodia. (Photo taken on 11 May 1970 by Richard H. Beveridge. National Archives, no. SC655663)

Recoilless rifle ammunition captured in The City, Cambodia. (Photo taken on 11 May 1970 by Richard H. Beveridge. National Archives, no. SC655664)

Expert on communist equipment SFC Vincent Delgrosso explains how to disarm a VC explosive to members of the 25th Infantry Division's A Troop, 3-4 Cavalry, which they found in the Cambodian jungle. (Photo taken on 18 May 1970 by SP4 Hinton, 221st Signal Co. National Archives, no. SC655570)

Troopers of C Company, 1-5 Infantry, of the First Cavalry Division examine a captured Chinese antiaircraft gun at Firebase Terry Linn, in Cambodia about eighty miles northwest of Saigon. Weapons such as these could shred any helicopter that flew into range. (Photo taken on 11 May 1970 by SP4 S. McFarland, 221st Signal Co. National Archives, no. SC656170)

A ninety- to one-hundred-man auditorium in The City, Cambodia, with training aids and trenches. (Photo taken on 7 May 1970 by SSG W. Bryant, 221st Signal Co. National Archives, no. SC655512)

An NVA structure found in a base camp near Firebase Phillips, Cambodia, thought to have been an officers' conference room due to the quality of its construction, 1970. (Photographer unknown. National Archives, no. SC655639)

A cache of rice in 250-pound bags found by A Company, 5-12 Infantry, 1st Cavalry Division, about three miles north of Fire Support Base Brown and four miles inside Cambodia. Bomb blasts damaged the roofs and sacks. (Photo taken on 19 May 70 by SP4 Lundee, 221st Signal Co. National Archives, no. SC655598)

A front-end loader from the 31st Engineer Battalion dumps rice into a truck for transport to South Vietnam. The rice was found by A Company, 5-12 Infantry, 1st Cavalry Division, three miles north of Fire Support Base Brown. (Photo taken on 19 May 1970 by SP4 Lundee, 221st Signal Co. National Archives, no. SC655600)

A ten-ton-capacity flatbed truck leaves Fire Support Base Brown, carrying 250-pound sacks of rice back to South Vietnam. (Photo taken by Bert Kasprowicz. National Archives, no. SC655674)

Sacks of captured rice at Fire Support Base Brown, waiting transport to South Vietnam. (Photo taken by Bert Kasprowicz. National Archives, no. SC655672)

Vietnamese stack confiscated rice from NVA stockpiles in a warehouse in Tay Ninh, Vietnam, to be given to Cambodian refugees in the IV Corps area. (Photo taken on 19 May 1970 by SP4 Gaynor, 221st Signal Co. National Archives, no. CC66402)

Aerial view of Fire Support Base Jay, operated by the 1st Cavalry Division near the Cambodian border. Six 105mm howitzers are in the circular berms in the foreground; six 155mm howitzers are visible in the top of the photograph. (Photo taken on 29 June 1970 by SP4 James Ensign. National Archives, no. SC656107)

A 175mm gun of C Battery, 2-32 Field Artillery, prepares to depart from Fire Support Base Sharon. The chain-link fence in the background is to protect the gun and crew from rocket-propelled grenades. (Photo taken on 19 May 1970 by SP4 K. Essen, 221st Signal Co. National Archives, no. SC655596)

Mess hall of 1-8 Field Artillery, 25th Infantry Division, after heavy rains in Cambodia. Cases of C rations support the tables and benches. (Photo taken on 19 May 1970 by 1LT N. Royce, Detachment C, 221st Signal Co. National Archives, no. SC655607)

Helicopter landing pad used to resupply the signal site on Nui Ba Den Mountain operated by B Company, 125th Signal Battalion, 25th Infantry Division, 1969. Note the density of FM antennae. (Photo taken by SP5 D. R. Goff, 125th Signal Battalion, 25th Infantry Division. National Archives, no. SC652881)

Radio relay site atop Nui Ba Den Mountain operated by the 39th Signal Battalion. The pyramid-shaped objects in the top left of the photograph are microwave antennae, which require line of sight to other stations. The vertical whips are for FM tactical radios, with omnidirectional transmission. Sandbags protect against VC mortar fragments. (Photo taken on 15 August 1969 by SP4 Timothy Fease, 53rd Signal Battalion. National Archives, no. SC651806)

Photographer SSG William Bryant passes out gum to Cambodian children outside Fire Base Terry Linn, Cambodia. (Photo taken by SP4 S. McFarland, 221st Signal Co. National Archives, no. SC656172)

6

The First Cavalry Division
Expands into Cambodia

In Washington the administration followed the incursion's start with great interest. Visiting the Pentagon on 1 May (2 May in Vietnam) for an update on Shoemaker's progress, Nixon decided he would "take just as much political heat for taking out two sanctuaries as [he] would for taking out six." He therefore ordered Wheeler to tell Abrams to "'Knock them all out so they can't be used against us again, ever.'"[1] Abrams instructed Davison accordingly, and new missions went to Roberts and Major General Edward Bautz of the Twenty-fifth Infantry Division.

As the incursion progressed, Roberts realized it had grown too big for Shoemaker's small staff to effectively control. On the afternoon of 5 May he disbanded Task Force Shoemaker and assumed direct command of all the division's activities in Cambodia.[2] This was appropriate, if belated, since the task force was never intended to replace division headquarters. Further, Task Force Shoemaker consisted of combat units and lacked the logistics and administrative specialists necessary to operate unsupported across the border in the sanctuaries for any length of time. The First Cavalry Division headquarters had such people, experienced at controlling and supporting multiple units spread over wide areas.

Soon after the division headquarters took charge, actions waned involving multiple brigades. The brigades moved into new areas, but their emphasis shifted to battalion-level searches for caches and the disposition of any materials captured. As daily operations settled into routines resembling those in Vietnam, the largely unnoticed supporters, engineers, supply, and transportation troops became relatively more important in fully exploiting the border sanctuaries.

On 6 May 1970 the First Cavalry Division's Second Brigade opened the division's second major action in Cambodia, TOAN THANG 45. This attack was against Base Areas 350 and 351, in the mountainous region along the northern borders of

Binh Long and Phuoc Long Provinces. Roberts's intelligence staff believed that these sanctuaries contained two infantry regiments' headquarters, two Rear Service Groups that handled NVA logistics, and at least one infantry battalion.[3] As the Second Brigade advanced against little opposition, however, the analysts realized that the two sanctuaries were about fifteen kilometers deeper inside Cambodia than they had suspected.[4] Though this meant lighter U.S. casualties, it also meant the extra days of looking for caches along the border were largely wasted.

To cover the division's expanding area inside Cambodia, Roberts had to include more units in incursion-related operations. Initially excluded from cross-border preparations and actions, the First Brigade had continued its searches throughout the northwest corner of Tay Ninh Province. Meanwhile, the Third Brigade rooted north and east across the Fishhook, and the Second Brigade shifted east and prepared to capture Base Areas 350 and 351. As its sister brigades moved across the border, the First Brigade assumed responsibility for much of the area in South Vietnam they had vacated, as well as helping search the Fishhook.

Normally commanding three infantry battalions, the First Brigade commander controlled eleven U.S. and ARVN battalions moving into the Fishhook behind the Third Brigade. This force was simply too big and complex for many brigade commanders to effectively direct, and the commander's lack of recent troop duty before taking command did not help matters.[5] Roberts relieved him just four days after the brigade had entered Cambodia.

While reliefs are always disruptive to the unit involved, the First Brigade commander's firing initiated a ripple effect that directly affected two other brigades in the division. On 8 May, after the Third Brigade had been in the Fishhook for a week, Roberts ordered Kingston to assume command of the First Brigade. He complied, turning over his Third Brigade temporarily to Colonel Kenneth D. Martel of the division's Aviation Group (a brigade-sized command) until Colonel Joseph Franklin took formal command on 4 June. Thus, in one morning three of Roberts's six brigades got new commanders.[6]

Fortunately, there was only light NVA activity at the time: such extensive changes in the face of determined resistance could have led to higher U.S. casualties. Kingston immediately got his new staff together, castigated them for not doing more to prevent his predecessor's failure, and announced that a like fate would not happen to him.[7] Though appropriate, the harsh tone and content of Kingston's initial remarks only added to the brigade's stress at the relief and their gaining a new commander with Kingston's abrasive reputation.

The relief and command shifts did not affect the operation's outcome, Base Areas 350 and 351 falling to Second Brigade without incident. Soon after taking over First Brigade, Kingston moved its headquarters across the border, making it the only U.S. brigade headquarters to operate inside Cambodia. It worked in the Fishhook until 20 May, when Major General George Casey, the division's new commanding general, sent it farther north along the border to help search Base

Areas 351 and 350. By then U.S. and ARVN forces had been in the Fishhook for almost three weeks, the rate of new finds had dropped, and Casey believed the First Brigade would be more valuable in searching fresh areas alongside the Second Brigade.

Kingston made a smart decision in moving his command post and supply base to O Raing, about fifty kilometers east-northeast of Snuol. Lieutenant Colonel Joe Anderson's First Battalion Fifth Cavalry had just established a camp there; by colocating with Anderson's infantrymen the brigade headquarters gained better security. Such roads as existed from Vietnam were at best poor, so the brigade's resupply would be almost entirely by air. The grass airfield at O Raing could handle C-7 and C-123 light cargo aircraft, greatly aiding the logisticians' efforts to sustain the force. Between 23 May and 30 June, 169 C-7 sorties delivered almost 246 tons of cargo and 328 passengers to O Raing.[8] Airplanes could carry supplies faster than helicopters and left the division's eighteen CH-47 medium-lift helicopters free to respond to unexpected developments. As the engineers realized, however, "a grass strip at the beginning of the rainy season was really going to be a SOB to maintain. . . . As the rainy season approached, that thing kept several of us in a sweat most of the time."[9]

Remaining in Cambodia and looking for caches required the division to protect and sustain its forces there. This would ordinarily have been hard enough, but three factors complicated matters. First, the division had to help supply other units as well, particularly the ARVN Airborne Brigade and the 11ACR. As one battalion commander noted, "It is an *incredible* strain on the artillery and engineers and the signal of the 1st Cav to have *all* the brigades conducting airmobile operations at the same time, much less having some responsibility to support the Vietnamese Airborne Brigade, the Vietnamese Armored Cav, and having the 11th ACR pulling resources from you, too."[10]

Additional friction came from the turmoil in division headquarters. Most of the key staff officers were finishing their yearlong tours of duty and departing in the annual personnel rotations. Between 15 and 27 April, Roberts got a new chief of staff, personnel officer, intelligence officer, operations officer, and civil-military affairs officer; only Lieutenant Colonel Lewis Williams, Roberts's supply officer, remained. Although most of these men came directly from other jobs in the division, their transitions to service as Division Staff principals briefly reduced the headquarters' overall efficiency as they became familiar with their new duties, subordinates, and their interplay with the other staff elements. Their learning period coincided with preparing for and launching both TOAN THANG 43 and 45. Fortunately, the First Cavalry Division was full of extremely gifted leaders: for example, besides division chief of staff Colonel Edward Meyer retiring years later as the army's chief of staff, the G-2 Lieutenant Colonel John Galvin likewise retired as a four-star general, the supreme allied commander of NATO in the late 1980s. Such officers' competence and experience greatly mitigated the disruption of the job changes.

Concurrently to the staff turnover was the division's change of command. Roberts was to have passed command to Casey on 3 May, but to preclude disrupting the initial assault into Cambodia, Davison had delayed the event until the twelfth. Casey took command, with little break in the division's rhythm: as a colonel he had commanded the Second Brigade, then served as chief of staff. Tragically, on 7 July he died in a helicopter crash, en route to visit wounded soldiers at Cam Ranh Bay.[11] Brigadier General John Burton, Casey's successor as one of the two assistant division commanders, became acting commanding general until Major General George Putnam could assume command. Putnam, commander of the division-sized First Aviation Brigade, had two years earlier served as division artillery commander and then division chief of staff; he succeeded Casey as commanding general of the First Cavalry Division about three weeks after the latter's death and shortly before the division left Cambodia. Thus, during the two-month-long incursion, the First Cavalry Division had three commanding generals and one acting commander.

A final serious problem was the virtual absence of any infrastructure on either side of the border, particularly roads big enough for trucks. Because units needed fire support bases for artillery and shelter and the area had few roads, engineers were particularly important. The division engineer, Lieutenant Colonel Scott Smith, directed all engineering projects in the division's sector. This caused some tensions, since IIFFV's Twentieth Engineer Brigade had sent Colonel Ernest Denz's Seventy-ninth Engineer Group (consisting of the Thirty-first and 588th Engineer Battalions) to support the division's operations. One rank junior to Denz, Smith could not give him orders, but his position as division engineer obligated him to direct Denz's efforts within the First Cavalry Division's area of responsibility. Smith shrewdly resolved matters by dividing the work geographically, his Eighth Engineers working inside Cambodia and Denz's Seventy-ninth Engineers inside Vietnam.

Smith's decision was both politically expedient and militarily practical, best using each unit's capabilities. The Eighth was a light organization that could move quickly by helicopter. For his 500 men Smith had about 300 chainsaws, which, used with explosives, knocked down trees to create landing zones for the helicopters and infantry to follow. Smith also had a few small bulldozers and backhoes to build fire support bases. The Seventy-ninth's equipment was different and included such heavy earthmoving machinery as road graders, front-end loaders, and dump trucks; it also had access to crushed rock for making or repairing roads. The Seventy-ninth thus improved and maintained the forward airfields within and supply routes across northern Tay Ninh and Binh Long Provinces.

Building roads through forests and jungles was a major undertaking, Denz splitting his forces to carry it out. In the east the Thirty-first Engineers opened the existing unimproved road from Loc Ninh north to Snuol and made it capable of handling heavier traffic. To the west the 588th Engineers expanded and maintained Katum's airfield and new supply depot.[12] The 588th also spent thousands of hours maintaining the fifty kilometers of Highway TL-4 between Tay Ninh and Katum, one of the major routes toward the border. Denz's biggest job was digging numerous drainage ditches and raising the road surface in low-lying areas.[13] Without this the monsoons would have flooded and closed critical supply arteries. The Seventy-ninth Engineer Group was indispensable in providing the roads and airfields necessary to sustain Roberts's presence in Cambodia.

When the Eighth Engineers were not cutting landing zones or blowing up NVA supplies during TOAN THANG 45, its men cut timber beams and built prefabricated bunkers to speed up construction of new firebases. Troops searching for or through caches relied on the firebases to provide both artillery support and a secure "home" from which to patrol farther. When a unit occupied an area for a firebase, a bulldozer scraped a perimeter ring and pushed up a low dirt wall while a backhoe dug holes in the middle of the circle and along the wall. Helicopters then carried assembled bunkers to the base and dropped them in the holes.

Normally, a firebase would need bunkers for the commander and operations staff, the artillery fire direction center, the communications center, the medical station, and strongpoints along the perimeter. Radios and telephones (if installed during the bunkers' construction) meant that the base's "central nervous system" would be functioning before nightfall. Preparing defenses rapidly was crucial. As Smith, who retired as a major general, later recalled,

> If you are truly disastrous in your reconnaissance way, [and] you land on a hot LZ, you're in shit from the get-go. If your luck is middling, you get hit some way or other that night. And if you're very fortunate . . . you have one night to work through, and the second day to work through, and get *nailed* the following night. So, to the extent [engineers] can, forty-five minutes after combat insertion you start piling in.[14]

A firebase's defenses often meant survival to the troops inside, and the bunkers were critical to its strength. Although the Eighth Engineers normally built them in advance of units' moves, the size of Shoemaker's force, the short notice before entering Cambodia, and the fast pace of operations for the first few days meant that Smith had far fewer prefabricated bunkers ready than he would have liked.[15] Fortunately, there was little serious enemy resistance until later in the incursion. By early June the NVA began contesting U.S. and ARVN control of the border sanctuaries, and night attacks became increasingly common. The engineers' berms and bunkers often made the difference between repelling such assaults or being overrun.

The supply effort followed closely behind the combat engineers. To preserve surprise, Davison had launched Shoemaker's attack without building up forward stockpiles. However, Lieutenant Colonel Williams's hasty logistical preparations of late April became the basis for much larger efforts by the First Cavalry Division in May and June. Several brigade-sized units had support facilities at Tay

Ninh and Quan Loi, so the division simply expanded its existing capabilities at those places.

Aerial resupply was essential, as Shoemaker's planners had assumed. Since runways at Katum and Tonle Cham were nearest the Fishhook and could handle air force C-130 cargo planes, beginning on 29 April they became the main forward supply points, supplemented by Tay Ninh and Quan Loi. Because the area's sole helicopter refueling and rearming point at Tonle Cham was insufficient, the First Cavalry Division built two more at Katum and Loc Ninh.[16]

As 1 May approached, division logisticians had pushed as many resources as possible to locations closer to the border. Units not essential to launching the attack were told only at the last minute and left to do their best. The division's Fifteenth Medical Battalion learned of the attack so late it did not begin redistributing its assets to better support Task Force Shoemaker until 1 May.[17] Not having the doctors ready would have cost more U.S. lives had the NVA and VC defended from the start, but light enemy resistance, tactical surprise, and adequate resources compensated for incomplete preparations. This gave the logisticians time to correct initial shortfalls, which included building more forward supply points as the incursion progressed.[18]

The nature of the First Cavalry Division's logistics changed in early May. At first each support unit and facility was affiliated with specific combat forces, regardless of their location within the division's area of responsibility at any moment. As forces moved or were reassigned from one brigade to another, though, it became increasingly hard for combat units to receive what they had ordered and for their designated support units to get those materials to them.

The commanding general from 12 May on, Casey approved a different procedure. In this new arrangement the support units were responsible for specific regions rather than units. Supporting everyone in a given area eased matters for the infantry and artillery but significantly complicated them for the supply personnel.[19] Not knowing with any certainty whom they were to help in the next few days, or what those units had ordered previously, logisticians could not accurately predict what supplies would be needed where.

Accordingly, the logisticians turned to a "push" system, sending forward without first being asked those items experience had shown most likely to be needed: for example, bullets, grenades, food, and radio batteries for the infantry. This was more inefficient than providing a particular item or quantity in response to a unit's request but was faster for the infantry company that wanted something. Time was limited; supplies, by comparison, were not. The U.S. Army in Vietnam had enough logistical capability to make the "push" technique work for the Cambodian incursion so long as heavy fighting elsewhere did not increase demands on the supply system.

There were some persistent stresses on the supply system, however. One came from the First Cavalry Division's view of itself as warranting special treatment. Initially something of a "fire brigade" for MACV upon its arrival in South Vietnam in 1965, ever since it had received its supplies directly from the U.S. Army, Vietnam (USARV). Such an arrangement made sense in the early days of U.S. involvement: the First Cavalry Division shifted frequently across corps boundaries in response to tactical dictates, and its supply requests often failed to keep up with the unit's location. With supply requests going directly to USARV, the First Cavalry Division had fewer lost requisitions, but it also tended to be less affected by the supply constraints imposed by corps-level headquarters on the other divisions. This changed on 1 May 1970, IIFFV ordering it to route all its supply requests through Davison's headquarters. The division complied but complained that doing so hurt its supply responsiveness.[20] The cost in time was comparatively minor: what irked the division most was that Davison treated it like all other American divisions. The division adapted and continued to fight.

A more significant logistical problem throughout the incursion was the resupply of artillery ammunition. Demand for shells remained high because of the rates of fire of 105mm light howitzers (up to ten shots per minute), their numbers (fifty-four in the Division Artillery, plus almost that many in the ARVN units it helped supply), and the infantry's readiness to shoot first at targets with artillery before investigating with foot patrols. The tonnages involved could quickly mount: in the Fishhook on 1 May alone, the First Cavalry Division, ARVN, and supporting IIFFV units fired 140 tons of ammunition that they needed replaced before nightfall.[21] As the incursion lengthened and major movements yielded to searches, NVA resistance increased. The more frequent firefights meant more shells were needed inside Cambodia and along the border.

Prompt resupply was essential, since most soldiers and commanders rightly regarded their lives as more valuable than ammunition. This was particularly true in the First Cavalry Division, relying as it did on firepower from artillery and the air to compensate for its lack of armor. By 1970, domestic pressures and declining troop strengths made firepower even more important in keeping U.S. casualties low. Unlike planes or helicopters, which weather conditions could hinder or halt in the pre–GPS satellite days of the Vietnam War, artillery was always available. Because the monsoons virtually precluded most air activities, artillery support usually meant life or death for infantrymen. Ammunition was thus an issue senior leaders took very seriously, especially given their reliance on aerial resupply.

To sustain heavy rates of firing, supply units set up forward ammunition dumps. Air force transports flew the shells from Long Binh and other major U.S. stockpiles to Bu Dop, Bu Gia Map, and later O Raing, Cambodia. Helicopters then moved the ammunition to fire support bases along the border and inside Cambodia.[22] The mountains around Bu Gia Map made the weather there less predictable than elsewhere, however, with rain and heavy usage occasionally forcing closure of the airstrip. Ammunition deliveries failing to arrive on time could cause backlogs to quickly develop in the First Cavalry Division's overall supply system. Division Artillery headquarters normally required its battalions to submit hourly ammunition status reports so the staff could determine priorities for more shells and coordinate with cargo helicopters to move the loads before dark. Such close management indicates the thin margin of error in this crucial area.[23]

Another major problem was the evacuation of captured supplies. Although Shoemaker expected to capture some supplies, he thought his staff could handle their disposal with little trouble. He, like all other observers, was stunned at the vast quantity of war materials ultimately seized, on a scale beyond what the division's units could easily handle unassisted.[24] These supplies had first to be inventoried and then either destroyed or moved back to South Vietnam. Because the infantry was searching for more caches, with the artillery standing by their cannon to provide protection, the hard work of evacuating enemy materials fell chiefly on support units such as truck companies and quartermasters. Doing so, however, made them less available to move friendly supplies forward to the U.S. and ARVN combat units. Fortunately, light NVA resistance during most of the incursion kept U.S. and ARVN supply demands (less artillery ammunition) small enough that the airplanes and helicopters could handle most of the shipments, with occasional convoys of large trucks moving the rest.

A unique and highly sought-after asset was IIFFV's 273rd Aviation Company. Equipped with CH-54A heavy-lift helicopters ("Flying Cranes"), the only such unit in the southern half of South Vietnam, the 273rd moved a huge amount of heavy material for the First Cavalry Division. This included 380 bulldozers, backhoes, road graders, and bridge sections, 429 medium howitzers and artillery trucks, twenty APCs, eight helicopters, and a crashed air force ground attack plane.[25] Ground transportation units could have eventually moved the engineering and artillery equipment, but their diversion to evacuate captured enemy supplies and poor roads would have taken too much time. With Nixon's deadline of 30 June for all U.S. forces to be out of Cambodia, time was Casey's scarcest resource; the 273rd's heavy helicopters gave him more than he would have otherwise had.

Time, though, was ultimately on COSVN's side. Inside Cambodia, initial NVA/VC resistance was sporadic and uncoordinated, the result of communist surprise at the scale of the assaults and their decision to preserve manpower at the risk of losing stockpiled materials. Trying to put their people ahead of their supplies, the communist leaders often lost both. As one of Casey's infantry battalion commanders observed, "[COSVN's] supply people ran away. We killed most of them."[26] Any located caches then became subject to seizure.

Enemy activity in the division's sector back inside South Vietnam fell off quickly as well. In early May communist artillerymen rocketed the division headquarters and Second Brigade and Third Brigade base camps, trying unsuccessfully to divert Casey's attention to his rear areas. These attacks virtually ended by late May, NVA artillerymen in III CTZ having shot their remaining rockets without any resupply.[27]

In mid-May, however, the NVA began to recover its balance and resume attacks against allied forces inside Cambodia. Ambushes and mining of roads were the most frequent actions; because most rural roads were dirt, the enemy could easily plant mines in them at night. These roads required daily sweeping, requiring a "special kind" of individual. As the First Cavalry Division's engineer commander Lieutenant Colonel Smith later commented, "Few things in life surpass the clarity that comes from walking up the road with a marginally operational mine detector in your hands. . . . I do not know *how* the hell people did [it]."[28]

Company- and battalion-level night assaults took place as well. One such attack, typical of actions as the United States began withdrawing back to Vietnam, occurred in mid-June against Fire Support Base (FSB) David. The FSB contained Lieutenant Colonel Anderson's First Battalion Fifth Cavalry, as well as supporting artillery tubes and the Third Brigade headquarters.

The assault on 14–15 June by several battalions of the Fifth VC Division's 174th Regiment was a major one but was poorly executed. FSB David was on a slight rise, with ravines leading off to the northeast and northwest. The spring monsoon having begun, ground fog formed by 0300 at higher elevations and often persisted until late morning; this hid NVA forces as they advanced.[29] Apparently they had planned on attacking simultaneously up both ravines in the fog but failed to coordinate their movements. One assault began well before the other, permitting the U.S. troops to mass their fires against each in turn. Anderson shot into both ravines with artillery and mortars, breaking up most formations moving toward the base. A few enemy troops got into the firebase's interior but died before dawn.[30]

As Nixon's sixty-day clock was running and units searched for caches during early and mid-June, Casey's thoughts turned to his division's withdrawal. Given its dependence on movement and resupply by helicopters, the spring monsoon would make such operations increasingly difficult. The rains normally began around the third week in May, but in 1970 they were about ten days late and did not start until 28 May. This gave Casey extra time for seeking and removing captured materials.

The unexpectedly clear skies also helped mitigate problems with keeping the First Cavalry Division pilots properly certified and safely flying. Once the monsoon began, pilots often had to be able to fly by instruments instead of sight, and among its 577 pilots were only two qualified instrument flight examiners, far too few to test the hundreds of others in time to maintain their army aviation standards for certification and proficiency.[31] Firmly established by 3 June, the monsoon thereafter "appeared to be making up for lost time" with heavier than normal daily totals.[32] Casey became increasingly concerned with the weather's effects on his pullout, and after 20 June his morning and afternoon briefings included weather forecasts for the vicinity of each firebase to be shut down and evacuated.[33]

As June progressed, Casey began to return his units to South Vietnam. The ARVN Airborne Brigade closed its fire support bases without incident, artillery commander Brady and his ARVN counterpart watching from his helicopter ready to intervene with fires if necessary. The U.S. withdrawals proceeded equally smoothly, accompanied by Brady's pounding the areas around each site to suppress any enemy troops who might be preparing to attack the units as they departed.[34] On the other hand, the communists had lost heavily in the two-month incursion and lacked the ability to launch a major offensive to drive the Americans out of the base areas. They knew of Nixon's 30 June deadline, could see the Americans pulling back, and generally limited their own actions to harassment.

There were a few rough spots for the First Cavalry Division during June, such as one between Colonels Brady and Kingston. Both possessing aggressive and domineering personalities, the two colonels detested each other. Brady wanted to put on a firepower demonstration in Cambodia to show ARVN the power of massed artillery when properly employed. However, the area Brady wanted to use as a target "belonged" to Kingston, who felt Brady was simply trying to show off. Brady was incensed at Kingston's refusal and got Casey to approve the shoot, making Kingston even angrier. The demonstration went off well but, being beyond the ARVN artillery's capabilities at the time, was thus of limited value.[35]

As with the division's experiences in TOAN THANG 43 there were dozens of small caches, as well as several major finds (see map 6). Of these the biggest was "Rock Island East," which, like The City, was first spotted by a helicopter pilot from the First Squadron, Ninth Cavalry. An infantry company sent to investigate on 8 May, the third day of TOAN THANG 45, found the single greatest trove of all the operations into Cambodia. In an area 1 kilometer long by 500 meters wide were 326 tons of ammunition and supplies, all on pallets on the ground. This included more than 1,000 Soviet-made 85mm artillery shells for the D-44 howitzer, as well as shells for tank guns.

Neither artillery nor tanks had yet appeared, but the presence of their ammunition strongly suggested that Hanoi was preparing to use them against III CTZ.[36] Either would have been a significant escalation in the North's war effort, marking a further shift toward conventional war. Little attention seemed to attach to their discovery at the time or among most historians since, and the shells were simply destroyed since ARVN had no use for them. As at The City, the engineers cut a road through the jungle for the trucks to haul the other captured supplies back to South Vietnam.

About two weeks later, on 23 May, an infantry patrol from the Fifth Battalion, Seventh Cavalry, was going up a hill some twenty kilometers northeast of Rock Island East when its point man (nicknamed "Shaky") spotted buried metal peeking through the surface. He was killed soon thereafter by NVA defenders, but his comrades drove them off and overran the complex; in his memory they called it "Shaky's Hill." A search uncovered fifty-nine buried bunkers, all with tin roofs and containing thousands of cases of weapons and ammunition. The troopers carried them out one at a time, wondering why they did not simply blow them up in place. The answer was that the equipment was heading for FANK, but no one told the men that.[37]

Map 6. 1st Cavalry Division's Major Finds and Fire Support Bases in Cambodia

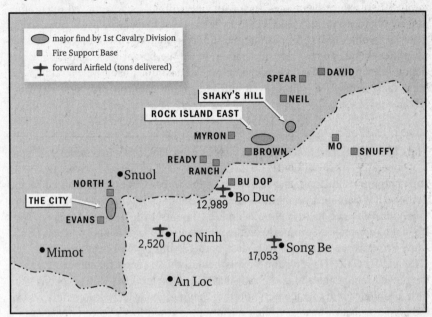

The First Cavalry Division inflicted substantial losses on Hanoi's efforts against III CTZ. These included some 2,600 enemy killed or captured, 6,900 individual or crew-served weapons, 2,200 tons of rice, 4,600 shells and rockets, more than 10 million bullets for machine guns, rifles, and pistols, and about thirty-six tons of explosives.[38] These were all munitions that Hanoi could no longer use against Saigon and the Americans, and would have to replace before mounting a new offensive.

The losses in troops were more significant than the numbers indicated, since fleeing NVA or VC often took their wounded but left their dead. At the then-typical NVA/VC divisional strength of 4,500 men, the death of 2,574 meant the B-2 Front lost the equivalent of half of a division to Casey's soldiers.[39] Most of these casualties were the result of the helicopter gunships, air strikes, and artillery that preceded infantry movements.

Many of the dead were specialists, such as medical, administrative, logistics, and communications personnel, more difficult for Hanoi to replace than infantrymen. It would first have to determine who was needed where, then identify, train, and dispatch the replacements from North Vietnam. Once in the right area of the South, they would have to be supplied with the necessary tools and equipment, yet another complication.

Hanoi had to send everything its troops needed, infantry and technician alike, through Laos, since Kampong Speu (Sihanoukville) was now closed to communist freighters. With the Ho Chi Minh Trail under air attack, even *more* scarce materials would have to be put into the supply system to ensure that the required quantities would survive the trip south to reach the border areas and thence into South Vietnam. This would be done but would take time, usually several months, and time for the U.S. withdrawal and the Vietnamization program was what Abrams most wanted.

The Cambodian operation led to the First Cavalry Division's making a small shift in its operating areas within III CTZ. Previously it had operated across Tay Ninh, Binh Duong, Binh Long, and Phuoc Long Provinces, generally to the north and northwest of Saigon. Upon returning from Cambodia, it turned over its sectors in Tay Ninh Province to ARVN units and the Twenty-fifth Infantry Division. This freed it to concentrate primarily on the northern regions of Binh Long and Phuoc Long Provinces, along the Cambodian border south of the boundary between II CTZ and III CTZ. The division was particularly well suited for this sector, since the rugged mountains and poor roads that would hinder other U.S. divisions were little problem for its helicopters. Further, having about forty kilometers less of the border to patrol near Tay Ninh meant pilots could focus more intensely on a smaller area, looking for infiltrators bringing supplies across from the Ho Chi Minh Trail. The First Cavalry Division stayed busy, but until its departure from Vietnam, none of its subsequent actions would match its work in the Cambodian incursion.

7

TOAN THANG 44:
The Twenty-fifth Infantry Division

Crossing into Cambodia soon after the First Cavalry Division was its sister American unit in III CTZ, the Twenty-fifth Infantry Division. Major General Edward Bautz, the Twenty-fifth's commanding general, had served with Abrams since World War II and had watched with interest Shoemaker's attack on the Fishhook on 1 May. Five days later Bautz's soldiers were themselves destroying border sanctuaries that threatened Saigon and could imperil the U.S. troop withdrawal.

More so than other units in III CTZ, the Twenty-fifth Infantry Division was stretched thin in spring 1970 by the U.S. withdrawal. The departures of the First and Ninth Infantry Divisions had greatly increased the area it had to cover. However, unlike other U.S. divisions in Vietnam in 1970, the Twenty-fifth had four infantry brigades. Three were regularly assigned to the division, while the fourth had previously been the Ninth Infantry Division's Third Brigade (Third/Ninth), briefly left in Vietnam to help guard III CTZ as Vietnamization progressed.

Four brigades gave Bautz a tremendous punch were he to attack en masse. The combat portion of his mission in early 1970 was essentially defensive, though, to help pacify and secure the western third of III CTZ. To do this he had to spread his units to secure the largest possible area against the most frequent threat, groups of ten to thirty NVA or VC who would fire a few shots and flee before U.S. troops could bring in their firepower. Further reducing his offensive potential, IIFFV detached the Second Brigade from Bautz's operational control in April and moved it east of Saigon near the coast.

Although Bautz had only one helicopter battalion compared with the three that gave the First Cavalry Division such mobility and flexibility, four of his twelve infantry battalions were mechanized with M113 armored personnel carriers (APCs).[1] The M113s were generally more useful in Vietnam than the 11ACR's M48A3 Patton tanks. Much lighter, they were thus less likely to get bogged down in soft ground; smaller, they could weave between trees more easily. Unlike helicopter gunships that were limited by fuel, darkness, and little armor, the M113s had "staying power." They mounted a .50-caliber heavy machine gun and carried ample ammunition, gave some protection against bullets, mortar fragments, and mines, and could transport about eight soldiers at speeds of up to thirty miles per hour.

When the Twenty-fifth Infantry Division attacked into Cambodia in early May, it usually assigned the mechanized battalions to whatever brigade was leading the assault. Doing so greatly increased that brigade's firepower and offensive power, since the mechanized infantry's speed, light armor, and heavy machine guns were hard for enemy soldiers to counter when armed only with assault rifles and grenades.

Bautz's Division Artillery also reflected the division's unique structure. It had fifty-four 105mm howitzers, in three battalions supporting the three infantry brigades. With the Third/Ninth came eighteen more 105mm howitzers, while the battalion firing for the division as a whole got a fourth firing battery of four 8-inch heavy howitzers to reinforce its eighteen 155mm medium howitzers. Colonel Harry Buzzett, the artillery commander, had these extra cannon because of the larger-than-normal area the division covered; at full strength he directed the fires of ninety-four cannon. Further support from IIFFV Artillery 155mm, 8-inch, and 175mm units was usually available if needed.[2] Buzzett also had a sixth battalion with mobile antiaircraft weapons; because there was no air threat in South Vietnam, it instead helped escort convoys and protect fire support bases. Buzzett typically deployed its weapons in pairs, keeping with the division's task of covering the maximum area possible.

The air defense battalion had three major weapons. The Vulcan was a six-barrel 20mm Gatling gun firing up to 3,000 slugs per minute from atop an M113 APC, while the Duster was a tank chassis carrying twin 40mm cannon together firing 240 two-pound high-explosive shells per minute. Finally, several cargo trucks carried "quad-.50s," four .50-caliber heavy machine guns rigged to fire at the same target. Any one of these weapons could tear an ambush or attack to shreds and had more firepower than a helicopter gunship at the expense of the latter's speed and mobility.

Unlike the First Cavalry Division, which Abrams and Davison had included in the Cambodian planning from the beginning, the Twenty-fifth Infantry Division became involved only after Nixon ordered the incursion expanded beyond the Fishhook and Parrot's Beak. Conducting its normal operations in III CTZ as TOAN THANG 43 began, it obeyed Davison's orders to support Shoemaker as the latter requested. On 1 May the division sent the First Cavalry Division an infantry battalion and two tunnel dogs with handlers to help with the attack on the Fishhook. Davison told Bautz to have his divisional cavalry squadron assume responsibility for part of Roberts's sector to compensate for the First Cavalry Division's commitment to the Fishhook.[3] Bautz was covering Roberts's back and wondering what else might happen, but he had no instructions concerning Cambodia.

Map 7. 25th Infantry Division in Cambodia

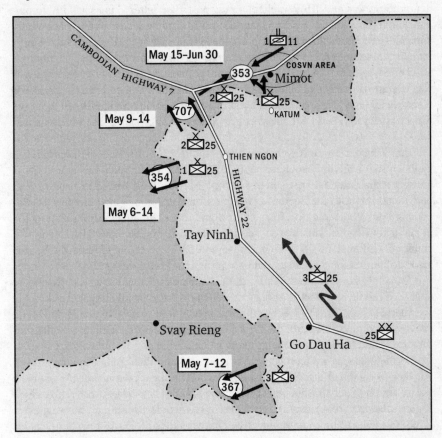

This soon changed. On 2 May, Davison gave Bautz three new missions (see map 7). The division was to attack Base Area 354 on 6 May to find and destroy the NVA Ninth Division's 95C Regiment, then seize whatever supplies it could find. His second task was to destroy Base Area 707, near Krek, and across the border from the area known as the "Dog's Head," while the third was to plan an attack on COSVN's suspected headquarters near Memot, Cambodia, a few kilometers west of where Shoemaker's forces had advanced in the opening assault on 1 May.

Bautz was to execute the first two orders and be ready to brief Abrams on the third.[4] He never got written orders on how his division was to attack the Cambodian sanctuaries, Davison instead simply saying what he wanted done. Bautz wrote Davison's guidance for an attack involving more than 20,000 soldiers onto one of the three-by-five-inch note cards he regularly carried in his pocket.[5]

Bautz needed additional troops in order to perform these tasks while continuing to protect the division's sector inside South Vietnam. He asked for and got back his Second Brigade and his divisional cavalry squadron, as well as Cambodian interpreters and IIFFV helicopter support. The latter was especially important, since the division's aviation battalion was sufficient only to lift one infantry company at a time.[6] Extra helicopters meant the Twenty-fifth could insert more infantry companies faster, which was safer for both the troops and the pilots.

Time was critical, since Bautz had only about sixty hours until the first attack was to start. He met briefly with Roberts; the two commanders quickly agreed on when the Twenty-fifth Infantry Division would assume responsibility from the First Cavalry Division for the western part of War Zone C and what Roberts could do to help Bautz.[7]

Bautz next flew to Tay Ninh and met with his First Brigade commander, Colonel Paul Mueller. Mueller was to relieve the First Cavalry Division units in the sector that night and plan an attack for 6 May on Base Area 354.

Bautz next told the Second Brigade's Colonel Ennis Whitehead that he was coming back under the division's control and would be attacking Base Area 707 in about four days.[8] This was something of a challenge for Whitehead, who was about 150 kilometers from his objective and on the "wrong" side of the Saigon metropolitan region. Whitehead did not have time to properly secure the areas he was vacating, he and Bautz taking the calculated risk that the enemy would be unable to mount an effective threat on such short notice while under attack in the sanctuaries. The Third Brigade continued patrolling Hau Nghia and Binh Duong Provinces, while the Third/Ninth got ready to support Tri's attacks into the Parrot's Beak and the Angel's Wing.

As the brigades were preparing for their new missions, Bautz had to consider whether to establish a forward division-level command post nearer the areas he was to attack, much as Shoemaker had done at Quan Loi in late April. He decided against this, knowing his units would be in Cambodia for only a relatively short time. Further, existing communications networks (particularly telephone cables and microwave relay stations) in the north and west of III CTZ connected those places where the units already were, rather than where they were moving; signal troops would be busy enough keeping First and Second Brigades talking to the division headquarters without the latter moving as well. Finally, since the division's cross-border operations would largely reflect tactical developments after the opening moves, a smoothly functioning division headquarters was essential. The division headquarters could communicate well with its brigades from where it was, so it would remain in its Cu Chi base camp.

Bautz and his two assistant division commanders, Brigadier Generals John R. Thurman III and Michael Greene, would supervise as necessary from their helicopters and Thien Ngon. On the morning of 6 May Greene oversaw the First Brigade's attack on Base Area 354, Thurman monitored the division's units supporting the First Cavalry Division as well as the Third Brigade, and Bautz briefed Abrams and Davison at Cu Chi on the Second Brigade's plan for assaulting Base Area 707 and COSVN.[9]

In preparing for his attack, Mueller had to consider both the forces available and the best place to start from. He had his "normal" four infantry battalions, two mechanized and two light, as well as the support of an artillery battalion. For the assault on Base Area 354, Bautz gave him D Troop/Third Squadron, Fourth Cavalry, on 5 May, and the bulk of the Third Squadron, Seventeenth Air Cavalry, on the sixth.[10] Although First Brigade's home camp at Tay Ninh West was only about thirty kilometers east of Base Area 354, Mueller decided to launch his operation from the abandoned village of Thien Ngon, about twenty-five kilometers to the northwest.

Thien Ngon had several advantages for such a role. It was far enough away from communist spies and sympathizers among the civilian populations of Tay Ninh West and Tay Ninh City, as well as the enemy observers in the caves on the sides of Nui Ba Den, the "Black Virgin," a solitary and ancient volcanic core just northeast of Tay Ninh City which towered 3,000 feet above the surrounding region. It was only twelve kilometers from where Mueller would cross the border, which meant shorter supply lines. From Thien Ngon the First Brigade could attack to the southwest (Base Area 354), northwest (Base Area 707), or north (Base Area 353). This multiple threat could confuse any NVA commander wanting to concentrate his forces, since doing so to protect one sanctuary would expose the other two. Finally, the old dirt airstrip could be refurbished, to help logistics operations.[11]

Thien Ngon and its airstrip played a critical role in the Twenty-fifth Infantry Division's attacks into Cambodia. From a deserted village it quickly became the forward base for First Brigade, and then the Second Brigade as well. It and Katum were the South Vietnamese airfields nearest the Tay Ninh Province–Cambodian border. Accordingly, the air force flew C-123 and C-130 "bladder birds" into these two airstrips, cargo aircraft carrying huge rubber bags filled with JP-4 high-octane aviation fuel. The fuel was then unloaded and pumped into army helicopters, permitting them to spend more time in the air over Cambodia. Planes were the safest and fastest way to get the volatile JP-4 forward: tracer bullets during an ambush could make a tanker truck explode, and ground targets were easier to hit than aircraft in flight. The airfield was also valuable for bringing in troops by C-130 airlift, an infantry battalion arriving in less than seven hours. Thien Ngon's airfield gave the First Brigade the logistical means to sustain itself.

Mueller had little time to prepare his attack, which led on occasion to errors. One unit was sent on a roundabout 150-kilometer road march, to finish just 50 kilometers from where it had started; this led the cavalry squadron commander to conclude the planning was "pretty rudimentary and done on horseback."[12] Such moves, almost 100 miles over poor roads, were hard on armored vehicles and required extensive maintenance to fix the broken or loosened parts. Better staff work would probably have prevented such wasted time and effort, thought the squadron commander years later.[13]

The logisticians' rapid response was vital to Mueller's attacking on schedule. One key issue was physically turning Thien Ngon into a forward base for launching his attack. While the engineers built the camp, logistics units brought up supplies and equipment. Troops from the division's supply and transportation battalion were at Thien Ngon by dusk on 4 May. They brought two days' worth of food and fuel for the brigade's upcoming attack, two 6,000-pound forklifts, five 10,000-gallon fuel bladders, and pumps and nozzles to set up a fuel supply system. More than thirty maintenance battalion mechanics set up a repair point to fix any vehicles and key equipment that might break. On 6 May the Division Support Command headquarters at Cu Chi sent a ten-man control element, including the assistant division transportation and ammunition officers, to Tay Ninh West. This team coordinated all the Twenty-fifth's logistical assets for the attacks on Base Areas 353 and 354 and COSVN. Bautz approved the division using a "push" supply system like that used by the First Cavalry Division in the Fishhook, where supply officers would send forward commonly requested items and amounts without waiting for them to be requested and then "pulled" forward.[14]

As units of all types poured into Thien Ngon, the congestion became unmanageable. A Company of the Sixty-fifth Engineer Battalion (habitually in support of the First Brigade) was working to establish the new base, but was fast running out of room. Accordingly, at suppertime on 5 May the First Brigade asked for five Rome Plows from IIFFV's 984th Land Clearing Company, the giant bulldozers needed to widen and lengthen the airstrip and clear fields of fire around the base itself.[15] A few hours later Muller's staff told division headquarters that he did not want any more artillery at Thien Ngon: twelve guns and howitzers were already there, the danger areas from their blasts and low trajectories precluding him from otherwise using a space the size of two football fields within his already crowded perimeter.[16]

The forward ammunition supply point's operations exacerbated the overcrowding inside Thien Ngon. Artillery consumes tons of shells and powder; infantry, helicopters, tankers, and other forces likewise require bullets and explosives. On 6 May a sergeant from the Division Ammunition Office arrived to process ammunition requests but was quickly overwhelmed. Units were supposed to submit their requests a day in advance, to be filled that night by trucks and flatbed trailers from Saigon Support Command's Forty-eighth Group driving from Long Binh's ammunition dumps. This arrangement lasted only a few days before the Forty-eighth Group canceled it, objecting to its scarce trailers sitting at Thien Ngon awaiting unloading, taking up space, and remaining vulnerable to mortar and rocket attacks. To resolve the paperwork backlog, soldiers from the Division Band and the Division Support Command's Headquarters Company helped the sergeant, and the Thien Ngon ammunition point operated until 28 June.[17]

The steady arrival of units and their burgeoning requirements for space affected the airstrip as well. Because empty areas inside the perimeter were at a premium, many units parked their vehicles and piled their equipment along the sides of the runway. However, this so limited its usable width that by 6 May only the small C-123 cargo planes, and not the much more capacious C-130s, could land. Ammunition-laden flatbed trailers parked alongside the runway further increased hazards. This problem ended later that day when Colonel Linwood Mather, due to become head of the division's logistics units on 15 May, arrived at Thien Ngon to take command of the base and begin straightening things out.[18] Mueller was happy to let Mather run Thien Ngon; his concerns were destroying the 95C Regiment and taking Base Area 354.

The First Brigade's plan of attack was fairly simple. One of the two light infantry battalions would make a helicopter assault into the northern part of Base Area 354 on 6 May. Meanwhile, the division's engineers would build a pontoon bridge over the Rach Cai Bac River, across which the two mechanized infantry battalions would enter Cambodia. Once there, the mechanized battalions would advance west, link up with the infantry battalion inserted on 6 May, and turn south. Finally, the second light infantry battalion would move by helicopter to land between the two mechanized battalions. If the brigade found the 95C Regiment, it would fight. If not, it would seize the base area and search for caches and enemy camps. Should the NVA or VC try to flee south, they would run into South Vietnamese navy patrol boats blocking the Kampong Spean River.[19]

The First Brigade's assault began early on 6 May. Air force C-130s dropped two 15,000-pound Commando Vault bombs at 0330 and 0430 hours just inside Cambodia.[20] These bombs blasted helicopter landing zones for the lead infantry company to secure the far side of the crossing site, where South Vietnamese Route 20 reached the border and river. Hitting about 500 meters west and northwest of the chosen crossing site, the two bombs cleared fewer trees than expected; sixty-four more 750-pound bombs were dropped to flatten more trees before the helicopters could land.[21]

Following the air strikes, troops from the Third Battalion, Twenty-second Infantry, air assaulted into Cambodia at 0710 hours.[22] C Company secured the western end of the bridgehead, while the other three companies landed near Tasuos, a small village about five kilometers inside the border.[23] The 500 or so men near Tasuos were to cause any major NVA attack on the bridgehead to reveal itself by hitting them first, thus warning the rest of the brigade. Meanwhile, the two mechanized infantry battalions provided near-side security at the river while the engineers built the bridge.[24]

There were mistakes early on. In an unfortunate case of fratricide, U.S. artillery shelled the far side of the crossing site shortly before 1000 hours while the C Company troops were spreading out. Two U.S. soldiers died, while eight others and a Kit Carson Scout were wounded.[25] The casualties were evacuated, and the engineers began preparing the ground to withstand the expected heavy flow of vehicle traffic. A bulldozer hit an antitank mine a hundred meters east of the crossing site, slowing down but not stopping the effort. By 1930 a 225-foot long pontoon bridge spanned the river. The APCs crossed into Cambodia to reinforce the infantry company but found that the far-side shore and approach area first needed extensive bulldozing like the near side's to handle the waiting traffic. Engineers had the job done by midnight.[26]

With a bridge to get them and their supply columns over the river, the two mechanized battalions crossed and advanced west and southwest. By the evening of the seventh, Mueller's entire brigade of some 3,400 U.S. infantrymen was in the northern part of Base Area 354, supported by air force jets and several artillery batteries.[27] The light enemy contacts the First Brigade experienced on 6 and 7 May were generally scattered enemy units, cut down as they fled.

Bautz massed a good deal of Buzzett's firepower behind Mueller's assault. The First Brigade could call on thirty cannon on 6 May, and sixty-four by the next day. At one time, twenty-six cannon were at Thien Ngon alone, their firing trajectories clear of the airstrip's flight paths but complicating airspace availability for pilots and air traffic controllers. The artillery's demand for shells increased the number of resupply flights required, which continued through the attacks on Base Area 707 and COSVN.

To keep pilots from flying into shells' trajectories, a Division Artillery cell at the Tay Ninh West headquarters tried to warn aircraft of all ongoing fire missions. By 7 May, though, it was obvious that coordinating thirteen batteries and aircraft flight paths from thirty kilometers away was impractical. Buzzett sent a detachment forward to Thien Ngon to track fire missions against Base Area 354 and keep pilots informed. This worked well, approving all fires to a depth of thirty-five kilometers into Cambodia. By 9 May Mueller faced no real NVA threat, so Buzzett began to shift his guns north to support Whitehead's upcoming Second Brigade attack on Base Area 707.[28]

Not finding the 95C Regiment, Mueller began searching for caches. The brigade was reasonably successful, finding twenty-five. However, only seven were within the zone analysts had said marked Base Area 354's boundaries; most were up to five kilometers deeper in Cambodia.[29] On 6 and 7 May Mueller used the Third Squadron Seventeenth Air Cavalry's scout and gunship helicopters for reconnaissance over the brigade area and killing enemy troops seeking to escape. This was a role the aviators were well suited for and performed capably, but once the lunge was over and the battalions began searching for caches, Mueller split the squadron into small teams to cover more area and better help the infantrymen below.[30]

The best source of combat intelligence remained the soldier on the ground. Once a unit had found a cache, it scoured the surrounding area for signs similar to those that had tipped it off the first time. This was often successful, since many caches in a base area were fairly close together.[31]

Besides soldiers' searches, local Cambodians sometimes could be persuaded to point out caches. Some villagers took Buzzett to a hidden cache simply because his troops had been nicer to them than had some passing U.S. infantrymen.[32] Most useful of all for finding caches were Cambodian-speaking interpreters. Starting 9 May the division's units became far more successful, partly from becoming familiar with the area but mostly because the interpreters received information from the locals. To cover an area of more than 100 square kilometers, the brigade had only one Cambodian-speaking interpreter in the attack's first three days, during which the soldiers found seven caches. In the next three days, with help of interpreters, they found fourteen.[33] The interpreters were instrumental in First Brigade's neutralizing the sanctuary.

In addition to looking for the NVA or caches, U.S. forces sought to help Cambodians. Several infantry units set up temporary clinics to help the local civilians they were encountering. Medics from the two mechanized battalions treated more than 350 Cambodian villagers, giving them immunizations and the first basic medical care most had ever received. Medics also treated civilians wounded as a result of combat actions; Mueller authorized payments to Cambodians as compensation for death or injuries caused by the United States. Lacking Cambodian currency, the brigade substituted one 25-kilogram bag of rice for a minor injury, one 100-kilogram bag for a major injury, and two 100-kilogram bags for a death.[34]

Bautz was unable to give Mueller enough time to completely destroy Base Area 354. Ordered to attack Base Area 353 and part of the COSVN region, he had kept the Third Brigade and the Third/Ninth back to secure the division's sector in III CTZ. With just the First and Second Brigades available for the new assault, he had to curtail Mueller's work in Base Area 354. In hindsight Bautz probably could have risked using his Third Brigade in Cambodia, since the division's sector in Vietnam was fairly quiet. However, the Third Brigade was Saigon's main shield to the west, and were he wrong, the capital would be exposed. Further, on 7 May he committed part of Third/Ninth to a very brief raid on Base Area 367 with RVNAF forces to help clear out the Parrot's Beak. The Third Brigade and Third/Ninth thus stayed put inside South Vietnam for the most part, and Bautz limited himself to using his first two brigades and his artillery.

As First Brigade pulled out of Base Area 354 on 14 May to join Second Brigade's attack on Base Area 353 and COSVN, the division left remote sensors in key locations in the sanctuary. Soldiers set up six seismic and two acoustic sensors to monitor a rice cache and a transshipment point. Aircraft dropped another thirty-three, to cover infiltration routes, camps, and caches. All forty-one were inside Cambodia, most within five kilometers of the border, and transmitted their data to the sensor control station at Cu Chi until their batteries wore out.[35] The NVA knew the Americans might leave sensors behind, but the camouflaged devices were too difficult to detect in the dense vegetation.

The brigade also left for the NVA almost thirty-seven tons of powdered tear gas, dropped on thirty-three sites "well outside populated areas" between 16 and 30 May. The purpose was to deny those areas to the enemy and induce them to use other routes monitored by the remote sensors.[36] The chemicals' effectiveness was transitory, though, since the approaching monsoon rains would quickly wash away the powder.[37] Until then, analysts could determine patterns of activity, which helped with unit identifications and targeting for artillery missions or air strikes.

———————

Despite its short duration of only eight days, the attack on Base Area 354 inflicted moderate losses on the NVA. Mueller's men killed 283 enemy troops, captured 12, and received 7 defectors, against losses of 18 U.S. soldiers dead, 40 wounded who required hospitalization, and 133 with minor wounds who were treated and returned to duty.[38] The First Brigade captured 297 individual and 34 crew-served weapons, sending most back to South Vietnam along with more than 1,500 pounds of explosives. Two ten-kilowatt generators, fifty-eight sampans, and a machine tool shop were discovered and destroyed. More than 350 pounds of documents revealed that the NVA's medical capabilities were poor, malaria casualties were high, and dissension, desertion, and extremely low morale were prevalent among the soldiers marched down from North Vietnam.[39] For individual communist troops as for many Americans in 1970, the war appeared endless.

The 217 tons of rice was the most important material captured in Base Area 354. The U.S. troops evacuated 34 tons and gave 66 tons to Cambodian civilians and refugees, but destroyed 117 tons.[40] Destroying rice the refugee centers needed was a regrettable necessity. Mueller had entered Base Area 354 without a specified end date and, when pulled out to attack Base Area 353, lacked time to evacuate all the rice he had captured. Even with more time, he would still have lacked the means. The division's trucks and flatbed trailers were busy moving equipment and supplies north of Thien Ngon to support Second Brigade's attacks on Base Area 707 and COSVN (discussed later) and the attack First Brigade was about to begin against Base Area 353. Mueller also lacked the troops to leave behind to continue the evacuation or guard the rice for later recovery: his four battalions were all required against Base Area 353.[41] Without the means to remove the remaining rice or keep it from enemy hands, he correctly ordered it destroyed.

Destroying rice was difficult. The grains do not burn by themselves, and the troops lacked enough gasoline or diesel fuel to burn it all. Further, that amount of fuel was more valuable in U.S. vehicles than on rice bags. Wetting the rice would lead to mold within a day, the rice becoming totally inedible within three. However, infantrymen in the jungle carried only personal canteens and could not sacrifice their water to wet a few pounds of rice in a cache containing tons. Dumping it in streams worked best, but getting it there was hard: stacked in 100-kilogram bags, the rice was too heavy to carry without engineer equipment. To bring it to the border, the NVA had used trucks from Sihanoukville or modified bicycles from North Vietnam over the span of months; the U.S. troops had less than a week to remove or destroy what they found.

The most common way within the Twenty-fifth Infantry Division to destroy rice quickly became to scatter it on the ground over as wide an area as possible and hope that afternoon thunderstorms would induce spoilage.[42] This worked after a fashion, but the preferred solution whenever possible remained taking it back to South Vietnam to feed the refugees.

In South Vietnam rice meant political power, and the captured rice caused Bautz headaches. Charitable groups wanted him to give the rice to them, as did the Cao Dai religious sect. Instead, he let the South Vietnamese government decide who should get the rice. Civil affairs personnel from division headquarters were stationed on key routes along the border to ensure it went to the Twenty-fifth Infantry Division's forward rice collection points at Katum, Thien Ngon, and Tay Ninh West. From there they turned it over to the South Vietnamese Social Welfare Services chief to help refugees in Long An, Hau Nghia, and Tay Ninh Provinces.[43]

The Twenty-fifth Infantry Division's initial performance in Cambodia was generally solid, in part because once Shoemaker's troops entered the Fishhook on 1 May, other American commanders began preparing for the orders they expected to soon receive. The First Brigade had quickly relearned many lessons about brigade-level field operations in attacking Base Area 354 and subsequently applied them to good effect, while the Second Brigade did its job quietly and methodically. Bautz retained control of his division's operations rather than forming a task force under one of his brigadiers, as Roberts had done initially in the First Cavalry Division. Using existing staffs with established internal routines avoided many of the organizational problems Task Force Shoemaker had encountered in late April. Finally, division logisticians successfully adapted as the division shifted from the border below the Dog's Head eastward to the Fishhook, supporting it from bases at Thien Ngon and then Katum. In all, the Twenty-fifth Infantry Division gave a good showing in Cambodia.

The attention on Mueller's 6 May attack overshadowed the division's second offensive into Cambodia, the Third/Ninth's quick assault on Base Area 367 in the Parrot's Beak. Bautz's intelligence officers thought this base to be a regimental training area, supporting enemy units in Long An and Hau Nghia Provinces. Charging west through the Angel's Wing and Base Area 706 on 30 April on his way to the Mekong River, Tri had left Base Area 367 to be mopped up later. Likewise, the ARVN Ninth Division cavalry squadrons that passed through it during TOAN THANG 42 had not stopped to thoroughly search for caches.

On or about 4 May, Bautz told Colonel Walworth F. Williams, the Third/Ninth's commander, to attack the Parrot's Beak to destroy Base Area 367. A mixed force of a U.S. infantry battalion, two South Vietnamese Regional Force companies, and some Civilian Irregular Defense Group (CIDG) troops quickly overran the area on 7 May. Meeting little real opposition, Williams withdrew his

U.S. troops on 12 May to resume their security patrols in the division rear areas, leaving the South Vietnamese to continue searching for caches.[44]

Despite its small scale and short duration, the attack on Base Area 367 was worthwhile. The Third/Ninth killed 128 enemy troops and captured 10 prisoners and 1 defector at a cost of 7 U.S. dead and 31 wounded. The meager material results, though, seemed to confirm the predictions of Base Area 367's relative unimportance. Third/Ninth captured only thirty-three individual weapons and one machine gun, 300 pounds of ammunition, 100 pounds of rice, 75 pounds of medical supplies, and 50 pounds of documents. The South Vietnamese who continued searching after Williams's men left, however, discovered that most caches were buried in "huge watertight metal containers at the intersection of rice paddy dikes."[45] This knowledge helped them find more supplies than had Williams's men, by then back on routine patrols in southwestern III CTZ.

Events elsewhere kept Bautz busy. Just before Mueller's and Williams's assaults, he had to deal with leadership problems in the Second Battalion Thirty-fourth Armor, his division's sole tank battalion, which he had loaned to Shoemaker to help overrun the Fishhook. Its weak performance there led Bautz to relieve the battalion commander and one of the battalion's two tank company commanders. On 10 May Bautz ordered the tank battalion back to its camp near Tay Ninh. Under a new commander the battalion began maintenance and retraining programs lasting about two weeks; to improve their gunnery skills the tankers used as targets the VC-held caves on the sides of Nui Ba Den. By mid-June the battalion was escorting convoys across War Zone C, ensuring supplies for the infantrymen on the other side of the border and providing a suitable mission for tanks that were otherwise of little use in searching for caches.[46] The reliefs, repairs, retraining, and rear-area security duties, however, meant the battalion's tanks were not available to support the division's combat operations against Base Areas 354, 367, or 707 or COSVN.

Bautz was looking ahead to future missions even as Mueller's First Brigade started rooting through Base Area 354 on 6 May and elements of Williams's Third/Ninth overran Base Area 367 on 7 May. IIFFV had just returned the Second Brigade to the Twenty-fifth Infantry Division's control, to attack Base Area 707 and the COSVN headquarters area. The Third Brigade would secure the bulk of the division's sector inside South Vietnam while the First and Second Brigades were in Cambodia;[47] the Third/Ninth would pull back from Base Area 367 to guard western Hau Nghia and northern Long An Provinces.

Bautz's order for Second Brigade to attack came as a great surprise to Colonel Ennis Whitehead. He was due to relinquish command of the Second Brigade in early May, but Bautz delayed the change until the fifteenth so that he rather than his successor, a colonel with little combat experience, would lead the attack on Base Area 707.[48] Almost as much a shock to Whitehead was his realization of how badly his brigade was positioned for making the assault. Located near the coast, about 40 kilometers southeast of Saigon, he had to move about

1,500 men and their equipment 150 kilometers northwest. The Second Brigade had one artillery and two infantry battalions, an engineer company, and a Ranger platoon. Whitehead ordered one infantry battalion to close down the brigade's base camp to keep the VC from picking up any supplies left behind.[49] Everyone else moved to Thien Ngon, where the division cavalry squadron, an infantry battalion, and two mechanized infantry battalions joined his force over the next few days; this gave the brigade seven combat battalions plus smaller elements.

Years later Whitehead remembered his first sight of Thien Ngon: "When I got there with my [command post] one day there were about 50 of us there and the next day there were 500. . . . C-130s were coming in like clockwork bringing in supplies."[50] Reaching Thien Ngon without the logisticians with whom he routinely worked, Whitehead asked those working for Mueller to support him as well until Bautz could send more supply units. They agreed and provided for both brigades from 8 to 14 May.[51]

The Second was probably more used to sudden movements than the division's other brigades, in part due to its previous shifts. This early shakeout helped it avoid some of the problems that had earlier beset the First Brigade. Getting its orders directly from Davison in early April, the Second Brigade had moved thirty kilometers north from Cu Chi to a new base at Dau Tieng to assume the area of a departing brigade of the U.S. First Infantry Division. The next day Davison moved Whitehead 100 kilometers southeast to Phuoc Tuy Province, "to take over from *another* brigade of the First Division that was going home. . . . A battalion was going to take over my brigade tasks. . . . [W]e [were] getting strung out."[52] In Phuoc Tuy for only three weeks, the brigade had to repack and hustle northwest to Thien Ngon. Though exasperating for the troops, it was nonetheless good preparation for the field operations to come.

Whitehead's mission was to attack Base Area 707 and COSVN, the latter not captured by Shoemaker at the beginning of May. Because COSVN was more important, Whitehead decided to hit it hardest. While waiting for all his units to arrive and get in position, he struck Base Area 707 with what he could spare from the forces in hand.

The assault on Base Area 707 began on 9 May with the helicopter insertion of two infantry battalions into positions about five kilometers southeast of Krek, Cambodia, just north of Base Area 707. On the morning of the tenth one battalion pushed forward, found an enemy camp, and began searching for caches. Behind them the Third Squadron Fourth Cavalry, which had been working for First Brigade in Base Area 354 the day before, opened and secured Highway 22 from the border to Krek, giving the infantry battalions near the town a much better supply route.[53] On the next day, 11 May, the second battalion air assaulted about twenty kilometers northeast as part of the attack on COSVN; the first remained in Base Area 707 and searched until 14 May. Until he received a better location for COSVN to permit an attack, Whitehead kept his troops busy against Base Area 707.

Base Area 707 was "a sprawling way-station and trans-shipment point for infiltration groups coming in from North Vietnam . . . organized to support people rather than things."[54] In taking it, Whitehead's men killed ninety-four NVA troops and captured seven, while suffering fourteen wounded. The material seized reflected the sanctuary's role as a rest stop for units moving laterally along the border. U.S. forces found only three trucks, six weapons, 40 pounds of ammunition, and 20 pounds of medical supplies, but 210 tons of rice.[55] Most of the latter was in eight caches about four kilometers inside Cambodia.[56] This made the rice easily available to enemy troops moving west along the border from the Fishhook toward Base Area 354, the Angel's Wing, and the Parrot's Beak.

———————

As the Twenty-fifth Infantry Division steadily destroyed Base Areas 353, 367, and 707 west and northwest of Tay Ninh City, the First Cavalry Division was shifting its focus from the Fishhook along the border to the northeast. The latter had found tons of supplies in and around the Fishhook, but not the elusive COSVN headquarters that Nixon had identified in his television address to the nation as a key objective. Upon hearing Nixon's words, MACV's Intelligence staff immediately began an intensive search in the border regions adjacent to III CTZ, using every means it had, including radio monitoring and direction finding, reconnaissance flights, and the activation of "deep cover sources in Cambodia" by the 525th Military Intelligence Group and the CIA.

COSVN's general location, somewhere in the vicinity of Memot, was good enough for Bautz to alert Whitehead to start planning in that direction but not precise enough to permit detailed plans for an attack.[57] On 8 May, however, U.S. forces spotted elements of COSVN about twenty kilometers west-northwest of Memot. Because this was more toward the Twenty-fifth Infantry Division's area than the First Cavalry Division's, Davison gave the mission to Bautz, who ordered Whitehead and his Second Brigade forward.

The Second Brigade's attack on COSVN started with a massive air strike followed by a ground assault. The decision to begin with B-52s was Davison's and caused him considerable thought. He felt that if this actually was COSVN headquarters, "we could expect a hell of a fight trying to get in there," causing many U.S. casualties. On the other hand, "there might be a breach of security with respect to the B-52 strike, and we would give away the farm."[58] Balancing secrecy against more firepower for his soldiers, Davison thought about it for a day, then ordered the air strike.

Unlike Shoemaker's Fishhook attack on 1 May, where the bomber flights had been spaced an hour or so apart, this one was a "compression." Three flights of three B-52s followed each other at only twenty-minute intervals instead of the typical hour, making it far more intense.[59]

The results were not as good as the Americans hoped. According to Davison, "COSVN Headquarters had been there–at three o'clock in the afternoon of the day before we went in, they got the word that the B-52s were coming that night."[60] Despite an emergency evacuation, about a third of the enemy staff was still there when the bombs landed. Those COSVN forces hit were mostly postal and finance units, trying to save their records. Between 50 and 250 communist soldiers died, the survivors being "pretty groggy."[61]

Once the bombing ended, Whitehead planned to surround the suspected COSVN headquarters and push inward until he had overrun it. The First Battalion Twenty-seventh Infantry was busy in Base Area 707, but he could use the Fourth Battalion Ninth Infantry and the Third Squadron Fourth Cavalry for the COSVN attack. Because these two battalions were not enough to ensure the capture of COSVN, Bautz gave him three more the day before his attack: one from the Third Brigade, one from the First Brigade, and one that had been supporting Task Force Shoemaker.[62] The air force provided 956 tactical air missions of two planes each, less than used against the Fishhook but appropriate given the number of APCs the Twenty-fifth Infantry Division had available for ground combat.[63] With five light and mechanized infantry battalions, a cavalry squadron, fires from an artillery battalion and the air force, and the support of an engineer company, the brigade had sufficient combat power to attack successfully.

The encirclement Whitehead envisioned took advantage of his unit's differing abilities and locations. Because the Second Battalion Twenty-seventh Mechanized was already near Memot, it would simply advance westward on line to become the eastern side of the box. The Second Battalion Twenty-second Mechanized would drive north from the border and face east, while the Second Battalion Twenty-seventh Infantry and the Fourth Battalion Ninth Infantry would make helicopter assaults to the northwest and northeast corners of the box, respectively. Everyone would be in place by midnight on 11 May, facing the center of the box like beaters driving animals before them into the waiting hunters' guns. At daybreak, they would push forward any trapped NVA forces south to be captured or killed by the Third Squadron Fourth Cavalry.[64]

A good plan well executed, it did not achieve the desired results of capturing COSVN proper. Most of COSVN's agencies had left the border area in late March, leaving only a skeleton headquarters near Memot. After Sihanouk's overthrow and the start of ARVN's raids, its key elements and those of the B-2 Front and the NLF had pulled back deeper into northeastern Cambodia. COSVN was not a single location or target like the Pentagon, vulnerable to a concentrated attack as Nixon led people to believe in his address to the nation, but rather was loosely dispersed along the border. Though Second Brigade's assault killed large proportions of various staff sections, it did not destroy the whole organization. Finally, the gaps between Whitehead's forces were simply too large to make a completely effective barrier to communists seeking to escape on foot, given the area they sought to enclose.[65]

After the battalions linked up on 12 May, attention turned to looking for caches. The brigade searched a twenty-five-square kilometer area for about three days, Whitehead having much better luck against the COSVN area than against Base Area 707. Supported by air strikes and artillery, his soldiers killed 241 NVA troops, captured 11, and received 5 defectors. They found 127 individual and 30 crew-served weapons, more than 20 tons of ammunition, eighteen trucks, 48 pounds of documents, 270 pounds of communications gear, and 256 tons of rice.[66]

Having seized Base Area 707 and COSVN, Whitehead took care of his units. On 14 May he ordered the Second Battalion Forty-seventh Mechanized to Tay Ninh Base Camp for some much-needed maintenance, and the Second Battalion Twenty-seventh Infantry to Cu Chi to rejoin the Third Brigade. These shifts were appropriate, since the former had been in the field continuously since 1 May, and Third Brigade had loaned the latter to Whitehead on 10 May to help him attack COSVN. Their departure left Whitehead with two infantry and one mechanized battalions, the division's cavalry squadron, and the support of an artillery battalion, still a powerful force with which to hold and search an empty sanctuary.

Although the initial hunt for COSVN lasted from 11 to 14 May, it soon was obvious that the bulk of the headquarters had escaped and further combat was unlikely. There was thus no need for all of Second Brigade's battalions to remain there when the western part of Base Area 353, just a few kilometers away, was yet unsearched. Shoemaker had sent Kingston north through the eastern part of Base Area 353 on 1 May, but as the First Cavalry Division shifted northeast, Roberts and then Casey could not send forces back to examine the area more closely.

Davison therefore gave responsibility for searching Base Area 353 to Bautz. Bautz told Mueller to prepare to pull out of Base Area 354 and attack Base Area 353 in conjunction with Whitehead's troops. This sudden change of mission threw the First Brigade headquarters into action as it made its third move in little more than a week, this time to Katum.

Fortunately for Mueller, the division's logisticians had already been preparing to support Second Brigade's attack on Base Area 353. Because Whitehead's part of the operation was merely an extension of what he was already doing, the Second Brigade would continue to get its support from Thien Ngon.

The First Brigade, though, would need a new base of operations. Katum, just a few kilometers south of the sanctuary, was the logical choice, so the Division Support Command sent a forward support element there on 13 May. This detachment of two officers and twenty-three soldiers brought three flatbed trailers of C rations, two fuel trailers with 10,000 gallons of JP-4 for helicopters and 6,500 gallons of diesel for vehicles, equipment for setting up a pumping station, and assorted other useful items.[67] Other supplies would follow, but this first load was enough for Mueller's initial needs.

Mueller also benefited from good timing in his arrival at Katum. Having turned the onetime Special Forces camp into a support base in late April, the First Cavalry Division pulled out on 14 May to move northeast along the border. The Twenty-fifth Infantry Division's area of responsibility then shifted correspondingly to the east to include the Fishhook.[68]

Arriving at Katum, Bautz's logisticians made a deal with the First Cavalry Division that saved everyone time and effort. Rather than dismantle the helicopter refueling point they had established two weeks earlier, the First Cavalry troopers simply left it for the Twenty-fifth Infantry Division and took the latter's still-packed refueling equipment in a swap. This kept a working system in place and let the First Cavalry Division depart much faster. The Twenty-fifth Infantry Division promptly added a third 10,000-gallon fuel bladder of JP-4, but otherwise the refueling station remained the same, available for use by any helicopter in the vicinity.[69]

Besides supplies and fuel, Katum was also an ammunition point. Its operation initially resembled Thien Ngon's, with a clerk receiving requests and trying to have the ammunition available the next day. However, as had happened at Thien Ngon, he too was swamped by the paperwork. Musicians from the division band and administrative troops soon arrived to help and stayed until the depot closed on 3 July.[70]

The attack on Base Area 353 began on 15 May, the Second Brigade coming from the west and the First Brigade from the south. The actual number of troops directly involved was comparatively small, however, as was the scope of their movement. Whitehead had left forces to continue searching the COSVN region and could send only the Fourth Battalion Ninth Infantry and part of the Third Squadron Fourth Cavalry into the western side of Base Area 353. They went, but deliberately rather than in a bold thrust to the sanctuary's heart: by then Whitehead simply lacked enough troops to risk an overly aggressive lunge.[71] Further, later that day he was due to relinquish command of the Second Brigade, and to do so in the midst of a fast attack would be unduly risky for those units in action. Under the circumstances, the brigade's deliberate pace was appropriate.

The First Brigade's attack from near Katum was a bit more powerful. The First Squadron of the Eleventh ACR was fifteen kilometers north of Memot. Mueller got control of it from the First Cavalry Division and had it face south as the "anvil" to his "hammer" moving north. By the end of the sixteenth, his troops had secured their areas and the searching began.[72]

As the two brigades spread steadily across Base Area 353, it became apparent they needed help to find caches more efficiently. Nixon's deadline of 30 June to be out of Cambodia was only six weeks away, and the soldiers lacked time to search by trial and error. On 18 May Bautz asked Davison for any special equipment IIFFV could get for the division. Eleven days later a helicopter-mounted gradiometer arrived, which indicated metal objects by detecting changes in magnetic fields. In nine flights over Cambodia it reported thirty-five possible sites. Infantrymen investigated nineteen, finding minor caches at six. Although a P-3 Orion from the U.S. Navy flew as well, it "was too sensitive and would pick up empty C-ration and beer cans . . . only 10 percent of the readings proved fruitful."[73] Still, in the triple-canopied jungle, almost anything was better than luck, and time not wasted searching could be used for evacuating captured supplies and ruining sanctuaries.

Although the First Brigade's attack against Base Area 354 on 6 May had been fairly successful, its shift a week later to attack Base Area 353 meant the exploitation and destruction of Base Area 354 remained incomplete. By late May remote sensors and aviators' sightings were reporting enemy units moving back into Base Area 354.[74]

Unable to spare the troops and lacking the time to attack again, Bautz told Buzzett to make an artillery raid against the area, by then estimated to contain about 1,500 returning NVA and VC troops. Buzzett did so on 31 May, firing more than 2,700 shells in five hours. Aerial observers saw many secondary explosions throughout the target area, indicating the presence of either undiscovered caches or new stockpiles. Helicopters were to have flown in an infantry company immediately after the shooting to determine what damage Buzzett had caused, but a monsoon beginning in early afternoon canceled that insertion.[75] To have gone later after the fires would have given the NVA and VC time to recover from the shock and made any insertion more dangerous. Nonetheless, the barrage reminded the NVA that "no ARVN or US troops present" did not necessarily mean a base area was still safe.

The danger was not only to the communists: had they known about Buzzett's attack in time, they could easily have disrupted or precluded it. The shells he shot weighed more than 240 tons and had to be ready at Thien Ngon before the guns arrived. Twenty-one flatbed trucks took most of the twenty-ninth to drive the 140 kilometers from the Long Binh ammunition depot to Thien Ngon. Unloading and preparing the shells took up the next day, the guns reaching Thien Ngon at daybreak on the thirty-first and opening fire at 1000 hours.[76]

Because both the batteries and ammunition trucks moved by road, they and the schedule were vulnerable. Abrams was attacking COSVN and the B-2 Front's logistics system; the communists would have liked to do the same to his but could not mass enough troops without their destruction by U.S. aircraft and artillery. Mines, though, were a low-risk alternative, particularly when buried in the roads on which the U.S. supply effort moved. Most roads were hard-packed dirt or dirt sprayed with an oil coating to hold down dust, and planting mines in them was fairly easy.

As with the First Cavalry Division in the Fishhook, mines were not a problem initially. Bautz noted that the division "had more trouble with mines on the friendly side of the border than we did across the border." The Twenty-fifth Infantry Division had no mine casualties for the first two weeks, which changed after the NVA regained its balance.[77] To beat this threat, Bautz's engineers put a new mine-clearing roller on the front of a Combat Engineer Vehicle (CEV). After hitting mines on three successive days, "each larger than the preceding one," they realized the VC were trying to determine the amount of explosive necessary to blow up the roller. The engineers preferred the roller to manual sweeps but thought it should go on one of the division's forty-four tanks instead of one of the four CEVs. The engineers felt that sooner or later the enemy would shift to "time delay or command detonated mines" to beat the roller's detonating simple pressure-activated ones; when that happened, they preferred that the tankers get blasted. They also recommended the roller's irregular use on any specific road, to keep the VC from using ever-larger mines.[78] For the most part, though, the engineers did a good job keeping the roads open for the convoys carrying supplies forward and captured materials back.

As the engineers maintained and improved roads, the infantry looked for more caches. The two brigades remained in Base Area 353 for more than a month, finding 249 small arms, 66 crew-served weapons, and 18 tons of ammunition. Even better were the 5,300 pounds of communications gear and 13,000 pounds of medical supplies. Best of all were the 854 tons of rice and 1,000 pounds of documents.[79]

Evacuating the captured materials was as much a problem in Base Area 353 as it had been in the other sanctuaries. Hundreds of tons of communist supplies were "found in jungle too dense even for armored personnel carriers. The rice had to be carried by hand to clearings where it was loaded on anything available–trucks, armored personnel carriers, tanks–almost anything going to the rear."[80] However, unlike the First Brigade's hurried disposition of captured rice in Base Area 354, the troops in Base Area 353 had time to evacuate nearly all their find to the South Vietnamese refugee centers.

The locations of many of these discoveries and their contents make clear that the incursions caught COSVN and B-2 by surprise. For example, on 17 May an infantry company overran the B-2 Front's signal school, located three kilometers north of the border. On 25 May another company uncovered a major NVA field hospital two kilometers inside Cambodia, just west of the Fishhook area. (Kingston's Third Brigade of the First Cavalry Division had driven right past it in the forest on 1 May.) On 9 June a third company found 175 tons of rice barely a hundred meters away from where Highway 22 crossed into Cambodia.[81] Such sites, and dozens of others like them, were far too vulnerable and valuable to risk unless Hanoi and its top commanders in the south had been convinced there was no danger in placing them so close to the border.

Captured documents produced an intelligence windfall. Postal and finance records helped MACV determine COSVN's and the B-2 Front's subordinate units, locations, strengths, activities, and individuals' names. Besides aiding the analysts and planners, such details let interrogators verify what they were being told. Of the fifty-four prisoners and twenty-two defectors, several were midlevel officers whose information complemented that in the documents.[82]

Most valuable of all were the cryptographic materials. Lacking telephone or teletype lines, COSVN and the B-2 Front depended on couriers or radios to pass orders and information to the divisions and regiments. Couriers were secure but very slow by comparison, so the NVA often used encoded transmissions to communicate along the border. By studying captured codebooks and frequency lists, U.S. radio monitors could listen in more effectively. Knowing major units' intentions and plans in advance, even if only in general terms, made it easier to counter them, a critical advantage when declining U.S. strength meant ever-smaller margins of error.[83] Without the codebooks, broken communist messages, and the insights resulting from their analysis, the American withdrawal from Vietnam during 1970–1971 would have been more risky.

The successes in Base Area 353 were not without cost. By mid-May the initial shock had passed, and the NVA was starting to fight back. Knowing it could not match U.S. forces in open combat, it mounted "ambushes, extensive road-mining and stand-off mortar/rocket attacks on fire support bases," which killed 89 U.S. troops and wounded 678, against 329 NVA dead, 14 captured, and 9 defectors.[84] This ratio, of about 3.5:1, reflected that NVA regulars and Main Force VC troops were fighting near their supplies rather than as scattered and hungry guerrillas inside III CTZ.

The Second Brigade's change of commanders may have influenced U.S. casualty rates. Whitehead turned over the brigade to his successor soon after attacking Base Area 353. On the way back from visiting units in Cambodia, Davison stopped by the Second Brigade command post for a briefing. The commanding general of IIFFV found that "what was going on out in the battalions bore no relationship to what [the commander] told me."[85] Bautz was dissatisfied as well with the colonel's performance and relieved him on 7 June after three weeks heading the Second Brigade. The Third/Ninth's Williams took temporary command of the brigade until 21 June, when Colonel Joseph R. Ulatoski arrived from the United States and formally assumed command.[86] While getting a new commander is often unsettling to a military unit, having four in five weeks probably affected the brigade's efficiency in fighting an increasingly aggressive NVA. United States losses were painful, but the damage the division inflicted on the NVA's ability to operate against III CTZ for the rest of 1970 and 1971, likely prevented higher casualties inside South Vietnam later.

By mid-June the division's operations within Cambodia were winding down, and Bautz wanted to conceal his intentions as he started pulling out. Having learned from captured documents how skilled enemy monitors were at collecting intelligence from U.S. radio traffic, frequently broadcast in plain language or with only elementary encryption, the division signal staff issued a new codebook for the withdrawal. Bautz put a much greater emphasis on not sending plain-language messages and ordered units to make sudden changes of frequencies and call signs.[87] The Division Artillery, for one, was already adhering to proper radio procedures. After some suspicious "coincidences" in early 1970 made him think the NVA was listening to U.S. tactical radio nets, Buzzett had started using couriers to carry orders to each battalion headquarters, imposing radio silence during battery moves. In early May he moved his battalions into position "by word of mouth," allowing only normal traffic.[88] These measures reduced his vulnerability accordingly: no radio traffic meant communist listeners could garner no information on the artillery's operations.

Because the Twenty-fifth Infantry Division would take longer to get out of Cambodia than the First Cavalry Division (due in large part to the former traveling chiefly by ground and latter primarily by helicopter), Davison appointed Bautz to command the withdrawal to South Vietnam of all IIFFV forces. Bautz was to focus in particular on two areas: "the movement of units and fire support coordination associated with the movement."[89] It was appropriate that a division commander head the pullout: to coordinate the many unit movements was complex, complicated by the infantry's continued search for caches, the engineers' need to clear land as long as possible to permit better future observation of enemy base areas and routes, the increasing frequency of firefights, and Nixon's firm withdrawal date of 30 June.

Considerations of Nixon's deadline and the monsoon increasingly decided matters, and getting U.S. troops and equipment out took precedence over finding more caches. As units moved toward Vietnam, the artillery's relative importance grew. By forcing enemy troops to fall back or take cover, artillery fires helped U.S. units withdraw with fewer casualties. More fires meant higher ammunition requirements, however, which sometimes exceeded the 180-tons-per-day capacity of the ten trucks and flatbed trailers the Forty-eighth Transportation Group had loaned Bautz; he had to augment them with some of his own cargo trucks for twelve days in June.[90]

As the monsoon set in, weather conditions hindered all movements. Pilots had harder times flying, while creeks flooded and became obstacles for ground transportation. Despite the weather, Nixon's end date was nonnegotiable. Williams brought the Second Brigade back into South Vietnam on 12 June, Mueller following with the First Brigade. By dusk on 28 June the Twenty-fifth Infantry Division was out of Cambodia.[91]

As Mueller had done upon First Brigade's leaving Base Area 354, Bautz sought to hinder the NVA's reclaiming and using Base Area 353. He had the division scatter almost eighteen tons of powdered tear gas on targets across the sanctuary between 26 and 29 June to force the NVA and VC to use other sections seeded with remote sensors.[92] Davison realized that the region had not been completely cleared and directed Bautz to develop plans to attack it with artillery and airstrikes after 30 June.[93] These plans formed the basis of subsequent U.S. actions that did not involve troops crossing the border.

Its units back inside South Vietnam, the Twenty-fifth Infantry Division returned to its previous mission of securing III CTZ's western and northern borders. Though the First Cavalry Division's shift northward into Phuoc Vinh Province meant the Twenty-fifth Infantry Division had an even bigger area to secure than before, the reduced level of enemy activity following the incursion made this less dangerous than it otherwise would have been.

The Twenty-fifth Infantry Division's achievements in Cambodia were substantial. Overrunning Base Areas 353, 354, 367, and 707, as well as part of the COSVN region, Bautz's forces killed 1,075 NVA and VC. They captured more than 1,500 tons of rice, bringing more than 900 tons back to South Vietnam to feed refugees. Finally, they seized almost seven tons of medical supplies and three-fourths of a ton of documents, the latter of great interest to intelligence experts. The division's cost was not cheap, though: 119 American soldiers died, with thirty-nine APCs and seven helicopters among the major items of equipment destroyed.[94]

Bautz's intelligence analysts were enthusiastic about the incursion's effects. Like their counterparts at MACV, IIFFV, and the First Cavalry Division, they predicted COSVN and the B-2 Front would need six to eight months to determine their losses and partially rebuild their capabilities; ARVN's presence in Cambodia after 30 June might delay communist recovery even longer. On 28 June, South Vietnam held provincial elections without any major interference by the communists, a measure of how badly Hanoi's efforts had been set back.[95]

Despite its solid performance, the Twenty-fifth Infantry Division got less recognition than the First Cavalry Division. This reflected Bautz's attitude toward the 1970-era media, since, like his mentor Abrams, "the further [he] could stay away from the media the better."[96] Other division leaders had similar attitudes: encountering correspondent Garrick Utley at Katum the day before the attack on Base Area 353, Buzzett turned and drove away without a word.[97]

Such behavior, however understandable given the adversarial state of media-military relations in 1970, was counterproductive, since reporters would get *some* story, if not from senior officers then from less-informed junior officers and troops. After the incursion the division staff concluded that while journalists "were frequently aware of the future operations, there were no security violations and no release of embargoed information."[98] This was too late, however, to get media coverage during the incursion itself.

Bautz made some provisions for accommodating reporters but did not go out of his way to help them. The First Brigade's dealings with the press in its attack on Base Area 354 were fairly typical of media support during the incursion. Mueller left his public information officer, a lieutenant, at Tay Ninh to brief visitors on his activities and upcoming operations so they could decide what units to visit the following morning. While the reporters slept at the Holiday Inn motel in Tay Ninh City, the lieutenant arranged their transportation forward through Thien Ngon into Cambodia. This setup worked reasonably well, but unexpectedly large numbers of media forced the division to ask IIFFV's and MACV's Offices of Information for help.[99]

More detrimental to the Twenty-fifth Infantry Division's coverage, Tay Ninh was the northern terminus of the province's public telephone lines. Reporters with the division in Cambodia had to return to Tay Ninh to file stories with their editors in Saigon. Reporters tended to go where their job was easier, the pictures were flashier, and the finds were bigger; in May 1970 this generally meant the First Cavalry Division, with its bigger press office, telephone lines reserved for media use, and helicopters that could fly photographs and film to Saigon for couriers to take them to the news bureau offices. Not surprisingly, then, most reporters within III CTZ during the incursion focused on the First Cavalry rather than the Twenty-fifth Infantry Division.

Bautz's division made some effort to tell its story, but it was generally of limited scope and too long after the given event. Battalions and brigades, using the fastest means available, sent their own pictures back to Cu Chi, where the negatives were developed and carried by courier to MACV's Offices of Information. MACV released the better pictures directly to reporters or transmitted them by satellite to Washington.[100] The photographs were rarely accompanied by news stories, however, since unit "journalists," normally the adjutants or the personnel clerks, spent their time on their administrative duties rather than writing for the division news magazine or the commercial press. This problem was so serious that the division's newspaper had to run pre-Cambodian stories until mid-June because it had received no articles from units about their activities in the sanctuaries.[101]

More interested in matters of immediate importance than in its public image back home, the division (re)learned many useful lessons in Cambodia. One such concerned tactical mobility, in particular that of brigade staffs deploying to the field. Stationary at Tay Ninh West for several years, the First Brigade headquarters had dismounted its communications gear from its vehicles and installed the equipment in various bunkers inside the base. As time passed, the unused mounting kits and cables were neglected, pieces becoming lost or corroded. The staff grew accustomed to running the brigade's operations from their bunkers. Bautz's order of 3 May to move west and assume control over what had been part of the First Cavalry Division's sector threw Mueller's headquarters into turmoil. It hastily set up a forward command post at Thien Ngon, the new headquarters becoming only partially operational before Mueller attacked Base Area 354 on schedule.[102]

Communications were poor for most of First Brigade's attack against Base Area 354, degrading its effectiveness. Before late April there had been no major U.S. outposts in War Zone C except a small Army Special Forces camp at Katum. Consequently, there was no established telephone network linking Thien Ngon to anywhere else.

Without wire lines or microwave towers, radio (both VHF/FM and AM teletype) was critical, in particular the relay site atop Nui Ba Den.[103] A radio-telephone switchboard reached Thien Ngon on 5 May but did not become operational until the following afternoon due to operator inexperience and equipment failures. As the infantry battalions moved west toward the border, the brigade had to use a radio relay in a UH-1H helicopter for its first days in Cambodia to talk with them and with division headquarters.[104] There were also not enough microwave circuits between Cu Chi, Tay Ninh West, and Thien Ngon when the attack began on 6 May, additional microwave gear only reaching Thien Ngon two days later.[105]

Unfortunately for Mueller and the First Brigade headquarters, their initial problems caught Davison's attention. He was unhappy with the brigade's difficulty in shifting to field operations and told Bautz to "'keep moving [them] until they learn how to do it.' And he [Bautz] moved them three times before . . . they finally got into the swing of things and could adapt themselves to this change."[106] Like Roberts's changing brigade commanders in the midst of the First Cavalry Division's advance, Davison could afford to make Mueller's headquarters move repeatedly chiefly because NVA resistance at the time was so light. Had the NVA or VC launched coordinated counterattacks during one of the headquarters' relocations, the consequences could have been serious for the First Brigade.

Communications support never quite caught up with First Brigade headquarters' multiple moves during the Base Area 354 attack. On 8 May it shifted three kilometers southwest of Thien Ngon to a new fire support base but did not get telephone lines to the division operations center until the eleventh.[107] Until then their teletypes stayed at Thien Ngon, and a courier shuttled between brigade headquarters and Thien Ngon's communications center. Telephone messages often had to wait for telephone lines to clear while nearby teletypes were silent, the inefficiencies further adding to delays.[108]

Because of the shifting center of the division's activities from the provinces around Cu Chi toward the northwest, the 125th Signal Battalion had moved more communications assets toward Tay Ninh. Unfortunately, it was only prepared to support one brigade's move to the field, not a second to the same area very shortly after. The existing telephone and VHF channels could not handle two brigades plus all the supporting elements.[109] Further, frequency interference problems atop Nui Ba Den like those that had plagued IIFFV and the First Cavalry Division also affected the Twenty-fifth Infantry Division.[110] To lessen the reliance on Nui Ba Den's station and help the First and Second Brigades the 125th Signal built a communications tower at Thien Ngon on 11 May, raising FM antennas 120 feet higher and greatly extending their range.[111]

The tower came too late to be of much help, however. On 14 May the First Brigade moved to Katum to attack Base Area 353. It cut its radio links with division headquarters before establishing contact from Katum, leaving it out of touch for several hours.[112] The heavy reliance on FM radios instead of telephones or teletypes meant Mueller's staff had to talk on more channels than they had radios. Accordingly, they might switch from one frequency to another, but then forget to go back to the first. Two channels they often left were the division's command and spot report/intelligence radio nets, which, with the early disconnect during the move to Katum, meant the brigade was frequently out of touch with division headquarters for several hours at a time. These mistakes greatly irritated Bautz.[113]

Bautz ordered changes as a result of the First Brigade's difficulties. The Second Brigade's headquarters had routinely operated in the field and so had few problems executing its attack on COSVN and Base Areas 707 and 353. However, Bautz felt the First and Third Brigades had become "comfortable" in their compounds at Tay Ninh West and Cu Chi and had lost their mobility. He therefore decreed that every brigade headquarters would spend at least one night each month in the field.[114] The field time quickly helped the First and Third Brigade headquarters regain their mobility, to the benefit of their subordinate units and the division.

The operation against Base Area 354 was successful but "rough," the result of few mobile brigade-level operations after years of almost exclusively conducting company- and battalion-level operations; subsequent attacks went much better. Initial problems in deploying headquarters, communications, aviation procedures, intelligence, and the lack of forward depots could all have become serious had the NVA stood and fought. Commanders soon corrected these shortcomings, aided greatly by Thien Ngon becoming a well-organized logistics base within easy reach of all the targeted base areas.

———————

The Cambodian incursion reinforced several key lessons for the Twenty-fifth Infantry Division's leaders. One of the most important of these was the critical need for good communications: effective command and coordinated operations were impossible if units and leaders could not talk. Terrain and thick vegetation complicated matters: "On occasion, enemy actions or darkness would find a unit in an area where FM radio communication was virtually impossible."[115] These companies and platoons had had to rely on airborne FM relays, limited in the time they could stay aloft and provide continuous radio links. Oftentimes signal troops at brigade and battalion headquarters did not know what equipment was working at any moment, a problem they solved by making and using equipment status boards.[116]

Many units in the incursion's early days were unfamiliar with proper aviation operations. These included not knowing CH-47 loading procedures, being unready to load when helicopters reached their locations, and failing to use correct radio frequencies.[117] Resupply requests late in the day by infantry units meant the division had to use helicopters to get the materials there before dark. As a result, the division exceeded its allocated helicopter flight time and had to abuse IIFFV's aviation priority guidelines to get the extra flight hours they needed. As combat units gained familiarity with aviation operations, their mistakes grew steadily fewer.

Intelligence procedures also improved as the incursion went on. Many units at first did such a poor job tagging captured documents and equipment that items arrived at division headquarters without any indication of who had captured them where, when, and under what circumstances. Some units also failed to report promptly enemy contacts or sightings, or, if they did, to update initial reports with more accurate information as they got it. Information from prisoners of war was not available until they reached the division collection point several hours later. This delay forfeited the value of much of the tactical intelligence, particularly anything of fleeting worth. The division intelligence staff corrected this matter by moving the interrogation teams down to the brigade headquarters (and occasionally to company level). Common sense helped resolve some intelligence problems. Since MACV regulations said only South Vietnamese citizens could get cash bonuses for information, field commanders circumvented the rules by using their captured rice to loosen Cambodian and Laotian tongues.[118]

The artillery underwent some changes resulting from Cambodia. "Harassing and interdiction" fires, blindly shooting at such likely targets as a trail intersection that the enemy might be using, ceased after Bautz and Buzzett concluded they were wasting ammunition.[119] Another change involved the artillery's deployment. Before the incursion Buzzett had usually sent out his cannon in three-gun platoons to maximize the area he could cover with fires. However, this meant less officer supervision and therefore more firing safety incidents and close calls. Bautz's order, that the division artillery's smallest fire unit be the six-gun battery, was smart. It let three officers oversee one battery, rather than being split between two separated platoons, and led to better fire control, greater accuracy, and fewer mishaps. Massing the guns increased their effectiveness dramatically, while a battery could protect itself better against attacks than could a platoon. By defending a firebase chiefly with cannon, the battery largely freed an infantry company from guarding the perimeter to conducting patrols.[120] Buzzett's troops applied these changes to their operations in III CTZ after the division's return from Cambodia.

A final lesson was the need to plan for refugees. There were more than 21,000 in the division's area of operations in May and June, mostly Vietnamese who had fled their homes in Cambodia for fear of local mobs. Refugees were technically Saigon's problem, but field commanders encountering them had to act on the spot. Sometimes ethnic Vietnamese from Cambodia had to be moved to refugee centers in Tay Ninh Province, or Cambodian refugees from the An Loc Refugee Center back to the vicinity of Memot.[121] Although Abrams's missions to his divisions emphasized fighting enemy units by attacking logistics systems, it was all part of his bigger goal of protecting the South Vietnamese population. In trying to kill NVA and VC forces and find caches, units had to avoid alienating the civilians they were supposed to protect and thus creating even more refugees or enemies.

The best way to do this, Bautz's men found, was to be themselves. The Cambodian peasants were at first scared, but they slowly lost their fear as troops helped build new community structures, set up medical clinics, and handed out captured rice. With the end of major movements and air strikes, "By the end of May the villagers were out and about, [and] young women were no longer hiding in the woods."[122] A civil affairs officer working with the Second Brigade described the Twenty-fifth Infantry Division's performance in Cambodia: "We haven't done too much damage to the Cambodian people. We left them pretty much unscathed. And leaving the Cambodian people unscathed, and getting rid of the VC is about as good as you are going to do, anywhere, anytime."[123]

The Twenty-fifth Infantry Division's operations helped cripple COSVN's ability to attack Saigon and its surrounding provinces. Bautz did well, his three separate brigade-level operations destroying five distinct objectives spread across a 120-kilometer front.[124] These successes occurred even as the division continued to guard Saigon's western and northern approaches, and its area of operations expanded significantly without a comparable increase in its helicopter assets to provide additional mobility and flexibility. Overcoming all obstacles, the Twenty-fifth Infantry Division's efforts helped secure Saigon and III CTZ for months to come.

8

Supporting Operations

The infantry searches through the border sanctuaries were the high point of Abrams's efforts to drive the NVA out of South Vietnam by hitting its logistics system, gaining time for pacification and the American withdrawal. However, the American and RVNAF operations against enemy bases and caches were possible only because of Abrams's *own* logistics system and supporting forces. As the old military saying goes, "The logistician draws the line beyond which the general dare not tread"; in the Cambodian incursion, that line was both figuratively and literally far enough across the border that the commanders were able to accomplish their missions at acceptable levels of risk. Without the substantial efforts of thousands of allied logistics troops, the campaign would have been harder to execute and less successful in its results.

The Cambodian incursion was "a major challenge" to logisticians and other support elements, with the equivalent of three U.S. and ARVN corps-sized forces conducting virtually simultaneous cross-border offensives.[1] Several factors greatly complicated the task. For large combat units to operate in Cambodia for more than a few days, a support structure had to sustain them. Such a system did not exist in spring 1970 along or across the border. To build and man refueling points, ammunition dumps, repair facilities, and transshipping areas in advance of the attack would tip Abrams's hand. Preparations for moving the support system up to the border, then across, could therefore only begin at the last minute; the logistics system would have to supply the attacking troops even as it took shape. The secrecy surrounding the assault also caused difficulties, since those few leaders who knew what was about to happen were forbidden to explain to their subordinates why they were giving certain orders. As the incursion progressed, the vast quantities of captured materials created new problems, of what to do with it all, and how to best help the Cambodian army in its efforts against the NVA, VC, and Khmer Rouge. That MACV could support the units in Cambodia at all was due to the huge military infrastructure within South Vietnam created since 1965, an infrastructure built to sustain both the RVNAF and American forces.

MACV's responsibilities included advising the RVNAF on its logistic efforts and assisting them as required. III Corps' TOAN THANG 42 generally went well, without too much direct U.S. involvement in the forward areas. The JGS in Saigon planned and set up a forward depot on the Mekong River near Moc Hoa, Cambodia, run by about 200 ARVN troops. Supplies reached Moc Hoa by ship, then were sent by truck to ARVN units as needed. This solution was sophisticated, since using the river to move his initial supplies let Tri keep the roads clear behind his assault formations until he had secured the area. Reducing "battlefield clutter" meant easier movement for the combat forces and less chance of either gunners killing friendly forces by accident or supply convoys getting ambushed by remnants of NVA or VC units. ARVN logistics troops followed his second-echelon infantry units to set up the bigger supply bases III Corps' forces would need to sustain themselves inside Cambodia.

As III Corps pushed deeper, ARVN established a second forward supply point farther inside Cambodia and a small depot in the northern part of the Angel's Wing. These three bases sustained both III and, later, IV Corps.[2] Moc Hoa continued to receive boat-delivered materials even after ARVN gave priority to its main overland supply route northwest from Saigon on Route 1 to Go Dau Ha, then west to Moc Hoa on the Mekong River.[3]

Although ARVN logisticians kept III and IV Corps adequately supplied during the incursion, MACV was not entirely confident in their abilities. Major General Ray Conroy, MACV's top supply officer, recalled that his main concern upon learning Abrams's plans for the incursion was the South Vietnamese. "They'd been in wars for years, but I don't think they'd ever got in anything as big as this. . . . Certainly the biggest thing we [at MACV] worried about was ammunition."[4]

Conroy's concerns were well-founded. ARVN's sudden shift to large offensive operations invalidated planning assumptions about the quantities of ammunition its units would need, and thus would have to order in advance to ensure sufficient stocks were available beforehand. As III Corps moved deeper into Cambodia in early May, its soldiers almost ran out of.50-caliber machine gun ammunition. Conroy and his staff scrambled, calling American depots and bases around the world before finally locating crates of the .50-caliber bullets in southern Japan that they could airlift to South Vietnam.[5] This was admittedly an extreme case, but indicative: ARVN conducted its own tactical operations but depended on MACV to supplement its logistics affairs.

The American support effort was smoother in large part because of Abrams's far greater resources. These assets generally fell under control of the U.S. Army, Vietnam (USARV), MACV's army component headquarters overseeing logistic and administrative matters for the ground war. Because the ARVN attacks would be important tests of Vietnamization's progress as well as a part of Abrams's strategy, USARV devoted additional assets to help ensure their success. A week before the incursion, maintenance teams from the U.S. Army's Saigon Support Command (SSC) began working with tactical units that would be crossing into Cambodia, or supporting from just within the South Vietnamese border. These teams concentrated on mechanized and armored forces, such as the wheeled and tracked vehicles of ARVN's Fifth Infantry Division and the U.S. Second Battalion Thirty-fourth Armor and Second Battalion Forty-seventh Mechanized Infantry, to ensure the largest number of vehicles could move on schedule.[6]

The incursion's opening attacks would depend on mobile operations by III Corps and IIFFV, so logisticians correctly expected needing new transmissions, engines, and final drives to replace those damaged in the assaults.[7] By the time the U.S. forces and many of the South Vietnamese troops left Cambodia just two months later, SSC had issued 169 engines and 59 transmissions for tracked vehicles, as well as 245 truck engines.[8]

Given the requirement that all pieces of equipment, however badly damaged, be withdrawn to South Vietnam before 30 June (to prelude their use in communist propaganda), the supply system had to replace and evacuate dozens of major items. USARV issued 126 tracked vehicles from its stockpiles to replace destroyed or badly damaged weapons, including seventeen tanks, eighty-three APCs, two 8-inch self-propelled howitzers, and two mobile bridges.[9] Though the United States could afford such losses in light of the gains achieved, they still entailed manpower, time, and money in their repair or replacement.

The logisticians were likewise responsible for delivering ammunition. Infantry units' resupply was fairly predictable, perhaps three or four trucks filled with bullets, grenades, mortar rounds, and claymore mines. Artillery batteries were another matter, due chiefly to the weight of the shells: to fire just ten 8-inch howitzer shells required the supply system to move more than a ton of ammunition.[10]

Of all the helicopters in Vietnam, only the medium-lift CH-47 or heavy-lift CH-54 helicopters could carry such loads. Several were usually necessary, since UH-1 "Hueys" were simply too light to carry the quantities involved. For example, on the afternoon of 30 April the 11ACR needed 3,000 155mm shells to ready its batteries for the next morning's opening barrage into the Fishhook. Moving the 142 tons of artillery shells and powder required twenty CH-47 sorties. IIFFV Artillery made similar requests, as did the Twenty-fifth Infantry Division. Neither had its own CH-47s like the First Cavalry Division and so had to rely on IIFFV and USARV aviation units.[11]

The artillery's organization complicated matters for the logisticians. "Medium" artillery battalions consisted of 155mm howitzers, which made their resupply easy by comparison. However, "heavy" artillery units, the 8-inch howitzers and the 175mm guns, used shells of two different calibers, and heavy batteries were often deployed by platoons. In a typical case, during part of the incursion B Battery, Seventh Battalion Eighth Field Artillery's 175mm guns were ten kilometers east of the Fishhook, while its 8-inch howitzers were fifty kilometers away at Bien Hoa on the same firebase as C Battery, Seventh Battalion

Eighth Field Artillery's 175mm guns.[12] Though the tactical dictates of the moment might have made such deployments valid at a given time, the mixing of calibers, units, and locations made it hard to keep all unit ammunition stocks full.

The cannon of both IIFFV and III Corps, including divisional and corps-level battalions, fired steadily throughout the two-month incursion in support of the infantry. The totals the logisticians had to move forward to the guns were staggering: 534,789 rounds of 105mm; 109,575 of 155mm; 9,575 of 175mm; and, 10,013 of 8-inch.[13] The shells alone weighed almost 9,900 tons, not counting powder, fuses, or packing materials. Every pound came by boat from America through South Vietnamese ports, then by truck, plane, or helicopter to the front.

The high demand led SSC to prudently increase the ammunition it kept on hand in South Vietnam. Stockpiles grew from 71,906 short tons (STON) in April to 78,598 in May and 90,000 in June. At times it had to draw on reserves at Qui Nhon, Cam Ranh Bay, Da Nang, and various "off-shore locations," such as ammunition ships kept as floating depots in several military ports.[14] The Long Binh ammunition depot set a new record for itself when it "received more than 2000 STON daily for four consecutive days," while movements by air "averaged 250 STON daily throughout May."[15]

The tempo for the supply troops could be numbing, the Third Ordnance Battalion having to load as many as 150 flatbed trucks with ammunition every night. The busiest single day for ammunition was 1 May, with logisticians issuing more than 2,300 STON.[16] Accounting for and moving almost 5 million pounds of ammunition, plus all other types of supplies, was a monumental task, one replicated day after day for much of May and June.

Regulations governing ammunition handling added to the strain. To speed the flow and avoid depending on convoys from distant ports, SSC officers tried to get permission to unload ammunition at Newport, Saigon's waterfront area. Appalled at the thought of fully laden ammunition ships sitting in their port, the capital's civil authorities vetoed the request. The logisticians instead had to unload the bullets and shells fifty miles away at Vung Tau, a port on a small peninsula jutting into the South China Sea. There, "for two five-day periods, thirty trucks of the 48th Transportation Group cleared the cargo and transported it to Long Binh."[17] This unforeseen requirement of 300 truck-days to drive an extra 160-kilometer round trip put a further burden on the strained supply system: those same flatbed trucks were therefore unavailable to carry ammunition from Long Binh forward to Tay Ninh and Quan Loi.

Transportation remained a headache throughout the incursion. When Westmoreland set up the logistic structure in Vietnam in 1965–1966, he kept the biggest-capacity ground assets under USARV's control. Field Forces, divisions, and brigades were fighting commands, with organic logistics units which USARV assisted as necessary. During the 1960s, tactical operations were generally on a small enough scale (most commonly at company- and battalion-level), and the overall intensity of fighting moderate enough, that the supply system was able to shift assets from one operation to the next with little difficulty. For Cambodia, though, having two corps attacking out of III CTZ at the same time, plus those secondary assaults out of II and IV CTZs, required using nearly everything available. Trucks in particular were in high demand by the light infantry battalions that constituted about half the total forces in Cambodia.

To help move supplies to the units across the border, USARV sent reinforced medium-truck platoons to both Tay Ninh and Quan Loi, two key supply sites in northwestern and northern Tay Ninh Province. The transportation offices at these two sites were changed from final destinations to midpoints, handling trucking requests from tactical units, coordinating convoy route security, and transloading from the Forty-eighth Transportation Group's tractor-trailers onto medium trucks to continue forward. SSC experienced further strains when the units over the border sent their own trucks back on errands to III CTZ and then asked for (or commandeered) USARV's trucks for use in Cambodia.[18]

Not only did SSC have a hard time keeping its trucks under its control while carrying supplies toward the border and the tactical units, but the movement itself increased its problems. When the divisions went into Cambodia, their own trucks went with them. This meant that SSC's tractor-trailers and heavy trucks had to go progressively farther forward than before, taking more time for each trip. The one-way road distance from Saigon to Tay Ninh was about 100 kilometers; to Quan Loi, almost 120. Although the main roads were good by Vietnamese standards, a one-way trip could still take three to four hours, assuming no wrecks, mines, or ambushes delayed the journey. This also assumed the trucks would be unloaded promptly at the forward destination and would not be appropriated by combat units wanting more trucks for their own use. These two assumptions were often false, and the cumulative effect of the delays played havoc with SSC's planning, scheduling, and deliveries.

Still another consequence of using trucks to carry supplies to the border region was that they were not available to bring cargoes from the seaports to major USARV depots such as Long Binh. Port support and local hauls declined some 40 percent as SSC committed both the Forty-eighth Transportation Group and Peril, a commercial trucking contractor, to move materials for the Cambodian operation. Noncritical supplies steadily piled up in the harbors and ports, the backlog at Newport rising from a normal 7,000 STON to 30,000 STON. This problem lasted until after the initial phase of the incursion, when the Forty-eighth returned to port and beach clearance and reduced the backlog to a high but manageable 17,000 STON.[19]

Abrams was fortunate: had the NVA fought for the sanctuaries instead of fleeing, U.S. and ARVN units would have rapidly consumed the bullets and fuel SSC trucks had brought up. After that, the supplies in southern South Vietnam would be sitting in the Long Binh depots or piled up in the ports, blocking further unloading. Ground units would have been at greater risk while waiting for supplies to reach them. Sustaining U.S. and ARVN troops in Cambodia without having forward stockpiles near the border was thus a major accomplishment by MACV's and USARV's logisticians.

Washington also ordered MACV to consider Cambodia's needs. National Security Council staff member Al Haig went to see Lon Nol in Phnom Penh immediately after the incursion began, in part to mend fences from the latter's not being told of the operation in advance. Besides the dangers posed by the Khmer Rouge and the NVA/VC takeover of Cambodia's eastern provinces, Lon Nol also feared that the NVA and VC would simply avoid the allied thrusts by moving deeper into Cambodia. Haig promised him that Nixon would do the best he could to help Lon Nol's government.[20] Soon thereafter, Abrams sent Major General Conroy to Phnom Penh to "find out what these guys [Cambodians] can do to help themselves."[21]

Conroy's initial impression upon arriving at Phnom Penh's airport was that the Cambodians had little common sense, stacking ammunition next to aircraft fuel. He and his assistants also found FANK had issued, seemingly at random, weapons from communist, U.S., and French sources (mostly the latter).[22] An infantry company might have five types of rifles, requiring different bullets for each; fast and efficient ammunition resupply by FANK during combat was clearly impossible.

Conroy quickly concluded the top Cambodian leadership had neither combat experience nor any idea of what stocks and supplies were in their own warehouses. They did not know how to run an army, nor were they seemingly concerned about their ignorance in the face of the mortal threats they faced.

Lon Nol's attitude set the tone for the rest of the country. One evening at his lightly guarded home in the country, outside Phnom Penh's defensive perimeter, he and Conroy talked. In answer to Conroy's question of how he planned on feeding his troops in combat, Lon Nol airily replied that all they had to do was stick their finger in the ground and things would grow. Conroy left with the feeling that Lon Nol had no clue of the difficulties he and his government were facing.[23]

Returning to Saigon, Conroy told Abrams that the only way the Cambodian supply system would work was for the Americans to completely reequip FANK. In peacetime this would be a monumental task, but with Lon Nol under attack from the NVA, the VC, and the Khmer Rouge, too few competent leaders at every level, and untrained soldiers and support personnel, it was hopeless. MACV nonetheless began shipping arms to Lon Nol.

Even before Lon Nol's earlier appeal for help, MACV had already begun preparing to give several thousand excess American M-2 carbines to the South Vietnamese People's Self-Defense Forces. These small semiautomatic rifles were cheap, ammunition was readily available, and they were about to be flown in to Indochina from the United States. The carbines, though, did not end up with the South Vietnamese. Arriving in early May at Tan Son Nhut Air Base just north of Saigon, they were instead put in unmarked boxes and loaded onto Vietnamese Air Force C-119 cargo planes at a remote corner of the airbase. Crews in civilian clothes flew them to Phnom Penh in postmidnight airlifts.[24] Though giving FANK thousands of M-2 carbines might appear to only complicate the ammunition mess, a major advantage was that entire companies could be armed at once, the uniformity of each company's weapons thus easing resupply concerns for those units.

Far better than the World War II era carbines were the modern automatic weapons captured in the base areas, particularly the AK-47 assault rifles. These communist bloc arms did not have the same overt taint of U.S. involvement that came with the M-2s, were fully automatic, and shot far more powerful ammunition. Though the United States and ARVN could not themselves use the tons of communist bullets captured in the sanctuaries, giving that ammunition to Lon Nol solved several problems at once. By the end of August, FANK had received 15,732 individual and 1,565 crew-served weapons, plus 461 tons of ammunition for those guns.[25]

A seemingly insignificant problem with the captured weapons caused the MACV J-4 officers considerable headaches and delayed some arms shipments to FANK. In leaving the border areas in April and May, the NVA had taken with them thousands of the AK-47 magazines, it being easier to hide or move empty magazines than crates of rifles. AK-47s comprised the bulk of the small arms Abrams wanted to give Lon Nol, but without magazines the rifles were virtually useless.

MACV logisticians inquired around the world for several weeks before the South Koreans agreed to make replacements. Despite the apparent simplicity of an AK-47 magazine, "It wasn't an easy thing to build. It had a certain tenseness, certain resiliency in [the internal spring] that had to be measured. . . . And then the thing had . . . twenty-some spot welds . . . there was a certain sophistication in manufacturing those things."[26] When the Korean magazines arrived, MACV could begin AK-47 shipments to Cambodia. The AK-47s and ammunition increased FANK's combat power while maintaining the appearance of limited American involvement; given FANK's organization, leadership skills, and level of training, the small arms were probably the most effective military equipment MACV could have provided at the time.

Just as the various theater support units under MACV were essential to the incursion's success, so too were the contributions of the U.S. and South Vietnamese Air Forces. Airlift in particular made it possible for MACV and the corps-level commanders to execute plans on short notice.[27] During an average month in early 1970, the air force's cargo aircraft carried about 84,000 STON of people, supplies, and equipment throughout South Vietnam. As ARVN made its mid-April raid and Tri's and Davison's incursions became imminent, the April total jumped to 88,000 and peaked at 113,000 for May. June's tonnage was less, 90,000, and from July through year's end, the monthly averages were back to those of early

1970.[28] This "spike" reflected senior ground leaders' use of air transport to compensate for the absence of forward stockpiles before the incursion's start.

Lacking until the second half of May a developed ground supply route to sustain them inside Cambodia, units relied on the U.S. Air Force to bring supplies to airstrips near the border for onward transport by truck or helicopter. Twenty-three such airfields handled 66,616 STON of cargo during the incursion; the most significant forward airfields were Song Be (17,053 STON), Bu Dop (12,989), DJAMAP (8,989), Pleiku (5,596), and Katum (5,194).[29] Though used extensively by all ground forces, tactical airlift was absolutely essential to the First Cavalry Division, which lacked enough organic trucks to haul its own requirements solely on the ground.

Airdrops (by parachute) were used when speed was essential or roads were blocked, but were nearly always less desirable than airlifting. For example, C-130s dropped forty-four tons of ammunition to Fire Support David on 27 May; aircraft likewise helped FANK units on occasion, dropping four tons of ammunition on 23 June and more than five tons of ammunition and communications gear to Kampong Thom on 29 June.[30]

The air forces also flew close air support (CAS) missions. Ground commanders from lieutenant general down to colonel had artillery battalions with which to mass fires on the battlefield; Abrams had the Seventh Air Force, which let him concentrate firepower across Indochina or parcel it out as he saw fit. General George Brown, MACV deputy commander for air and the Seventh Air Force's commander, ran twelve major air operations during 1970, the most important mission being to support friendly ground troops.[31] Because fighting within South Vietnam was comparatively light in early 1970, Brown felt airpower's biggest contribution would be interdiction, attacking the Ho Chi Minh Trail to reduce the numbers of men and material finally reaching the southern battlefields. He recommended Abrams allocate his air assets accordingly.

Abrams took his advice. From January through March about 55 percent of MACV's attack sorties went to interdiction, while 45 percent were for CAS within South Vietnam. This changed in April, interdiction dropping to 44 percent and CAS rising accordingly. The start of the Cambodian incursion caused a further shift, one-quarter of all air missions being CAS in Cambodia during May and June, interdiction targets in Laos getting 36 percent in May and 27 percent in June, and the balance going for CAS in South Vietnam.[32] In response to a JCS proposal on 16 May for an interdiction campaign in northeast Cambodia like that ongoing in southern Laos, MACV noted that in the absence of an identified line of communication or a clear logistics flow in the area, it would be better to use aircraft to hit targets closer to the battlefields.[33]

There was one noteworthy exception to the Seventh Air Force's focus on interdiction and CAS: a series of strikes in North Vietnam. President Johnson's ending the Rolling Thunder campaign in November 1968 had removed the American threat to the North Vietnamese homeland. This unilateral strategic change was unmatched by any comparable self-restraint on Hanoi's part. Instead, it had permitted North Vietnam to shift most of its mobile air defense weapons, particularly heavy machine guns and small-caliber quick-firing cannon like the ZU-23-2, out of the country and increase the density of those weapons along the Ho Chi Minh Trail.[34] Interdiction strikes on the trail accordingly grew steadily more hazardous.

In the spring of 1970 the U.S. strikes on North Vietnam suddenly resumed, with 128 planes hitting air defense sites in the country's southern two provinces on 1 and 2 May. Secretary of Defense Melvin Laird warned Hanoi on 2 May that the bombing would be resumed if the NVA crossed the DMZ in response to the Cambodian incursion. Laird's threat was never put to the test: Hanoi kept its forces north of the DMZ, but an immediate furor in Washington over the war's apparent expansion led to the raids' halting on 4 May.[35] The threat of American strategic bombing largely neutralized by political means, Hanoi was thus free to leave along the Ho Chi Minh Trail its forward-deployed antiaircraft units and to use the May bombing as justification to ask Moscow and Beijing to supply more and heavier air defense weapons.

Back in South Vietnam, once Abrams allocated CAS sorties, subordinate ground commanders decided where to use the strikes. During the incursion two major considerations were how long it would take planes to get to the border and how long they could stay there: the longer the first, the less time for the second. Jets from Bien Hoa air base twenty kilometers northeast of Saigon could be over the Fishhook in about seven minutes, while A-1 ground attack turboprops would take about twenty. Jets out of Binh Thuy, in the Mekong Delta, could reinforce Bien Hoa's aircraft but needed about fifteen minutes to reach the Fishhook. Once on station the planes could normally remain for half an hour and carried between 5,000 and 7,500 pounds of high explosives or napalm.[36] CAS was thus both readily available and responsive throughout the incursion, reassuring the infantrymen below.

MACV made a major effort to provide CAS to forces in Cambodia. The USAF flew 5,189 preplanned and 1,675 immediate air strike sorties, plus 193 gunship and 44 flareship sorties. The VNAF flew 2,691 strike sorties and 184 gunship missions. However, due to weak VNAF FAC skills, there were no reported VNAF immediate strikes in support of troops in contact.[37] By the end of July, airmen had flown 11,150 FAC-directed sorties in both Cambodia and III CTZ. Of these 3,864 were in support of III Corps units on both sides of the border, 6,736 were for U.S. troops, 196 were for the Thais, and 354 were for the Australians.[38]

One fundamental tenet of ground combat planning is to weight the main effort, concentrating both maneuver and firepower at the most important point. Abrams clearly did this with his tactical airpower, as did the JGS: sorties for the BINH TAY and CUU LONG operations combined totaled less than a third of the sorties in support of IIFFV and III Corps. This was appropriate, as Abrams con-

Table 1. Tactical Air Sorties during the Cambodian Incursion

Tacair sorties	By USAF/VNAF	Total
BINH TAY operations	1,094/423	1,517
TOAN THANG operations	5,631/2,118	7,749
CUU LONG operations	187/425	612

Source: CHECO, figure 25.

sidered the regions directly across the border from III CTZ to pose the greatest threat to Saigon's survival (table 1).

Because the incursion was the most significant action in Southeast Asia during May and June 1970, most CAS missions within the theater supported the ground and naval forces attacking the sanctuaries or communist forces inside Cambodia. As claimed by the FACs, major results of CAS in the incursion included more than 1,050 enemy killed, with almost 3,400 structures and about 9,800 bunkers damaged or destroyed.[39]

While the number of dead was probably fairly accurate (and doubtless included some unlucky civilians), the "structures" and the "bunker" numbers were misleading. Nearly all structures in the base areas were open-sided huts with thatched roofs, easily knocked down and almost as easily fixed. Though burning them was the only sure way to destroy them, the planes dropped more high explosives than napalm. As for the bunkers, direct hits were normally necessary to destroy them. Thus, those secondary explosions the FACs saw were mostly from ammunition stored in the open, not from bunkers, and certainly not almost 10,000 of them. As with previous conflicts, bomb damage assessment based on pilots' reports tended to be grossly overstated.

Besides bombing and strafing, the tactical aircraft unquestionably helped the ground forces by scouting in front of advancing units. Given the paucity of timely and relevant intelligence in the hands of the ground commanders, aircrew observations of terrain and possible enemy locations were a source of valuable real-time reports. For example, FACs spotting groups of refugees helped preclude accidental attacks on the civilians by air or artillery.[40]

One aircraft in particular operated independently of FACs: the B-52s. Designed as strategic bombers rather than CAS aircraft, the B-52s were surprisingly effective in the latter role. A B-52 typically carried sixty-six bombs weighing a total of about 21 tons.[41] Because of its speed and high altitude, each plane's impact area was three kilometers long by one kilometer wide; a flight of three planes could thus strike without warning an area three kilometers square. B-52 flights reached Indochina every hour or two throughout the day, but for special events such as Bautz's attack on COSVN a "compression" could hit a specific target area with more than 360 tons of bombs in an hour.[42] The effect was devastating. If not killed or wounded by the blasts, those in the target box were shaken so badly by the concussion they were largely ineffective for several hours thereafter and were easy prey for allied infantrymen arriving to search for survivors.[43]

The B-52s were Abrams's "theater reserve." With his U.S. ground forces committed or leaving Vietnam, he lacked sufficient numbers of troops in the event of a major NVA offensive to single-handedly reinforce battlefield success or avert defeat by soldiers alone. Accordingly, airpower, and the B-52s in particular, was Abrams's tactical trump card. Each day the MACV deputy operations officer would draft the next day's target list for B-52 Arc Light (CAS) missions, using guidance provided by the operations officer. When the list was complete, Abrams personally reviewed and approved each strike, using a two-by-two-foot map board annotated with stickers.[44]

Abrams used his "strategic" airpower extensively in Cambodia. In the first quarter of 1970 there had been 117 B-52 strikes in III CTZ, 86 of them in the north and west of Tay Ninh Province.[45] During the two months of the incursion, there were 643 ARC LIGHT sorties, spread along the border.

As was the case with the tactical airpower sorties, so too did the numbers and distribution of Arc Light sorties along the Cambodian border region prove unequivocally where Abrams felt the campaign's critical areas were: the base areas opposite III CTZ's sector (see map 8). The TOAN THANG operations out of III CTZ received some 550 B-52 sorties, compared with 72 for BINH TAY from II CTZ and 23 for CUU LONG from IV CTZ. By using massed airpower to disrupt or crush any potential or actual threats, Abrams ensured that his ground maneuver forces were able to move freely to accomplish their missions.

Also flying above Cambodia were the gunships, especially the AC-47, AC-119G, and AC-119K. Depending on the specific model, they carried an assortment of 7.62mm or 20mm Gatling-style miniguns and 40mm autoloading cannon and were particularly effective against NVA supply columns or infantry attacks.

The gunships were fortunate in several regards. First, in May 1970 the air defense guns moved out of North Vietnam during 1969 and 1970 were more in southern Laos and northeastern Cambodia, opposite II CTZ, than around the base areas opposite III CTZ. Second, these weapons were aimed optically rather than by radar; the gunships could thus operate at night at acceptable levels of risk. Finally, the Soviet Union's infrared shoulder-fired guided missile, the SA-7, was still a year or so away from its introduction into Southeast Asia; by 1972 it was inflicting painful losses on American aircraft. As the gunship crews knew too well, if the enemy was in range of the gunship's weapons, the gunship might well be in range of the enemy's.

Psychological warfare support was a secondary mission for the Seventh Air Force but was nonetheless used during the incursion. IIFFV printed 12 million leaflets weekly to persuade the NVA and VC to defect and to let the Cambodians know what was happening around them.[46] Efficient distribution on the ground was a problem, so starting 11 May Brown let Davison use two C-123 aircraft for leaflet drops. The C-123s made one flight a day each, carrying 5 million leaflets. The next day Brown added a C-130 for one drop per week of 12.5 million

Map 8. B-52 Arc Light Air Strikes during the Cambodian Incursion

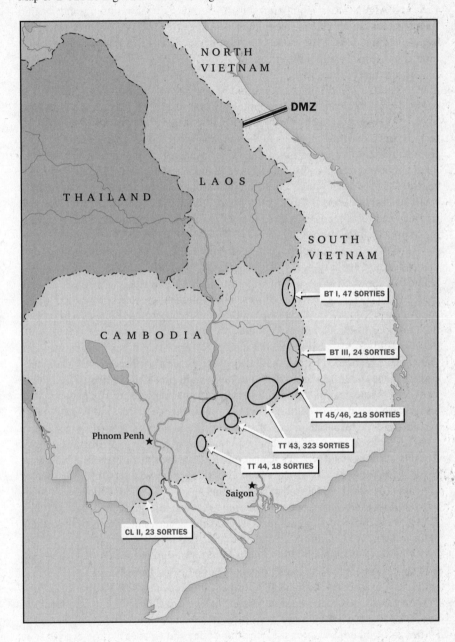

leaflets. Forty communists abandoned their cause and turned themselves in to U.S. and ARVN units; compared with the effects of the bombing and ground forces' attacks, the leaflets' role in their decisions to surrender was unclear. However, given the number of leaflets to those persuaded, it was apparent most communist troops were not quitting easily.

An air force asset with more immediately obvious effects was the Commando Vault, a 15,000-pound bomb rolled on a pallet out of the back of a C-130 cargo aircraft to create helicopter landing zones. The USAF dropped twenty during the incursion, sixteen of which detonated in the right places with good effects.[47] Since existing clearings in the jungles were often guarded, such clearings were extremely dangerous to use for troop insertions. While a few 250- or 500-pound bombs might possibly blow a hole in the forest big enough for a single helicopter, several helicopters could land and take off together in a Commando Vault's clearing. Inserting an infantry platoon all at once was safer and faster than putting in three squads one after the other, so pilots and ground commanders much preferred the mass entry.

There were some problems during the incursion in coordinating B-52s, Commando Vaults, artillery, CAS, and troop insertions. IIFFV later concluded that about two days' advance notice was necessary to plan such missions, and that most of its brigade staffs in 1970 were not proficient enough to give them direct control over B-52s. The shortest period between the end of the B-52 strikes and the dropping of the Commando Vaults was about fifty minutes, after which the troops could go in.[48] However, the intervals were often hours longer, meaning that an enemy stunned by the B-52 attacks might well have recovered when helicopters came in with infantrymen and might fight or withdraw as it suited them. A faster response would probably have let troops capture more prisoners with less fighting, but by 1970 many battalion and brigade staffs often struggled to synchronize the disparate pieces of such air-ground operations.

The focus of air activity changed considerably during 1970 as a result of Abrams's strategy and Nixon's decision to destroy the sanctuaries. When the year began, Cambodia was off-limits for all air strikes except the secret MENU bombing campaign, but by December 1970 flights against Cambodia and Laos constituted almost three-quarters of all missions starting in South Vietnam.[49] Further, CAS sorties dropped from 45 percent down to 25 percent, strongly suggesting that enemy activity within South Vietnam had declined comparably. Abrams and Brown considered the situation within South Vietnam secure enough to permit using airpower elsewhere, which meant Cambodia and Laos.

After CAS, Brown's highest priority was interdiction of the Ho Chi Minh Trail in Laos and Cambodia. On 6 June Operation FREEDOM DEAL formally began, an air interdiction mission that was to "maintain surveillance of enemy activities in Cambodia, east of the Mekong River, and to attack those activities as necessary to protect U.S. forces in the Republic of Vietnam."[50] Running from 1 through 20 June, the strikes included 414 preplanned and 224 immediate sorties.

FREEDOM DEAL's focus changed after 7 June, from hitting possible lines of communication to instead striking near major cities in northeast Cambodia to help beleaguered FANK forces try to repel NVA attackers. The aid was kept quiet: administration officials had "repeatedly said that the U.S. would not provide air combat support to South Vietnamese forces beyond the [thirty-kilometer] limit."[51] This support was thus technically not a lie: it was to FANK, not ARVN.

Due to the rising intensity of the NVA's assaults, on 17 June FREEDOM DEAL expanded into FREEDOM ACTION, hitting NVA and Khmer Rouge forces across the breadth of the country. This effort lasted until 30 June, when FREEDOM ACTION reverted to FREEDOM DEAL, the original area for air operations expanding slightly to the south. Southern targets were authorized for attack only if they posed a major threat to allied forces.[52]

By attacking NVA logistics with airpower far away from South Vietnam's borders, Abrams further delayed Hanoi's rebuilding its captured or destroyed base areas. Hanoi's inability to launch significant offensive actions gave Saigon time to strengthen its control over South Vietnam, and the United States more time to withdraw its forces without interference. The air strikes in northeast Cambodia also meant that fewer NVA troops would be able to attack the U.S. troops remaining in South Vietnam, and later rather than sooner. Given the American desire to leave Vietnam and the pressure from Washington to keep casualties low, interdiction helped to achieve those goals. Between interdiction, CAS, and logistics functions, airpower played a significant role in the incursion.

Naval forces played a useful if secondary role in attacking the sanctuaries. Their chief functions during the incursion were to aid the ground logistics units by carrying supplies forward, evacuate Vietnamese refugees from eastern and central Cambodia, and secure the Mekong River and other waterways while denying their use to the enemy. This latter task included interdicting and searching ships bound for Kampong Speu, the port previously named Sihanoukville.

The incursion's biggest naval action began on the morning of 9 May, in direct support of ARVN IV Corps' Operation CUU LONG I. As ground forces, including mechanized and armored units, penetrated west and northwest about sixty kilometers deep into Cambodia up the eastern side of the Mekong River, a combined force of 110 Vietnamese Navy (VNN) and 30 U.S. Navy vessels sailed up the Mekong.

Their initial objective was Highway 1's ferry crossing northwest of Prey Veng, which linked Phnom Penh and Cambodia east of the Mekong. Gaining control of this ferry site would permit IV Corps to move westward, to Phnom Penh, and to aid ethnic Vietnamese refugees seeking flight to Vietnam.

However, the two ferries normally there were missing and were not found until 12 May. They had been deliberately sunk in shallow water just north of the crossing, near the eastern bank; the deputy commander of the U.S. Navy, Vietnam, a rear admiral, took some glee in his old eyes spotting them from the air after younger pilots had repeatedly missed them. Salvage operations began immediately, and the ferries soon reentered service across the Mekong.[53]

With the Mekong River open as a line of communication, refugee evacuations afloat took place concurrently with combat operations on land. On 11 May a VNN force proceeded farther up the Mekong to pick up refugees; it consisted of two Landing Ship Tanks, three Landing Ship-Mediums, ten Landing Craft-Medium-8s, and fifteen escorting Patrol Craft Fast (PCF), also called Swift boats.[54] Naval and Vietnamese Marine forces quickly began evacuating Vietnamese refugees from Phnom Penh. By 18 May almost 20,000 had come out; thousands more wanted to leave, but because of Saigon's uncertainty regarding where to relocate them within South Vietnam, they and the naval convoy sent to carry them remained in Cambodia through the end of May. Over the next several weeks the Vietnamese and American navies evacuated about 35,000 refugees from as far north as Kampong Cham, about sixty kilometers farther up the Mekong from the capital.[55]

After the initial clearing of the Mekong, active naval roles subsided. The VNN provided most of the boats, did most of the work, and stayed on after 30 June; the U.S. Navy participated in steadily declining numbers until all U.S. naval and marine forces were back in Vietnamese waters or in Vietnam by midafternoon on 29 June.[56] Given the dictates of geography, with CUU LONG being ARVN IV Corps' operation without significant U.S. Army involvement, and IV Corps' drive into Cambodia deeper than Nixon's thirty-kilometer limit, it was thus inevitable that the scope of the VNN's participation was greater than the U.S. Navy's. Nonetheless, the naval role was important even if largely overlooked: every ton of war supplies carried by boat up the Mekong from South Vietnam, and every refugee evacuated down the Mekong to South Vietnam, meant that much more ground and air transport able to support the maneuver commanders and that much "cleaner" the area in the combat units' rear.

Just as the air and naval forces contributed significantly to the overall success of the Cambodian incursion, and the logistics and support units sustained the combat forces across the border, so too did secondary military operations aid the main assault originating out of III CTZ. The actions of IV Corps influenced and were directly affected by those of III Corps and IIFFV. This was not the case in the cross-border operations originating out of II CTZ.

Binh Tay I, II, and III were distinct ARVN and U.S. assaults into the border region of northeastern Cambodia. Binh Tay I, involving elements of the Fourth Infantry Division, targeted Base Area 702. Binh Tay II and III were ARVN affairs, beginning on 14 May against Base Area 701 and on 20 May against Base Area 740, respectively. The events of Binh Tay I are indicative of all three, with the strengths and weaknesses ARVN displayed in TOAN THANG and CUU LONG present in II Corps units as well.

As IIFFV and III Corps attacked at the beginning of May, Abrams told Lieutenant General Arthur Collins, the commanding general of IFFV, to make his own assaults. Fully aware that the bulk of MACV's assets were supporting Abrams's main effort, in the COSVN/Fishhook area, Collins gave the mission to the Fourth Infantry Division under Major General Glenn Walker. On the night of 2 May, Colonel Harold Yew of the division's First Brigade learned he was to seize Base Area 702, the traditional location of the B-3 Front headquarters and various support units, on 5 May; Yew began planning immediately.[57]

In the process of pulling out of the Central Highlands prior to departing for America, the division was poorly postured to make such an assault. Between mid-March and mid-April it had relocated most of its units from Camp Enari to Camp Radcliffe, a sprawling base with a perimeter of more than eighteen kilometers and enclosing twenty-eight square kilometers (almost eleven square miles).[58] Unfortunately, it was too far from the border, and assaults had to be launched from temporary sites at New Plei Djering. While marginally better, New Plei Djering left much to be desired: its own distance from the objectives made helicopters use too much fuel in travel and left them too little to tarry over the landing zones if needed.

Assaulting via helicopters on the morning of 5 May, the initial forces were driven back by fire from dug-in 12.7mm heavy machine guns. Returning four hours later after additional airstrikes, the troops from the Third Battalion 506th Infantry (Airborne) found "cold" landing zones and disembarked safely. Heavy fires from NVA defenders prevented their sister unit, the First Battalion Fourteenth Infantry, from landing at either its primary or alternate locations, and the battalion had to return to South Vietnam to wait until 6 May before trying again, this time successfully. Colonel Yew's third unit, the Third Battalion Eighth Infantry, inserted sixty men on the morning of the sixth at its alternate landing zone (LZ) before heavy enemy fire shut down the LZ and left the men stranded overnight in hostile country; one died and two were wounded before the rest of the battalion arrived on a now-cold LZ the next day.[59]

Over the next week the First Brigade searched through the northern part of Base Area 702, with fair success. During the operation 136 NVA troops died, and the brigade captured assorted minor supplies and 554 tons of rice.[60]

Two days after the First Brigade started its attack on the northern half of Base Area 702, the division's Second Brigade under Colonel William E. Conger Jr. attacked the center. Conger's three infantry battalions' insertions via helicopter were largely unopposed, in contrast to Yew's movement. Between 7 and 13 May the Second Brigade killed fifty-seven enemy soldiers (including the losses inflicted by aircraft and helicopter gunships) and captured about thirty-seven tons of rice. The meager results did not warrant a longer stay in Cambodia, and General Walker pulled it back to South Vietnam to help resume the U.S. drawdown;

the ARVN Twenty-second Infantry Division subsequently moved into Base Area 702 to continue the searches.[61]

———————

Just as MACV concentrated its resources to support the incursion, so too did IIFFV. Davison assigned some of his units in late April to help Tri's attack and other units to assist Shoemaker's. As the incursion's scope widened to include other sanctuaries, he put almost all his assets into ensuring the operation's success. This corps-level involvement was particularly important in the areas of engineer and signal troops, without which other units could have neither moved nor talked.

Engineers were critical to ground operations, in both getting units and supplies into Cambodia and getting captured materials out. In late April, when of all IIFFV only Task Force Shoemaker was to enter Cambodia, the corps engineer units' participation appeared minor. Two platoons with additional bulldozers, road graders, and front-end loaders went to Katum and Tonle Cham, along with thirteen demolition teams to destroy any bunkers the maneuver forces located. This small force was sufficient for the weeklong raid Shoemaker was expecting. However, as Abrams steadily expanded the area and duration of operations, the engineer effort grew proportionally. By the campaign's conclusion two months later, engineers had built (or reinforced) fifteen bridges and 163 kilometers of new roads while maintaining another 263 kilometers of existing roads and seven forward airfields.[62]

Four of IIFFV's engineer battalions ultimately supported the incursion. Two were "combat" engineers, helping the First Cavalry and Twenty-fifth Infantry Divisions' own engineer battalions and infantry brigades. Another was a construction battalion, with heavy earthmoving equipment to improve and maintain the major routes across Tay Ninh and Binh Long Provinces. The fourth was a land-clearing battalion, using teams of Rome Plows to cut swaths through the jungles and forests

The engineers' deployment was largely an outgrowth of the initial dispositions during Task Force Shoemaker's first days: the First Cavalry Division's Eighth Engineer Battalion worked inside Cambodia, and the corps-level engineers worked in the adjacent border region inside South Vietnam. This division of labor continued after the incursion expanded beyond the Fishhook. For example, the Thirty-first Engineer Battalion opened a thirty-five-kilometer stretch of Highway QL-13 north from Loc Ninh across the border to Snuol and cut a twenty-two-kilometer long spur through the jungle from QL-13 to The City.[63] The 588th Engineer Battalion was busy around Katum, keeping open roads along the border and north from Katum to Cambodian Highway 7, the asphalt road that linked Memot and Snuol.[64] The Ninety-second (Construction) Battalion worked behind the Thirty-first and 588th to maintain the area's major supply route, the road from Tay Ninh City north to Katum. Within their sectors the battalions also enlarged and kept the airfields repaired, since the heavy aircraft traffic at times was more than the packed-dirt runways could handle.[65]

The fourth IIFFV engineer battalion active in the incursion, the Sixty-second Land Clearing Battalion, had initially been working in northern Tay Ninh Province. Davison realized in early May that its Rome Plows might help find caches by thinning or removing the dense vegetation. Accordingly, he sent the Sixty-second north, where two of its companies spent the next month flattening almost 1,700 heavily forested acres in the Fishhook.[66] Other Rome Plow platoons worked in northwest Tay Ninh Province, pushing the jungle back from Highway QL-22 between Thien Ngon and the border, and in northwest Phuoc Long Province, opening Highway QL-14A to bring out captured enemy supplies.[67]

As the Rome Plows pushed through the forests and jungles, they were at risk from enemy infantry, so after seizing Snuol the 11ACR escorted them through the woods. Such a mission made sense, since tanks and ACAVs were less effective in helping search for buried or hidden caches than in protecting Rome Plows and smaller bulldozers. To further reduce the cover available in the border areas, IIFFV used chemical defoliants, such as Agent Orange, in limited amounts.[68] This, however, occurred toward the end of the incursion and was less immediately useful than the Rome Plows: the herbicides took time to kill the foliage, often a week or more.

Whatever the method, by clearing the jungle along the border, the engineers made it more difficult for the returning NVA and VC to hide their movements or positions from helicopter scouts inside South Vietnam. The Sixty-second's efforts, plus those of the three IIFFV and two divisional battalions, played an important role in the incursion's success. Without them the infantry and artillery would have had more difficulty searching and fighting, and the evaluation of captured supplies would have been far more difficult.

The other critical support IIFFV provided for the various ground units was communication. Telephones linked Field Force, divisional, and brigade base camps, but brigades' moves to field sites put them beyond the established phone network.

Radio immediately became the primary means of talking between headquarters. However, the multichannel VHF radios linking headquarters from brigade level up to MACV required electronic lines of sight, and tactical FM radios' limited ranges were further reduced in the jungle or in forests. Relay stations of various types were thus necessary; the most important in III CTZ was Nui Ba Den. The U.S. Army controlled the mountain's top and bottom, but VC holdouts in caves controlled the middle, forcing the army to travel to and from the top via helicopter. Realizing the mountain's value to radio communications, the U.S. Army had built a signal site on its top in 1965; by 1970 the peak was an antenna farm, regularly subject to harassing VC rocket and mortar fire.

The unit movements throughout III CTZ caused an increase in the number of radio transmitters crowded atop Nui Ba Den, leading to serious frequency management and mutual interference problems. With both ARVN and U.S. units using the same American-made radios, more users demanded pieces of a finite asset, the tactical radio frequencies between 30.00 and 79.95 megahertz (MHz). In 1968 more than 20,000 U.S. and ARVN users had been on 2,100 FM radio nets in III CTZ; the situation was comparable in May 1970.[69] Exacerbating this was many units' tendency to commandeer "unused" frequencies if their assigned one was too busy or was jammed; when the frequencies' assigned "owners" came up on the airwaves, they found themselves blocked out by the "squatters."

The interference problem became so severe that IIFFV signal officers had to divert electronic warfare units from monitoring the enemy to instead trying to identify or locate the "friendly" offenders. It turned out that most of the "jamming" was from mutual interference rather than deliberate enemy efforts, either the transmitters being physically too close together or their frequencies causing harmonics (as 35.00 MHz would do to 70.00 MHz). The more radios in a small area, the greater the odds of electronic interference.[70] Brigade and division headquarters from the First Cavalry and Twenty-fifth Infantry Divisions, an ARVN division, IIFFV, aviation, and MACV all used Nui Ba Den as a relay site, as well as for electronic warfare interception. There was very limited space available atop Nui Ba Den: "At one time as many as 77 stations were operating at the summit of the mountain," and only by cutting the number of stations to fewer than fifty could signal officers resolve the interference.[71] Doing so, however, meant that some units lost their radio relays, causing some poisonous and heated discussions.

Another serious problem was the need to create and maintain new communications networks where none had existed, and to do so between moving headquarters. American signal troops not only had to support ARVN's III Corps but likewise had to help U.S. brigades and battalions. For example, Abrams's Fifty-third Signal Battalion set up a VHF multichannel system to connect Shoemaker at Quan Loi to Roberts at Phuoc Vinh and Davison at Long Binh. It also opened an FM retransmission station on Nui Ba Ra, another mountain signal site thirty-five kilometers northeast of Quan Loi, to give Shoemaker a scrambled voice link to Davison, and set up a signal center at Quan Loi to support Davison's team monitoring Shoemaker's broadcasts. For the Twenty-fifth Infantry Division the Fifty-third put in two VHF multichannel systems between Katum, Dau Tieng, and Tay Ninh.[72] This was just one signal battalion's work, in less than two weeks; each division had its own signal battalion as well. The radio links they hastily created, eventually augmented by extending the area telephone network, gave commanders and staffs the indispensable "central nervous system" necessary to coordinate actions of the scores of units into coherent operations.

Complicating commanders' control was the incessant abuse of message priorities. Every message going through a communications center, such as VHF multichannel or teletype, had an assigned priority; higher-priority messages would "bump" lower-priority ones. With the tremendous number of signals during the incursion, staff officers often wrongly inflated their own messages' priorities to get them transmitted sooner. Though they knew this was improper, it quickly became a matter of self-preservation, since to not do so when everyone else was doing it meant guaranteeing one's own messages would never get transmitted in time.

By early June the abuse had become so bad that the Twenty-fifth Infantry Division asked IIFFV for five additional circuits so that lower-priority messages could get through without being cut off.[73] The messages most often overridden were administrative and logistics ones, as opposed to those concerning movements or real-time combat. Had IIFFV faced serious opposition inside Cambodia, the message bottlenecks would have eventually caused critical shortages of supplies and people.

Sometimes simpler problems added to the friction. For example, the night before he attacked, Shoemaker ordered a soldier he did not recognize, a telephone installer, out of his command bunker, resulting in his staff not getting some telephones they had requested. On 13 May Roberts had been unable to talk to Davison on secure FM radios; he had used the wrong scrambler code.[74]

Equipment shortages often caused a ripple effect as one unit borrowed from another, which was subsequently ordered into Cambodia but without its own "loaned" equipment; certain types of voice-encoding gear were especially scarce.[75] Generals and division headquarters could talk to each other on scrambled circuits, but companies and platoons, pressed for time during firefights, had to use a cumbersome manual coding process for anything like helicopter landing sites or their ammunition status.

A final complication came from making sure everyone had the correct signal codebook and frequencies, a nightmarish accountability and security problem made worse by the number of units involved and the need to replace every copy of a particular codebook whenever a single one was lost. By virtue of incredibly hard work, signal units kept the combat and support forces talking; their generally unheralded efforts were critical in whatever successes the incursion achieved.

———

Although there were problems resulting from the short time allowed to prepare for the cross-border attacks, overall the combat units had sufficient support to complete their missions with acceptable risks. The logistics system the United States had established in South Vietnam during the previous five years, sometimes criticized as having been excessively large or wasteful, had been built to sustain two armies, not just one. Thus, its vast capability gave Abrams and his subordinates the flexibility and resources to sustain major and simultaneous corps- and lesser-level offensives into Cambodia. Hanoi's far smaller system had been seriously weakened by the loss of the Sihanoukville Trail and the fighting across eastern Cambodia during late March and April, as well as by the Seventh

Air Force's strikes on the Ho Chi Minh Trail. When Abrams launched his assaults on the sanctuaries in May, the strain was more than COSVN and the B-2 Front could stand. Even had it wanted to fight, it lacked the mobility and resources to do so, with American and ARVN troops having captured their stockpiles and made organized conventional resistance futile.

9

Aftermath

The Cambodian incursion was, as Nixon correctly described it, "the most successful military operation of the Vietnam War."[1] Though it could not, nor was it intended to, prevent Hanoi's ultimate triumph in Vietnam's civil war, it had major impact on the degree of risk under which U.S. forces withdrew from Southeast Asia.

Abrams bought time for pacification and U.S. withdrawal by destroying the NVA's border sanctuaries. Had he not done so, Saigon would have been far more vulnerable to a major NVA attack out of Cambodia in 1971 or 1972 while U.S. ground troops were still in South Vietnam. Such a fiasco would have denied the United States either "a decent interval" or the fig leaf of "peace with honor." America's loss of life and prestige would have been much the worse, the United States never having had an army captured or destroyed as it lost a war. Other tools of statecraft, such as diplomatic posturing, economic inducements, or propaganda, could not have averted or mitigated such a catastrophe.

The incursion was thus militarily necessary and was reasonably well conducted despite its hurried nature. In its immediate aftermath, prospects in South Vietnam looked more promising than in years, thanks largely to the destruction of the border sanctuaries.

Such views were, and are, not popular in many circles. Those who in hindsight say the incursion was not worth the costs generally base their arguments on either of two unproved and unprovable assumptions.

The first, and primary, objection was that U.S. domestic opposition to the Nixon administration and the Indochina War would have been significantly less had the incursion not occurred. American college campuses would not have erupted, the protesters at Kent State and Jackson State would not have died, and the open warfare between the executive and legislative branches that strained the Republic throughout the 1970s would instead have been a passing spat.

There are certainly plausible grounds for this perspective: students protested violently, and six died, some 450 colleges and universities went on strike, and open dissent emerged within the federal government itself. Three of Kissinger's National Security Council staffers resigned, and 250 State Department employees signed a protest memorandum.

Nixon clearly felt the domestic pressure and tried to defuse or distract it. On 8 May he held a press conference at which he reiterated the incursion's temporary nature; he promised that most troops would be out by mid-June and predicted a gain of six to eight months of relative peace for Vietnamization. This did not stop an antiwar rally from taking place on 9 May in Washington, involving 60,000 to 100,000 protesters. On 11 May Nixon hosted a meeting in the White House, attended by forty-six state and territorial governors; it lasted four hours and addressed Cambodia and campus unrest.[2] Nixon was scrambling politically, dealing with the immediate threats; however, the longer-term problem of relations with "the Hill" was not amenable to such measures.

By 1970 Congress was seeking to redress the imbalance of power that had developed since the 1930s between the legislative and executive branches, the gradual shift having generally been in favor of the latter. World War II, Korea, the cold war, and Vietnam had seen power and initiative in matters of national security steadily concentrated in the presidency, at the Congress's expense.

Cambodia was arguably the straw that "broke the camel's back," but it was not the sole factor. News of the incursion made congressional opponents of the war livid; just days earlier Secretary of State Rogers had testified to the Senate Foreign Relations Committee that the United States had no plans for any operations in Cambodia.[3] Rogers was telling what he thought was the truth, unaware that Nixon and Kissinger had deliberately excluded him from all knowledge of the pending incursion. Congress, however, drew the obvious conclusion that Rogers, and by extension the Nixon administration, had lied to it. Its fury was thus the greater.

News of the attack produced immediate attempts to curtail operations through legislation. On 1 May, for example, two bills were proposed in the Senate: the McGovern-Hatfield Act would cut off all funds for U.S. military activities in Indochina by the end of 1971, while the milder Cooper-Church Amendment sought to prohibit all funds after 30 June for training FANK or fighting in or above Cambodia. Neither bill passed both houses, the congressional anger abating somewhat as U.S. troops withdrew from Cambodia during June.[4] However, the proposed legislation clearly indicated the depth and vehemence of congressional opposition to Nixon's war policies and was a harbinger of electoral pressures to come.

Had Cambodia not galvanized Congress into action, sooner or later something else would have done so. Nixon violated numerous laws, not solely due to the Cambodian incursion, and was ultimately held accountable by Congress.

Cambodia clearly accelerated movement down the path leading to Watergate, but did not cause it: Nixon's fundamental problem lay in his willingness, and in that of his closest advisers and aides, to put political expediency ahead of the law.

Even before U.S. troops had finished withdrawing from Cambodia, an initial assessment began at home. Leftist intellectuals and student radicals were frustrated, their protests making clear to them their inability to decisively affect the Nixon administration's actions: the incursion continued for almost two months despite their vehement opposition. In partial consequence, many protesters' subsequent calls for increased violence at home grew more strident and frequent: the American social fabric appeared to be unraveling.[5]

In part responding to widespread disquiet across the country, Nixon addressed the American public with an initial assessment as of 30 June, the day all U.S. forces were out of Cambodia. He summarized the background of the incursion and emphasized his administration's search for peace. He then listed four key points: North Vietnam had brought the war to Cambodia; NVA troops had contributed to Sihanouk's downfall; Sihanouk's government and the Cambodian National Assembly had deposed Sihanouk; and major NVA/VC base activity had led to action by the Americans and South Vietnamese, after the allies had endured blatant violations of Cambodian neutrality for five years.[6]

Nixon next detailed specific policies concerning U.S. involvement in Cambodia. No U.S. ground forces would remain in Cambodia, less the regular embassy staff; there would be no U.S. advisers with FANK; only air interdiction would take place, and then with the Cambodian government's approval; and the Cambodian government would receive captured war materials, U.S. military assistance, and American diplomatic recognition.[7]

The president's assertions and promises, though appropriate and valid, did little to repair the damaged trust between the administration and the media. When reporters asked why U.S. Air Force jets were flying CAS missions for FANK, Secretary of Defense Laird told them the strikes were, rather, interdiction attacks, but he admitted they might provide certain "ancillary benefits" for FANK.[8] The Vietnam-related misleading of the American public, begun in previous administrations, continued: whether deceptions of omission or commission, they remained lies.

A final point, overlooked or ignored by "domestic politics" opponents of the incursion, involved the cost of the incursion as measured in lives and damage to the American body politic. Six students died during campus protests in summer 1970, and there was serious turmoil across the United States. This was clearly a painful cost, with lasting consequences.

But what of the American lives spared, and those of the South Vietnamese soldiers and civilians who survived because the NVA and VC now lacked the bullets and explosives to kill them? Although trying to specify exact numbers would be speculative, based on previous months' casualty rates the numbers of U.S. and RVNAF troops escaping death thanks to the incursion must have been in the hundreds. Those soldiers' and South Vietnamese civilians' lives were no less valuable because they were not American college students, or had family backgrounds unlike the protesters'. The postwar historical focus on student protesters unfairly relegates by default the incursion's participants to anonymity and insignificance, at best an elitist perspective. Those soldiers, and their families, mattered every bit as much as did the students who were protesting, rioting, and refusing to share the burden of defending freedom by their own personal sacrifice.

A second major objection to the incursion presumes that the NVA would have stood passively by and watched the U.S. forces depart in peace rather than seek to drive them into the sea in defeat. This argument relies heavily on COSVN Resolution 9, which called for low-intensity conflict; its guidance was valid for 1970, but not necessarily for 1971 or later.

Given the absence of any trust toward each other by both sides by 1970, responsible American politicians and generals were unwilling to simply turn their backs on the communists and move to the ports and airfields: there had been too many dead to risk the NVA or VC not seeking revenge against departing U.S. forces. No soldier of any army has ever wanted to be the last one killed in a war, and no American leader wanted unnecessary deaths at the end of the nation's involvement in South Vietnam. Against this, the Politburo had shown itself willing to sacrifice its troops if it felt the political gains warranted the costs. Until Hanoi's archives are fully open, its true intentions for 1970 and 1971 must remain a matter of conjecture.

For Abrams to have not attacked the sanctuaries in 1970 would have left them in place, fully stocked and operational despite MENU's damage. They would have permitted COSVN and the B-2 Front to pose a mortal threat to the heart of South Vietnam in 1971–1972, and Saigon might have fallen before 1975. Nixon could have ordered a precipitous U.S. withdrawal and satisfied most of his domestic and international opponents, but doing so would have raised grave doubts about the value of American security guarantees elsewhere.[9] Global strategic dictates as well as domestic political imperatives necessitated the U.S. withdrawal, while doing it at the least risk to, or cost in, U.S. lives and credibility.

By 1970 Hanoi's efforts toward increasing the capacity and security of the Ho Chi Minh Trail were well advanced, unequivocally demonstrating by its actions the trail's critical importance; Cambodia's ports and the routes from them to the base areas were no longer available or necessary. In the absence of the incursion's destruction, perhaps Hanoi would have sat passively by throughout 1970 and 1971 as the United States departed, waiting and gathering its power to crush the isolated RVNAF. But as they showed during the 1975 offensive inside South Vietnam, the Politburo and the NVA were willing to accelerate their plans to take advantage of unexpected battlefield successes. To imagine they would have lacked similar initiative and resolve in 1971 or 1972 is foolish.

That Hanoi fully intended to seek a decisive and unambiguous military victory against a departing (but still not totally gone) United States was brutally apparent in spring 1972.[10] North Vietnam's entire army, the equivalent of twenty NVA divisions, smashed across the DMZ and out of southern Laos and northeastern Cambodia into the less-populated northern half of South Vietnam. No major units remained behind in North Vietnam: everything was committed toward the goal of a decisive victory in I and II CTZs.

The offensive did not erupt out of Cambodia to drive the mere sixty or so miles to Saigon and the Mekong Delta because after June 1970 there were no border stockpiles to support such large and sustained conventional attacks. Additionally, Washington's decision to curtail bombing of North Vietnam had permitted Hanoi to build up stockpiles in southern North Vietnam, closer to the DMZ, where they could support the cross-DMZ offensive.[11] Hanoi's focus on the more distant and less-populated I and II CTZs meant that South Vietnam had more strategic depth for the 1972 fighting than it would have possessed had the Easter Offensive started from the Fishhook and Parrot's Beak.

Such debates and deliberations were for those sitting in safety, across oceans or in later years; the immediate beneficiaries of the Cambodian operations were the U.S. and ARVN forces in South Vietnam in 1970.[12] As one American soldier commented, "'We caught them running across an open field and it seemed like the NVA just couldn't believe we were really here.'"[13] Davison was pleased with their work, saying that "if we hadn't gone into Cambodia there just would have been one hell of a lot of bullets and mortar shells that could have been shot at our troops and consequently would have made the course of Vietnamization more difficult than should now be the case."[14] After the incursion Bautz noted, "[We were] supposed to be so fat and sloppy . . . [the NVA was] supposed to be so slim and trim and mean in their support . . . but they had a lot more than anybody ever figured."[15] A battalion commander in the Twenty-fifth Infantry Division observed, "'We have destroyed in a very short time what has taken the enemy months, perhaps even years to build.'"[16]

The troops agreed wholeheartedly. One company commander reported that his unit had suffered three dead in capturing a cache during the incursion, but "'didn't receive another single shot'" before he gave up his command in November, almost five months later. Indeed, "'As we ran our patrols, we would find they were trailing us so they could eat our garbage.'"[17] Enemy soldiers without food or ammunition posed little threat, as Abrams had realized a year earlier (table 2).

Communist offensive capabilities declined significantly across III and IV CTZs. Kissinger quantified the drop: "In the twelve months before Cambodia, more than 7,000 Americans had been killed in action. In the year after, the figure was less than 2,500. The next year [1972] it fell to less than 500."[18] Those numbers were affected by the declining numbers of Americans in the country, as well

Table 2. Allied Operations in Cambodia, 29 April–30 June 1970 (selected results)

Operation	Dates	Days in Cambodia	Size of Force at Maximum Strength		Captured/Destroyed						GVN KIA	US KIA	GVN WIA	US WIA	KIA Exchange Rate
			GVN	US	NVA/VC KIA	NVA/VC POW	Individual Weapons	Crew-served Weapons	Ammo (STON)	Rice (STON)					
TT42 III Corps	29 April–cont'd. after 30 June	61	9,794	1,590	2,752	767	1,893	478	360	1,042	283	9	1,290	65	9
TT42 IV Corps	29 April–6 May	8	NA	NA	1,202	0	1,146	174	63	46	67	3	329	5	17
TT43 (1CD)	1 May–30 June	59	8,000	13,400	3,099	73	4,680	731	316	2,699	149	141	656	863	11
BINH TAY 1 (4ID)	5–25 May	26	2,463	8,016	276	8	842	37	13	602	16	30	98	72	6
TT44 (25ID, BA 354)	6–14 May	9		2,700	283	122	297	34	4	217		21		174	13
TT45 (1CD, BA 350/351)	6 May–30 June	55		10,900	1,189	12	3,069	449	804	1,584		126		332	9
TT46	6 May–30 June	55	3,160	32	70	9	325	41	10	79	27		147		3
TT44 (25ID, BA 367)	7–12 May (US) (SVN longer)	6	400	600	128	10	33	1	.15*	.05		7		31	
TT500/B16/645	7–11 May	5	900	900	(Results included under TOAN THANG 42 III Corps)										
CUU LONG I	9 May–1 July	53	11,696	2,364	1,431	61	2,738	157	23	41	148	6	473	5	9
TT44 (25ID, BA 707/COSVN)	9–14 May	6		4,000	335	18	133	30	20	466					
BINH TAY II	14–26 May	13	4,593	392	73	6	476	136	27	89	7	2	34	0	8
TT44 (25ID, BA 353)	15 May–30 June	45		5,000	329	14	249	66	18	854		89		678	4
CUU LONG II	16–24 May	9	10,260	346	613	40	792	84	65	44	36	0	122	7	17
BINH TAY III	20 May–27 June	38	3,615	272	141	1	587	133	40	412	26	0	67	7	5
CUU LONG III	24 May–cont'd. after 30 June	41	3,727	147	433	36	3,299	80	40	27	50		270	1	9
Totals			58,608	50,659	12,354	1,177	20,559	2,631	1,803	8,202.05	809	434	3,486	2,233	10

Sources: *CHECO*, figure 1; OB Logistics MACV; and 25th Infantry Division Combat Operations AAR, p. 10.

*TT44–BA367 – U.S. found 300 lbs of ammo; SVN found hundreds more after U.S. withdrawal.

as by less-aggressive tactics by both sides, but a key factor was indisputably the NVA and VC lack of adequate war material with which to fight. Indeed, the VC were particularly hard-hit and to obtain weapons and ammunition often had to attack RF and PF outposts as the "softest" targets that had stocks large enough to make the risks of such assaults worth taking.[19]

High during the incursion, morale stayed that way back in South Vietnam. U.S. troops were grateful for the chance to destroy the sanctuaries;[20] they realized it meant far less danger in the months to come, the enemy lacking the means to endanger them as they left Southeast Asia. ARVN, proud of its own performance during the invasion and aware of the NVA/VC's weakness, became more confident in its own abilities.[21] Not bound by Nixon's deadline of 30 June, the RVNAF kept about 34,000 troops in Cambodia for several weeks after the American return to South Vietnam to continue searching for caches and evacuating Vietnamese refugees.[22] President Thieu saw Lon Nol's survival as essential to his own nation's survival and accordingly deployed RVNAF units inside Cambodia for the remainder to the war, to help FANK and protect South Vietnam's interests.[23]

Although intangible, the increase in South Vietnamese morale and optimism was a significant step in the process of Vietnamization. Ambassador Bunker cabled Nixon that ARVN's performance had provided a big boost to the civilian population in general, and to the RVNAF in particular.[24] Before the incursion, ARVN had hesitated to fight without U.S. units alongside. Limited American involvement during the incursion, and the degree of success the RVNAF achieved in 1970, wrongly convinced many South Vietnamese they could stand up to the NVA. However, as one historian later commented, "Little more than a dozen South Vietnamese battalions had been involved in Cambodia at any one time, and the enemy response had been negligible. The real test was still to come."[25]

More obviously, ARVN had serious problems that warranted immediate attention.[26] Davison reported shortcomings in ARVN's "combined arms coordination, employment of mechanized and armored forces, use of supporting artillery and other fire support means, and first and second echelon maintenance."[27] Although ARVN overcame many of these weaknesses in the next two years, patterning its organization, doctrine, and equipment on those of the U.S. Army, with the latter's emphasis on firepower and mechanized forces, made it even more dependent on continued infusions of American money and supplies. In the short term, though, ARVN's performance in Cambodia seemed positive evidence of its progress since 1965.

The militia's enthusiasm matched that of the regular troops. With more than 70 percent of Davison's U.S. combat battalions and as much as 44 percent of Tri's rotating into or out of Cambodia during May and June, the RF and PF were responsible for security within III CTZ. Handling the few incidents that occurred boosted their self-confidence and pride in being trusted with the zone's defense.[28]

Confidence is a critical part of any unit's combat effectiveness, and Cambodia provided a much-needed dose of it to the RVNAF that lasted until the 1971 debacle of LAM SON 719 in southeastern Laos.

The incursion and the resulting drop in NVA and VC activity helped South Vietnamese society as well. The northern half of Tay Ninh and Binh Long Provinces had long been "war zones," where farmers and peasants lived only at grave risk. The danger had led most to abandon their homes and become refugees in greater Saigon, a trend that reversed itself in July 1970. ARVN planned to reopen the Michelin rubber plantation in northwest Binh Duong Province, closed for years because of heavy fighting. Many plantations in central Binh Long Province resumed operations as well, the town of An Loc's population trebling in the eleven months after the incursion. There had been only nine sawmills in Tay Ninh Province in April 1970, but by May 1971 there were almost a hundred.[29] People voted with their feet, indicating that the NVA and VC no longer posed enough of a threat to keep them away from their fields.

The incursion knocked COSVN and the B-2 Front badly off balance. Most caches found were within thirty kilometers of the border; by mid-June the rate of locating new ones had dropped off significantly.[30] Realizing that the Fishhook "had not been completely cleaned out" but unable to give the infantry more time to search in the face of Nixon's 30 June deadline, Davison hit suspected stockpiles and camps with B-52s, artillery, and tactical air strikes from 25 to 29 June.[31] These attacks also helped dissuade any surviving NVA units from returning too closely on the heels of the departing Americans.

As U.S. forces returned to South Vietnam, MACV resumed sending troops home. The reduced enemy threat and decreasing numbers meant commanders had to make the most of their dwindling resources. Davison realized, as had Ewell before him, that helicopter battalions gave him comparatively more mobility and firepower than did infantry battalions and tended to suffer fewer casualties. Accordingly, he tried to keep helicopter units longer, seeking whenever possible to send infantrymen and other soldiers home earlier.

Particularly important in the months following the invasion was IIFFV's Third Squadron Seventeenth Air Cavalry. Ewell had previously dispersed its helicopters in platoon-sized elements across III CTZ to cover the greatest area, a policy Davison continued when attacking the Cambodian sanctuaries. However, this meant the squadron could not mass against any single target and lessened the squadron intelligence and operations staff's effectiveness at coordinating their units' activities.

Davison changed this deployment during summer 1970 by having the unit fight either as a complete squadron or as air cavalry troops (companies), but nothing of smaller size. The advantages of massing attack helicopters were so clear that by the winter of 1970–1971 he had created a provisional air cavalry brigade under the control of the First Cavalry Division, composed of the First Squadron Ninth Cavalry (the First Cavalry Division's renowned reconnaissance unit) and the Third Squadron Seventeenth Air Cavalry. In one of III Corps' later battles near Dam Be in 1971, this brigade averted an ARVN defeat by killing or wounding a thousand NVA troops in one day.[32]

Abrams's top concerns after the incursion remained stabilizing Saigon's position and safely withdrawing U.S. troops. In large part, this meant departing U.S. units handed off their equipment to their ARVN counterparts, significantly increasing the latter's combat power even as it further strained the South Vietnamese economy by requiring more fuel, repair parts, and logistics effort. Likewise, giving captured weapons to Lon Nol was another expedient and effective way to advance these goals, since making Hanoi fight longer and harder to secure eastern Cambodia meant those NVA troops were not attacking South Vietnam or the departing American forces.

Despite a sharp rise in U.S. domestic opposition to the war, Hanoi probably considered the incursion a military setback for its war effort. Because the United States was leaving anyway, Nixon's loss of public support would not appreciably speed up the American withdrawal but would constrain his ability to support Saigon following the withdrawal's completion. Hanoi was confident it could defeat Saigon in the absence of U.S. ground forces.

U.S. leaders in both Washington and Saigon thought Hanoi's cost in both human and material terms delayed its schedule for conquering South Vietnam by a year, if not more. Following the military disasters of 1968, caused in part by having engaged American and RVNAF units more openly, COSVN and Hanoi fell back on a strategy of protracted war. In this approach time favored the communists and was a weapon with which to wear down the Americans' will to remain and Saigon's will to resist. However, communist personnel losses in 1968 and 1969, coupled with the material losses in Cambodia in 1970, badly constrained Hanoi's desire for a quicker, more decisive solution.[33] Its rebuilding efforts in southern Laos and in northeastern Cambodia gave Abrams the time he needed to complete the U.S. pullout and avoid a clear-cut military defeat.

Communist casualties overall were heavy during the incursion. MACV Intelligence claimed 11,562 enemy dead, with 215 NVA and 882 VC taken as prisoners of war.[34] Because combat typically results in two or more soldiers wounded for every one killed, Hanoi thus lost about 30,000 troops in two months. About 1,300 more defected to South Vietnam's Hoi Chanh program, and IIFFV heard of "NVA units being sent to the rear for refusing to fight." After the Cambodian incursion, only three NVA regiments remained scattered across III CTZ, none with more than 600 troops out of about 1,200 typically in a regiment.[35] New soldiers could be sent to the South, but the casualties' skill, training, and local knowledge could not be easily replaced.

The communists in the South had been shorthanded even before the events of late spring 1970. Constant fighting throughout South Vietnam had steadily worn down units' strength, while Abrams's logistics focus had made it increasingly difficult for COSVN to sustain those troops it had. Fighting FANK after Sihanouk's overthrow further stretched communist resources. The surprise incursion thus hit a dispersed, maldeployed, and weakened communist force, rendering it temporarily incapable of effective military action. Vietnamese communist leaders further reduced their numbers by infiltrating VC cadres from Cambodia into South Vietnam among the Vietnamese refugees fleeing ethnic violence in eastern Cambodia and Phnom Penh.[36] Although useful in the longer term, the immediate effect was fewer leaders to restore the Cambodian base system necessary for the sustained combat operations on which the rapid conquest of South Vietnam had depended.

Hanoi's material losses were equally painful. North Vietnam could come up with replacement infantrymen, but it lacked the manufacturing base to replace the war stocks captured by U.S. and ARVN forces. Such supplies as it captured from FANK in eastern Cambodia were valuable for sustaining the fight against Lon Nol but insufficient for major actions inside III CTZ. In due course the Soviet Union and China would send new equipment to help their "fraternal brothers" in their struggle against the mutual enemy, America. However, before Hanoi could use those supplies it would have to build new forward bases prior to moving the materials south under U.S. air attacks in southern Laos and northeastern Cambodia. This put an enormous demand on manpower, which North Vietnam could ill afford. It also cost time, which was what MACV most wanted.

The scale of Hanoi's accomplishments in Cambodia before the incursion surprised even Abrams. Shocked at the extent of the early discoveries, he called Davison to see if they were really finding as much as the U.S. Armed Forces Network radio news was reporting.[37] They were. During the incursion Hanoi lost more than 20,000 individual and 2,500 crew-served weapons, between 6,800 and 8,200 tons of rice, about 1,800 tons of ammunition, 29 tons of communication equipment, 431 vehicles, and 55 tons of medical supplies (including equipment for fourteen field hospitals).[38] Among the medical supplies were drugs from the United States, France, Britain, and Germany, some of which had been flown into Phnom Penh as late as 20 April.

Papers with most of the caches indicated the bulk of the supplies had arrived via the Sihanoukville Trail, confirming that MACV Intelligence had been correct in its debates with the CIA and State Department.[39] The tons of ammunition included some 143,000 mortar shells, rockets, and recoilless rifle rounds, most often fired in batches of seven or eight to cause a continuous (even if low) flow of friendly casualties.[40] Without them, communist attacks inside South Vietnam were much less lethal.

The vast quantity of rice captured further proved the importance Hanoi attached to operations against III and IV CTZs. There was enough to provide 25,000 enemy soldiers full rations of 1.5 pounds daily for a year, or 38,000 soldiers reduced rations of a pound per day.[41] Although ARVN and the United States tried to haul most of the rice back to South Vietnam, Nixon's 30 June deadline and the border region's primitive road system prevented a complete evacuation. Rather than permit its recapture, units destroyed what they could not take.[42] This was unfortunate, but the unacceptable alternative was to leave it for the NVA to recover and use.

Destroying the sanctuaries had an immediate effect on Hanoi's plans within South Vietnam. Communist documents captured inside South Vietnam during July told units to "economize on ammunition, intensify farm production, and emphasize capture of Allied materials." They were to expect issues of all types of supplies to be cut between 50 and 80 percent.[43] No matter how motivated the NVA or VC troops, they could not fight effectively without ammunition or while growing their own food.

The loss of the established Cambodian logistics system hurt. Phnom Penh's shift from "neutrality" to "belligerency" denied the NVA the use of Kampong Som (formerly Sihanoukville), as well as easy and safe movement across northern and eastern Cambodia to the South Vietnamese border without fear of U.S. air strikes. For the foreseeable future it would have to move everything over the longer and poorer roads of the Ho Chi Minh Trail, requiring far more manpower and materials and under the continuous threat of U.S. air attack. During Sihanouk's reign Hanoi had needed only a handful of supply officers to oversee moving its supplies inland from the port. After Lon Nol's coup it had to provide armed guards to move throughout northeast Cambodia.[44] Further, the thousands of NVA troops rebuilding and working on the logistics system were not fighting in South Vietnam, making Hanoi's ultimate victory more assured but also later rather than sooner.

Less than a week after the last U.S. troops left Cambodia, MACV Intelligence issued a report predicting how Hanoi would use Laos and Cambodia after the incursion. Enemy units in southern South Vietnam, it estimated, required 1,222 tons of all categories of supplies each month from outside sources to keep fighting. Of the 800 tons for food, 480 to 640 tons came from communist sympathizers in eastern Cambodia. Hanoi thus had to provide via the Ho Chi Minh Trail between 580 and 740 tons per month, or 6,960 to 8,880 tons per year, about 90 percent of which it moved during the six-month-long dry season.[45]

These figures indicated what the forces in southern South Vietnam needed to wage guerrilla war. The losses imposed by the Seventh Air Force's air campaigns against the North's supply lines, coupled with the logistics system's own requirements for food, fuel, and equipment, were costly: Hanoi had to send about 2.5 tons south to ensure that 1 ton reached the destination. To sustain the insurgency at low levels of activity required Hanoi to move some 22,000 tons annually, and much more for conventional battles.[46] Because the ever-expanding Ho Chi Minh Trail's capacity was even greater, allied air interdiction alone could not keep enough supplies from reaching South Vietnam to prevent guerrilla operations so long as Hanoi was willing to pay the cost in people, material, and time.

However, the stockpiles' loss meant that North Vietnam had to build new base areas and depots before it could again launch major offensives. Had the NVA wanted to attack the U.S. or ARVN forces in the second half of 1970 or early 1971, after the incursion it lacked sufficient ammunition and equipment. Abrams had thus gained perhaps a year before Hanoi would again be able to threaten withdrawing American forces and Vietnamization.

Hanoi had no choice but to fight Lon Nol and FANK to keep its routes south open. Though U.S. air attacks hurt the flow of communist supplies, ground operations would halt them entirely if unopposed. To reestablish its southern supply system after the U.S. withdrawal to South Vietnam, Hanoi opened a new fighting front in Cambodia.[47] This involved troops from four NVA/VC divisions and two sapper battalions from III and IV CTZs in South Vietnam.

The communist conquest of South Vietnam continued but more slowly: Hanoi's diverting combat units and those NVA replacements originally destined for South Vietnam into Cambodia reduced the threat within the South, allowing pacification and Vietnamization to proceed more easily. In 1969 and early 1970 it had taken infiltrators about four months to travel the Ho Chi Minh Trail from Vinh, in southern North Vietnam, to the vicinity of COSVN near Memot, Cambodia, and most of these soldiers had gone on to fight in III CTZ.[48]

With the loss of the logistics system's southern terminus to support this movement, plus the need to fight the Cambodians as well as the South Vietnamese and Americans, the calculations were significantly different. Hanoi had to determine how many men to allocate to combat against Phnom Penh, how many against Saigon, how many to move the supplies to replace those lost to the incursion, how many to expand the Ho Chi Minh Trail's capacity, and how many to build new base areas to hold such supplies as could be stockpiled to permit future operations. It then had to shift the people accordingly and sustain them with food and equipment in those new locations. Hanoi had not expected so many complications, and it needed time to address the radically changed situation.

COSVN put a brave face on the disaster. A directive it issued on 8 May 1970 on the party's role in Cambodia portrayed the events since Lon Nol's coup as "a golden opportunity to liberate all of Cambodia." To compensate for the closure of Sihanoukville, the communists had to enlarge the Ho Chi Minh Trail and add new routes across southeast Laos.[49] Although this would be difficult, COSVN said, once done it would prevent having to bribe the Cambodian government and army officers with weapons, supplies, and money. The result would be more materials reaching the border sanctuaries to use against Saigon.[50] The words were truthful enough, but they were poor substitutes for the food or bullets its troops in the field so desperately needed.

The incursion also hamstrung COSVN's ability to control its troops in III CTZ and coordinate operations between different units. Forced deeper into Cambodia, lacking twenty-nine tons of telephones and radios, and with its codebooks compromised by capture or loss of positive accountability, COSVN had to use messengers. Unable to contact either COSVN or the B-2 Front headquarters for instructions, many enemy units inside South Vietnam had to operate autonomously, making major or coordinated actions against ARVN and U.S. forces almost impossible.

Exacerbating the communications problems was these units' splitting into much smaller elements to find food.[51] Without clear and timely guidance, reinforcements, radios, or supplies, many became hesitant to fight, greatly reducing friendly casualties among civilians and soldiers alike. Scattered acts of terrorism became the norm, making it far easier for South Vietnamese forces to control the countryside and the American withdrawal to continue.[52]

Despite the tons of captured materials and thousands of enemy dead, there were debates within MACV on the incursion's effectiveness; its tools for measuring pacification's progress within South Vietnam gave mixed assessments. The Hamlet Evaluation System concluded that the decline in enemy activity in those provinces closest to the border sanctuaries had made things there more secure.[53] Likewise, the Terror Incident Reporting System, a monthly nationwide count of assassinations, bombings, woundings, and the like, showed a significant drop in enemy activity during and after the incursion. However, the decreases matched previous years' patterns, the VC being unable to sustain an intensive terror campaign.[54] MACV Intelligence thus concluded there was no definitive link between the incursion and terrorism inside South Vietnam, despite such a correlation appearing reasonable.

Studies of other pacification programs gave similar responses, indicating the incursion had only minor effects on their respective efforts.[55] These included the Territorial Forces Evaluation System, which looked at the Popular Forces and the Regional Forces; the Phung Hoang (Phoenix) Program; the Chieu Hoi Program; attitude surveys (public opinion polls of South Vietnamese); and inputs from U.S. advisers to the Civil Operations and Revolutionary Development Support (CORDS) program, the U.S. pacification effort's central headquarters, run by a civilian deputy to Abrams.

The pacification survey results are not surprising: the incursion most immediately and clearly affected conventional NVA/VC operations and capabilities, while the MACV metrics were more oriented toward guerrilla or terrorist incidents. Unable to fight as battalions, communist forces split up into smaller units and emphasized political recruitment and survival over combat. Previously hesitant to face NVA regulars, ARVN became more willing to fight scattered bands. Some units remained in Cambodia past 30 June, Saigon's sustaining them there showing a marked advance in the RVNAF's abilities. Reduced enemy activity inside South Vietnam and heightened South Vietnamese self-confidence and pride also meant there was less immediate need for U.S. troops to fight.

The military gains of the incursion, however valuable in the short term, did not produce comparable political advances for Washington. Rather, deteriorating political circumstances at home significantly constrained the U.S. ability to capitalize on the fleeting opportunities within Southeast Asia. American opinion, already polarized before Nixon entered office, increasingly opposed an indecisive and unproductive war. This limited Nixon's options but did not greatly alter the pace of America's withdrawal from what Nixon had started in 1969.

Things appeared better on the surface within South Vietnam in the months following the incursion. Saigon's internal security programs continued to decimate what remained of the VC. U.S. leaders in Washington and Saigon proclaimed South Vietnam was on the road to viability, needing time more than anything else.

Politicians' and generals' upbeat assertions were not entirely wishful thinking, but too often they ignored the significant economic, structural, and political problems that continued to beset South Vietnam. The economic picture remained bleak and was a serious threat to long-term viability. As the incursion was winding down, Ambassador Bunker reported, "Pressures are rising: retail food prices, for instance, have increased about twenty-two percent so far this year. The black market dollar rate continues high, although it dropped from the peak of 424 in Saigon April 21 to 378 in early June."[56] Morale was critically important, but it alone could not compensate for the country's near-total economic and military dependence on the United States.

Despite the successful results of the Cambodian campaign, the U.S. and RVNAF military performances showed several recurring weaknesses. Intelligence at the tactical level was generally a shortcoming, most units having only limited knowledge of where their opponents might be. They were lucky, in that for the most part surprised NVA units initially chose not to stand and fight, particularly from prepared defenses.

MACV had assumed during Westmoreland's years in command that, because Cambodia was off-limits for its overt military operations, it was more productive for its intelligence assets to focus inside South Vietnam than to collect and analyze information on events across the border. Covert efforts, such as SOG missions and U.S. Air Force overflights, yielded data for MACV's analysts, but tactical commanders often had little idea what was in front of them or where caches might be. This resulted partly from MACV Intelligence not having the information the incursion's searchers needed in as much detail as they wanted, and partly from excessive security policies that precluded releasing photographs and intelligence, at the expense of those units assigned to capture those very sites. American intelligence was adequate at Abrams's and his immediate subordinate commanders' levels, but all too often soldiers found caches by bumping into NVA guards or stumbling across the hidden supplies by chance.

A second noteworthy deficiency was linguistic: U.S. Army units crossed the border with almost no one who spoke the Cambodian language or understood Cambodian culture. Instead, they had to rely on the South Vietnamese, defectors, U.S. Marine Corps interpreters, and (for troops on the ground) simple hand signals. Such shortcomings meant the army could not take advantage of what Cambodians in the area might know or be willing to tell them. When interpreters finally joined units, the effectiveness of searches increased dramatically.

The logistics system had problems, even though its vast capacity allowed it to overwhelm many issues and continue to support U.S. and RVNAF forces simultaneously. Because of the need for secrecy before 1 May, logistics officers had been unable to push supply dumps nearer the border, subsequently making it take longer to fill units' requirements. No missions failed because of the initial absence of forward bases, but more effort had to go into distributing supplies to units on the move.

Two important consequences were increased inefficiency and the development of a tremendous backlog of cargo in the ports that lacked the trucks to move them to intermediate depots. Inclusion of more logisticians earlier in the planning process could have averted or reduced both these problems, albeit at a greater risk of the NVA's realizing what was to happen. However, since ARVN's April raids had already forfeited strategic surprise, this ought not to have been as significant a consideration.

The RVNAF remained dependent on U.S. assistance, particularly in its logistics at the highest levels and for fire support. Equipment maintenance was generally weak, both in the field with the units themselves and at the depot, and the flow of replacement parts to the units that had requested them was slow.[57] To its credit, though, the RVNAF demonstrated the "capability to plan and conduct mobile operations far from their home bases, [and did so] . . . without direct American combat intervention." As its lines of communication lengthened, the RVNAF kept its forces supplied with minimal U.S. help.[58]

A final weakness was in brigade-level operations by the U.S. Army and in division-level ones by ARVN. This was most apparent for the Americans in two areas, the reliefs of two brigade commanders in Cambodia so soon after their assuming command, and the difficulty with which several brigade headquarters shifted to field operations. With command tours frequently lasting only six months, to give more officers opportunity to command and thus help their careers, too many officers were reassigned about the time they achieved competence in the position; subordinate units bore the burden of their learning curves.

The physical movement from Vietnam into Cambodia was not particularly hard for most battalions and companies, the units being used to frequent shifts inside South Vietnam. However, over the years some brigade headquarters had become almost static in their areas of responsibility, having occupied positions far too long. Fortunately, IIFFV and the divisions ran their actions in Cambodia from their headquarters' "normal" locations. Had they tried to move and reestablish communications links with the brigades while the brigades were likewise moving and trying to control their battalions, the results would likely have been chaotic for the first several days.

In ARVN's case, shortcomings at division-level command augured poorly for the country's long-term survival against the NVA. Tri's use of regiment-sized task forces that he personally controlled, instead of relying on his divisions and their commanding generals, was indicative of his lack of confidence in their abilities. The situation in IV Corps was essentially the same.

Though some ARVN division commanding generals were good, many were not; of those in III Corps, Davison thought Major General Thanh of the ARVN Twenty-fifth Infantry Division was the best. However, in 1969 Thieu had relieved the Eighteenth Division's commander, Do Ke Giai, but replaced him with the equally incompetent General Tho. "Worst of the lot was the 5th Division Commander, General Hieu. Hieu's forces had been badly handled in the Snuol operation, and his troops, according to Davison, were close to mutiny." It was not until April 1971 that Thieu finally relieved him, after months of wasted opportunities and unneeded losses.[59]

Saigon's biggest setback in the entire Cambodian campaign was the loss of both the III and IV Corps commanding generals in helicopter accidents.[60] Tri's death in particular was a heavy blow to III Corps, and his replacement by Nguyen Van Minh left a distinct void. Given his weak division commanders, Minh continued Tri's practices of commanding regiment-sized task forces directly and bypassing division headquarters.

Overall, the positive elements of the two armies' tactical performances outweighed the negatives. There was little difference between searching for caches in Cambodia or in South Vietnam. For the most part, companies and battalions operated in the same ways they had before crossing the border, with the exception that support troops had to build an infrastructure up to and across the border while sustaining the combat units. This placed a particularly large burden on the engineers, signal troops, transportation units, and aviators.

The Americans did a good job of using firepower flexibly. From the complex fire plan for Task Force Shoemaker to the B-52 "compression" against COSVN's suspected location near Memot, artillery officers, aviators, and air force pilots successfully integrated fires with the movements of infantry and cavalry units to minimize friendly casualties. Though some headquarters were better than others at synchronizing air strikes with ground maneuver, all applied firepower as needed.

Operational security, keeping information about the pending incursion secret, was a success. This was largely Abrams's doing, having insisted on restricting to the bare minimum those who knew of the upcoming attack. While communist penetration of Saigon's military, intelligence, and security organizations doubtless cost some measure of surprise once Tri sent his plan for his late April attack to the JGS, the secrecy surrounding the U.S. Army's intentions and the complacency fostered by a "safe" border made the surprise that much greater once Shoemaker assaulted the Fishhook. The secrecy helped keep the communists from realizing their peril until it was too late to evacuate many of their documents, codes, and supplies.

American leaders at division and lower levels did well in planning on short notice and improvising as operations progressed. With less than ninety-six hours to form a headquarters, draft and brief a plan, and launch a major attack, Shoe-maker was not unduly disturbed by his lack of detailed intelligence, limited preparation time, or absence of specific guidance. He simply did what was neces-sary and trusted his subordinates to take care of whatever problems they encoun-tered. Other commanders did likewise. This characteristic was common to most American units participating in the incursion and goes far to explain why the army could successfully shift from small-unit patrols to a corps-level attack in under two weeks.

Also important to the outcome of the incursion was simple luck: timing was everything. As Bismarck is alleged to have said, "God looks out for children, id-iots, and the United States." This was clearly the case in Cambodia. Lon Nol's fortuitous coup presented the United States with a magnificent if fleeting oppor-tunity to achieve many of its goals, should Washington but act decisively. The fighting that broke out in mid-March between the North Vietnamese and the Cambodians had, by late April, led the B-2 Front to shift its NVA infantry regi-ments westward, from shielding the border region bases from the U.S./ARVN forces to moving toward Phnom Penh from the base areas. This left the sanctuar-ies completely exposed to a surprise attack from the east. Second, the spring 1970 monsoon was several weeks late, giving searching troops precious extra days of comparatively good weather to locate more caches.

Finally, by 1970 there were new people in the critical positions. In contrast to Johnson's aversion to any military actions that might interfere with the Great So-ciety, Nixon was willing to take the political heat he knew would result from such a controversial but essential decision. Westmoreland had been succeeded by Abrams, a pragmatic and aggressive commander with a clear idea of what he had to do to achieve American goals. The fortuitous confluence of timing, unit dispo-sitions on both sides, and key leaders resulted in the destruction of Hanoi's Cam-bodian base areas.

There was an overlooked party in the Cambodian incursion: the Cambodian people themselves. Caught between two vastly more powerful belligerents, they suffered the most, victims of Hanoi's willingness to sacrifice their welfare for its conquest of the South. The allied responses, of MENU and the incursion, were tragic military necessities, driven by self-defense against Hanoi's aggression. Any assessment of external influences on recent Cambodian history must lay pri-mary responsibility at Hanoi's door.[61]

While historians debate the political fallout of the Cambodian incursion, there can be no doubt of the military consequences. At a comparatively light cost in friendly casualties, the incursion crippled Hanoi's principal forward stockpiles along South Vietnam's borders. Hanoi's 1972 and 1975 offensives were conventional campaigns chiefly against Military Regions I and II (previously I CTZ and II CTZ) by combined arms units of the NVA trained, equipped, and organized in accordance with Soviet doctrine; guerrilla forces played only peripheral roles. Lacking sufficient food and ammunition, communist troops inside South Vietnam were unable to seriously hinder the U.S. withdrawal from Southeast Asia or disrupt Saigon's pacification efforts. Had U.S. units instead been compelled to fight well-armed and well-equipped NVA regulars, or even VC Main Force guerrillas, in the environs of Saigon and other major cities to reach and depart from the airfields and ports of southern South Vietnam, thousands more Americans and Vietnamese would have been wounded or killed than was the case.

That this did not happen and the United States avoided a bloody military defeat as it withdrew from Southeast Asia was the direct result of a two-month raid on the Cambodian base areas from which such an NVA offensive would likely have come. Rather than being a minor operation, deserving only passing mention in the rush to focus on American campus protests and congressional outrage, the Cambodian incursion was as great a military victory as Tet 1968, made possible by political leaders seizing fleeting opportunities and armed forces carrying out a mission they were ready, willing, and able to do.

War is a horrible thing, with few decisions easy or without painful costs paid in blood. However, given the alternatives Nixon and Abrams faced in 1970, the Cambodian incursion was clearly the lesser of several evils.

Notes

1. THE JOHNSON-WESTMORELAND ERA, 1965–1969

1. Throughout this study I refer to the People's Army of Vietnam (PAVN) and the fighters of the National Liberation Front (NLF) by the names most American readers would recognize: the North Vietnamese Army (NVA) and the Viet Cong (VC).

2. Lewis Sorley's *Honorable Warrior* (Lawrence: University Press of Kansas, 1998), *Thunderbolt* (New York: Simon and Schuster, 1992), and *A Better War* (San Diego: Harcourt, 1999) provide excellent insight into the personalities of senior American military leaders during the period. See also Richard A. Hunt, *Pacification: The American Struggle for Vietnam's Hearts and Minds* (Boulder, CO: Westview Press, 1995), 212–13; and Ronald Spector, *After Tet: The Bloodiest Year in Vietnam* (New York: Free Press, 1993), for more on the change in strategy.

3. William J. Duiker, in his foreword to Military History Institute of Vietnam, *Victory in Vietnam: The Official History of the People's Army of Vietnam, 1954–1975*, trans. Merle L. Pribbenow (Lawrence: University Press of Kansas, 2002), xvi, notes that Hanoi largely omits or downplays mention of Chinese or Soviet "fraternal assistance," particularly of their military personnel.

4. Henry Kissinger, *Diplomacy* (New York: Simon and Schuster, 1994), 660.

5. *Dau tranh,* or "armed struggle," is best explained in Douglas Pike's *PAVN: The People's Army of Vietnam* (Novato, CA: Presidio Press, 1986), 212–54. Phillip B. Davidson, in *Vietnam at War* (Novato, CA: Presidio Press, 1988), described the "mosaic" nature of the war in South Vietnam. Most scholars in the 1970s and 1980s did not adequately address the significance of *dau tranh,* as shown in the antithetical works of Harry Summers and Andrew Krepinevich. Since the early 1990s, Davidson's more nuanced and sophisticated perspective has steadily become the foundation of current assessments of the conflict's military aspects.

6. See William J. Duiker, *The Communist Road to Power in Vietnam* (Boulder, CO: Westview Press, 1981), for a superb analysis of the links between the NLF and Hanoi.

7. Military History Institute of Vietnam, *Victory in Vietnam,* 49–52.

8. For additional insight into Cambodia's role in North Vietnam's plans, see C. Dale Walton, *The Myth of Inevitable US Defeat in Vietnam* (London: Frank Cass, 2001), 71–84.

9. LTG (Ret.) Phillip Davidson, MACV J-2, interview at United States Military Academy (USMA), 24 June 1991. Davidson was MACV J-2 from May 1967 to May 1969. "Order of battle" most often means unit organization, manning, and equipping.

10. MACV Command History, 1970, vol. 3, Annex C, pp. C-1, C-32 U.S. Army Center of Military History (CMH), Washington, DC. Also, MACV J-2 briefing papers on the Cambodian incursion, accession number MACD1 31-2-4869/72, CMH Histories Division, Southeast Asia cabinet 9, p. 3. Dr. Christopher Goscha of the University of Lyons is doing pathbreaking work on the maritime aspects of the communist logistics system before 1966. Goscha, "The Maritime Ho Chi Minh Trail and the Wars for Vietnam, 1945–1975" (paper presented at the Vietnam Center's Fourth Triennial Vietnam Symposium, Lubbock, Texas, 11 April 2002). See as well Jonathan S. Wiarda's "The U.S. Coast Guard in Vietnam: Achieving Success in a Difficult War," *Naval War College Review* 51 (Spring 1998): 43–44. Interestingly, the flyleaf maps included in Robert McNamara, *In Retrospect: The Tragedy and Lessons of Vietnam* (New York: Times Books, 1995), do not indicate any North Vietnamese supply routes by sea or across Cambodia, only the Ho Chi Minh Trail.

11. MACV Command History, p. C-1.

12. GEN Michael S. Davison, oral history, p. 11, U.S. Army Military History Institute (MHI), Carlisle Barracks, Pennsylvania, MHI Archives, Michael S. Davison Collection.

13. CHECO Reports no. 52, *The Cambodian Campaign, 29 April–30 June 1970,* Honolulu, HI: HQ Pacific Air Forces, Tactical Evaluation Directorate, CHECO Division (Majors D. I. Folkman Jr. and P. D. Caine) (hereafter cited as CHECO), p. 4. Available on-line through the Virtual Vietnam Archive, Vietnam Center, Texas Tech University, Lubbock, Texas, item no. 0390102001.

14. Headquarters, U.S. MACV, Office of the Assistant Chief of Staff, J-2/ Combined Intelligence Center–Vietnam, "Special Study: Supply Lines through Laos and Cambodia into South Vietnam," 28 February 1969, pp. 81–90, U.S. Army MHI, Carlisle Barracks, Pennsylvania, MHI Vietnam Collection.

15. Message, GEN Abrams to GEN Wheeler CJCS and ADM McCain CINCPAC, 131121Z March 1970, Subject: Operation MENU, U.S. Army Center of Military History (CMH), Washington, DC, CMH Histories Division, General Creighton W. Abrams Papers. There was one exception to this trimonthly schedule, when an extra shipment arrived before Tet 1968.

16. CHECO, pp. 1–2.

17. MACV Command History, pp. 83, 87, C-1.

18. *Victory in Vietnam,* 464n24. The front's name was the Hak Ly Company, a fact known to MACV Intelligence at the time. CHECO, p. 1.

19. Tran Dinh Tho, *The Cambodian Incursion* (Washington, DC: Center of Military History, 1979), 21.

20. See Spector, *After Tet,* 312.

21. The idea of using ground forces to cut the Laotian Panhandle west of the DMZ was a recurring one within the U.S. military, argued most clearly in the war's aftermath in Bruce Palmer, *The Twenty-five Year War* (Lexington: University Press of Kentucky, 1984), 172–88; and Harry Summers Jr., *On Strategy: A Critical Analysis of the Vietnam War* (Novato, CA: Presidio Press, 1982), 166, 170–72.

22. *Victory in Vietnam,* 168–69, 264.

23. Ibid., 170, 227, 243. In addition to greater tonnages heading south, the U.S. decision to halt bombing of North Vietnam allowed the NVA to disband the 377th Air Defense Division and the 268th and 278th Missile Regiments. Elements of these units went south to take up static defensive positions in southern North Vietnam and along the Ho Chi Minh Trail. Ibid., 242.

24. Ibid., 182.

25. Richard Helms to Robert S. McNamara, 1 June 1967, and attachment, CIA Memorandum 196752/67, Subject: Evaluation of Alternative Programs for Bombing North Vietnam, June 1, 1967, in Country File, Vietnam, National Security Files, Lyndon Baines Johnson Library, Austin, Texas, quoted by McNamara in *In Retrospect,* 275.

26. On 31 March 1968 Johnson expanded the bombing of Laos. After 31 October 1968 Laotian routes were part of the U.S. Air Force's interdiction effort.

2. THE NIXON-ABRAMS ERA, 1969–1970

1. Henry Kissinger, *White House Years* (Boston: Little, Brown, 1979), 240.

2. Ibid., 245–47. See also Robert Mann, *A Grand Delusion: America's Descent into Vietnam* (New York: Basic Books, 2001), 629–31.

3. Willard J. Webb, *The Joint Chiefs of Staff and the War in Vietnam, 1969–1970* (Washington, DC: Office of Joint History, Office of the Chairman of the Joint Chiefs of Staff, 2002), 135–38; William Shawcross, *Sideshow: Kissinger, Nixon, and the Destruction of Cambodia* (New York: Simon and Schuster, 1979); Kissinger, *White House Years,* 247–48; Richard F. Newcomb, *A Pictorial History of the Vietnam War* (Garden City, NY: Doubleday, 1987), 224.

4. Kissinger, *White House Years,* 249.

5. Message, GEN Abrams to GEN Wheeler CJCS and ADM McCain CINCPAC, 131121Z March 1970, Subject: Operation MENU. Abrams Papers, CMH Histories Division.

6. For more on the Nixon administration's decision to begin U.S. troop withdrawals, see Henry Kissinger, *Ending the Vietnam War: A History of America's Involvement in and Extrication from the Vietnam War* (New York: Simon and Schuster, 2003), 81–95.

7. Interview, MG Edward Bautz, USA (Ret.), 18 March 1993.

8. Newcomb, *Pictorial History of the Vietnam War,* 232. See also A. J. Langgruth, *Our Vietnam: The War, 1954–1975* (New York: Simon and Schuster, 2000), 562; Mann, *Grand Delusion,* 656–57.

9. IIFFV Periodic Intelligence Report (PERINTREP) 17-70, 26 April 1970, p. 25, MHI Vietnam Collection. COSVN's Directive 7 was dated 3 April 1970; friendly troops captured a copy on 13 April 1970.

10. Dale Andradé's *Ashes to Ashes: The Phoenix Program and the Vietnam War* (New York: Lexington Books, 1990) is an excellent and detailed study of the program's effectiveness.

11. John J. Tolson, *Airmobility, 1961–1971* (Washington, DC: Department of the Army, 1989), 209–13.

12. Hunt, *Pacification,* 217–18. For a more detailed treatment of the First Cavalry Division's tactical operations during the first half of 1969, see J. D. Coleman's *Incursion* (New York: St. Martin's Press, 1991), 59–91.

13. IIFFV PERINTREP 17-70, p. 19. Cut off from their homes and families, NVA soldiers were particularly vulnerable to morale problems. Northern troops sent south knew their journey was often a one-way trip.

14. Pacification was the policy emphasizing internal security of rural areas, seeking to gain villagers' support of the Saigon government. Its main opponents were the VC. After Tet 1968, pacification made significant gains throughout South Vietnam. See also Hunt, *Pacification,* 219.

15. IIFFV PERINTREP 17-70, p. 14.

16. HQ USMACV Strategic/Tactical Study: Study of the Comparisons between the Battle of Dien Bien Phu and the Analogous Khe Sanh Situation, 10 March 1968, available on-line at the Virtual Vietnam Archive, item no. 7390101003, John M. Shaw Collection.

17. James H. Willbanks provides a good review of COSVN's April and July 1969 change of strategy from large, conventional attacks to small-scale guerrilla operations, prolonging the conflict and preserving communist forces. James H. Willbanks, *Abandoning Vietnam: How America Left and South Vietnam Lost Its War* (Lawrence: University Press of Kansas, 2004), 67–68.

18. Peter MacDonald, *Giap: The Victor in Vietnam* (New York: Norton, 1993), 327.

19. Sorley, *Thunderbolt,* 237–38, 255–57. Charles F. Brower IV concludes Westmoreland sought to change the American strategy in 1967 and 1968 but failed to convince the JCS and Secretary of Defense Robert McNamara that such a shift was necessary or viable. Brower, "Strategic Reassessment in Vietnam: The Westmoreland 'Alternate Strategy' of 1967–1968," *Naval War College Review* 44 (Spring 1991): 20–51.

20. Spector, *After Tet,* 225–26.

21. Ibid., p. 236.

22. Kissinger, *White House Years,* 272, 276, 433–36.

23. MACV/Joint General Staff (JGS), "Combined Campaign Plan, 1970," 31 October 1969, p. 2, U.S. MHI Vietnam Collection. The JGS was South Vietnam's equivalent to the U.S. Joint Chiefs of Staff.

24. Ibid., pp. II-4, II-7.

25. Ibid., pp. A-15, A-16. Small arms are basic infantry weapons, such as pistols, rifles, submachine guns, and assault rifles. Crew-served weapons are machine guns, recoilless rifles, mortars, and other such infantry weapons. They need two or more men to fire and use more and heavier ammunition than small arms, but they greatly increase a unit's firepower. A forty-man platoon will normally carry about thirty small arms and two or three crew-served weapons (most often machine guns). One machine gun has the equivalent combat power of roughly ten riflemen, but at the cost of using more ammunition.

26. MACV/JGS Combined Campaign Plan, 1970, pp. A-15, A-16.

27. Message, GEN Abrams to ADM McCain CINCPAC and GEN Wheeler CJCS, 131133Z March 1970, Subject: Force Planning, Abrams Papers, CMH Histories Division.

28. MACV/JGS Combined Campaign Plan, 1970, p. A-16. A superb work on the Ho Chi Minh Trail is John Prados, *The Blood Road: The Ho Chi Minh Trail and the Vietnam War* (New York: Wiley, 1999).

29. Message, GEN Abrams to ADM McCain CINCPAC and GEN Wheeler CJCS, 131133Z March 1970, Subject: Force Planning, Abrams Papers, CMH Histories Division.

30. See also Ambassador Ellsworth Bunker's telegram to President Nixon, eighty-fifth message, 27 March 1970, pp. 1–2, available on-line at Virtual Vietnam Archive.

31. MACV/JGS Combined Campaign Plan, 1970, items 3–6, pp. A-26, A-27. For more

detail on NVA/VC logistics, see James W. McCoy, *Secrets of the Viet Cong* (New York: Hippocrene Books, 1992), 51–71.

32. Donn A. Starry, letter, 5 July 1992; William Colby, in Sorley, *Thunderbolt*, 290; Ray G. Hatmaker, phone interview, 18 August 1994. See also Prados, *Blood Road*, 298–99.

33. Fifth Special Forces Group OR-LL, 1970, p. 13, MHI Vietnam Collection.

34. IIFFV PERINTREP 17-70, p. 15.

35. CDEC Bulletin no. 33,129, 12 May 1970, National Archives, College Park, Maryland, Record Group (RG) 472, 270/76/11/box 68.

36. IIFFV PERINTREP 18-70, 3 May 1970, p. 13, MHI Vietnam Collection.

37. IIFFV PERINTREP 19-70, 10 May 1970, pp. 27–28, MHI Vietnam Collection. At full strength an infantry regiment has more than 1,200 men.

38. Military History Institute of Vietnam, *Victory in Vietnam*, 250.

39. CDEC Bulletin no. 35,219, dated 18 June 1970, NA, RG472, 270/76/11/box 72.

40. Document captured 23 April 1970, dated 20 February 1970, from Rear Services Staff, SR-1, to Rear Services Staff, COSVN, IIFFV PERINTREP 18-70, pp. 16-7, B-4, B-5.

41. IIFFV PERINTREP 18-70, p. 18. The source was a communist defector who had been a recruiter.

42. Bunker telegram to Nixon, eighty-fifth message, 27 March 1970, pp. 22–23, Virtual Vietnam Archive.

43. IIFFV PERINTREP 18-70, p. 21. Andradé's *Ashes to Ashes* and William Colby's *Lost Victory* (Chicago: Contemporary Books, 1989) show the pacification program was breaking Hanoi's grip on rural South Vietnam in 1969 and 1970.

44. Bunker, eighty-fifth telegram to Nixon, 27 March 1970, p. 3, Virtual Vietnam Archive.

45. At a press conference on 13 May 1969, Sihanouk said that "'in certain areas of Cambodia there are no Cambodians,'" the closest he came to admitting NVA troops were in his country. Prince Sihanouk, 13 May 1969, in Kissinger, *White House Years*, 251.

46. MACV Command History, p. C-3.

47. Ibid., pp. C-3, C-5.

48. Intelligence report based on the written notes of a VC cadre who had recently studied "COSVN Directive on the Role and Responsibilities of the Lao Dong Party in Cambodia," dated 8 May 1970, Issued at Bien Hoa, RVN, 18 May 1970, Field no. FVS-22,222, CMH Histories Division, Southeast Asia Cabinet 9, p. 3.

49. See Arnold R. Isaacs, *Without Honor: Defeat in Vietnam and Cambodia* (New York: Vintage Books, 1984), 195–99; see also Stanley Karnow, *Vietnam: A History* (New York: Penguin Books, 1984), 589–90.

50. Karnow, *Vietnam*, 604.

51. Kissinger provides additional insight on the Cambodian coup in *Ending the Vietnam War*, 126–41.

52. CHECO, p. 5. Under Sihanouk the military was known as FARK, its acronym in French for the Royal Cambodian Armed Forces; after his deposition it was the Cambodian National Armed Forces (FANK).

53. MACV Command History, p. C-9; MACV J-2 briefing paper, p. 6; Thomas C. Thayer, ed., *A Systems Analysis View of the Vietnam War 1965–1972*, vol. 1, *The Situation in Southeast Asia* (Washington, DC: Department of Defense, Office of the Assistant Secretary of Defense [Analysis and Evaluation], Asia Division, n.d.), 178. See also Hal Kosut,

ed., *Cambodia and the Vietnam War* (New York: Facts on File, 1971), 71–85, for more on the widening fighting in March and April 1970.

54. CHECO, pp. xiv, 34.

55. CDEC Document Log no. 06-1647-70, copy in Indochina Archive, UCB (file: Cambodia, 1970), quoted in Stephen J. Morris, *Why Vietnam Invaded Cambodia: Political Culture and the Causes of War* (Stanford, CA: Stanford University Press, 1999), 50.

56. Truong Nhu Tang, with David Chanoff and Doan Van Toai, *A Vietcong Memoir* (San Diego: Harcourt Brace Jovanovich, 1985), 180.

57. A discrepancy exists between these dates from the Fulbright Committee's "Cambodia: May 1970–A Staff Report" (Committee on Foreign Relations, U.S. Senate, 7 June 1970, pp. 2–4) and Truong's assertion of 30 March as the date of the ARVN attack on the PRG's Ministry of Justice. There may have been more ARVN raids than just these four.

58. Thayer, *Systems Analysis View of the Vietnam War,* 177.

59. Ibid., 178–79, 191. Tran Dinh Tho, *Cambodian Incursion,* 32.

60. Thayer, *Systems Analysis View of the Vietnam War,* 191, 194; MACV Command History, p. C-111. For more on FANK's unpreparedness, see Denis Warner, *Certain Victory: How Hanoi Won the War* (Kansas City: Sheed Andrews and McMeel, 1978), 163.

61. MACV J-2 briefing paper, p. 5; MACV Command History, p. C-27; IIFFV Operational Report–Lessons Learned (OR-LL) for period ending 31 July 1970, dated 14 August 1970, p. 105, CMH Histories Division. Despite the Fifth's and Ninth's "VC" designations, both were composed of NVA regulars sent south after the losses of the 1968 Tet Offensive.

62. Thayer, *Systems Analysis View of the Vietnam War,* 191. MacDonald, in *Giap,* 326, concurs that about 50,000 NVA troops attacked Cambodia.

63. "COSVN Directive on the Role and Responsibilities of the Lao Dong Party in Cambodia," pp. 4, 6.

3. MACV'S INITIAL PLANNING, SPRING 1970

1. MACV J-2 briefing paper, p. 3; MACV Command History, p. C-32.

2. MACV Command History, p. C-32.

3. Willbanks, *Abandoning Vietnam,* 70.

4. Ibid., 71–72.

5. Message, GEN Abrams to ADM McCain CINCPAC and GEN Wheeler CJCS, 131133Z March 1970, Subject: Force Planning, Abrams Papers, CMH Histories Division.

6. Ibid.

7. Ibid.

8. Henry Kissinger discusses the planning from the National Security Council perspective in *Ending the Vietnam War,* 147–63.

9. Message, GEN Wheeler CJCS to GEN Abrams COMUSMACV, 260126Z March 1970, Subject: Plan for ground strikes against base camps in Cambodia, Abrams Papers, CMH Histories Division. "Higher authority" meant President Nixon. See also Webb, *Joint Chiefs of Staff and the War in Vietnam,* 131–60.

10. Message, GEN Wheeler CJCS to ADM McCain CINCPAC and GEN Abrams COMUSMACV, 261941Z March 1970, Subject: Plan for ground action against base areas in Cambodia, Abrams Papers, CMH Histories Division.

11. Message, GEN Wheeler CJCS to ADM McCain CINCPAC and GEN Abrams COMUSMACV, 271736Z March 1970, Subject: Plan for ground action against base areas in Cambodia. Abrams Papers, CMH Histories Division.

12. Message, GEN Abrams to ADM McCain CINCPAC; INFO to GEN Wheeler CJCS, Subject: Plan for Ground Action against Base Areas in Cambodia, 301014Z March 1970, Abrams Papers, CMH Histories Division. In a follow-up message two hours later, Abrams added that MENU would be compromised on the first option, because aviation and ground troops would see signs of past bombing missions. Message, GEN Abrams to GEN Wheeler CJCS and ADM McCain CINCPAC, Subject, Plan for Ground Action against Base Areas in Cambodia, 301242Z March 1970, Abrams Papers, CMH Histories Division.

13. Interviews, Bautz, 18 March 1993 and 15 November 1994.

14. Message, GEN Wheeler CJCS to ADM McCain CINCPAC and GEN ABRAMS COMUSMACV, 011716Z April 1970, Subject: Increased MENU Activities, Abrams Papers, CMH Histories Division.

15. MACV Command History, p. C-32, "The Vietnamese . . . had always been eager to undertake cross-border operations within their capabilities. . . . When US planning was authorized in March, JGS participated with professionalism."

16. Shawcross, *Sideshow,* 140–41.

17. Taped memoir of MG Raymond C. Conroy, (USA, Ret.), received 28 December 1992. Conroy did not recall the exact date of this meeting. Abrams's remarks suggest it was before 20 April. Because Abrams had not yet received Nixon's order to attack, he was preparing for what he felt was inevitable.

18. Message, GEN Wheeler CJCS to GEN Abrams COMUSMACV, 261954Z March 1970, Subject: Planning Cambodia Actions, Abrams Papers, CMH Histories Division.

19. Kissinger, *Ending the Vietnam War,* 153. Rogers visited Saigon only twice (mid-May 1969 and early July 1970) during 4.5 years in office and stops in 119 capital cities. http://www.state.gov/r/pa/ho/trvl/ls/13036pf.htm, accessed 29 January 2003. Laird was not in favor of actions in Cambodia. http://www.defenselink.mil/specials/secdef_histories/ accessed 29 January 2003.

20. Message, LTG Ewell IIFF to GEN Abrams COMUSMACV, no subject header, 080640Z April 1970, Abrams Papers, CMH Histories Division.

21. Message, LTG Ewell IIFF to GEN Abrams COMUSMACV and GEN Rosson Dep COMUSMACV, no subject header, 130807Z April 1970, Abrams Papers, CMH Histories Division.

22. In a 1 May 1970 meeting with President Thieu, Abrams assessed LTG Tri as "a very independent officer . . . not a team player. He does not accept well the decisions of the JGS. He is critical to the Americans of all the JGS does and to the Americans critical of his own government." Abrams to GEN Wheeler, TS Eyes Only, 031017Z May 1970, Abrams Papers, CMH Histories Division.

23. COSVN might have received some advance warning of Tri's attack. ARVN officers made several trips to meet Cambodian counterparts beforehand, and ARVN reconnaissance units crossed the border two days before the attack began. Hanoi's intelligence agents had deeply penetrated South Vietnam's government, security, and military organizations. Any of these factors could have forfeited surprise. Tho, *Cambodian Incursion,* 47.

24. HQ, USA Advisory Group III CTZ, Report, "SUBJECT: Operation Toan Thang 41," 7 June 1970, Inclosure 1: Task Organization, pp. 1–2, CMH, Histories Division.

25. U.S. Army Advisory Group, III Corps, USMACV, "Combat Operations After Action Report, III Corps," 24 July 1970, p. 1, CMH Histories Division. Tho's book *Cambodian Incursion,* 47, says the rice total was 200 tons.

26. "COSVN Directive on the Role and Responsibilities of the Lao Dong Party in Cambodia," p. 6.

27. Message, GEN Abrams COMUSMACV to GEN Westmoreland ACJCS and ADM McCain CINCPAC, Subject: Situation in Cambodian [*sic*], 221111Z April 1970, Abrams Papers, CMH Histories Division.

28. Interview, LTG Phillip Davidson (USA, Ret.), 24 June 1991, at U.S. Military Academy. Another factor affecting the quality of intelligence analysis was the one-year length of most tours in South Vietnam. About the time a U.S. intelligence specialist at MACV would fully understand the issues, he would return to America.

29. John L. Plaster, *SOG: The Secret Wars of America's Commandos in Vietnam* (New York: Simon and Schuster, 1997), 95–97.

30. Charles F. Reske, *MAC-V-SOG Command History, Annex B: The Last Secret of the Vietnam War,* vol. 1 (Sharon Center, OH: Alpha Publications, 1990), 23, 29–32, 48. See also Plaster, *SOG: The Secret Wars of America's Commandos in Vietnam,* 95–97; Wilfred P. Deac, *Road to the Killing Fields: The Cambodian War of 1970–1975* (College Station: Texas A&M University Press, 1997), 45–49.

31. Reske, *MAC-V-SOG Command History,* 361, 366–69, 380.

32. Message, GEN Abrams to ADM McCain CINCPAC; INFO to GEN Wheeler CJCS, 100831Z September 1969, Subject: SALEM HOUSE Evaluation, Abrams Papers, CMH Histories Division. Abrams's enthusiasm was not universal: then-colonel Donn Starry, commander of the Eleventh Armored Cavalry Regiment, had a total lack of faith in any report from SOG teams. Letter to author, Starry, 5 July 1992.

33. Plaster, *SOG: The Secret Wars,* 247.

34. Ibid., 239. Even if the estimates were twice as high as the actual numbers might have been, SOG's effectiveness was still several times that of the average for U.S. infantry units.

35. MACV J-2 briefing paper, p. 3.

36. Ibid., p. 6.

37. "Directive on Security Maintenance in the Cambodian Border Area," captured 6 February 1970 southeast of Katum. Report number 6 028 0185 70, dated 2 April 1970, MHI Vietnam Collection. Translators in MACV's Captured Document Exploitation Center thought it was from the 95C Regiment, Ninth VC Division.

38. MACV Command History, p. C-15.

39. See Willbanks, *Abandoning Vietnam,* 72–76, for more on internal Nixon administration debates.

40. Kissinger, *Diplomacy,* 491. Another account is in his book *Ending the Vietnam War,* 153–54.

41. Kissinger characterized the decision as "not a maniacal eruption of irrationality . . . [but rather] taken carefully, with much hesitation." *Diplomacy,* 502. He also recounts Nixon's decision and the immediate aftermath in *Ending the Vietnam War,* 155–63. For another view of events in the White House, see Langgruth, *Our Vietnam,* 563–66.

42. Richard M. Nixon. *RN: The Memoirs of Richard Nixon* (New York: Grosset and Dunlap, 1978), 448–51.

4. ARVN'S OPENING ATTACK AND FINAL U.S. PLANNING

1. "A Perspective on Cambodia: An Interview with LTG Michael S. Davison," *The Hurricane,* newsmagazine of II Field Force, issue no. 35, September 1970, pages unknown, personal collection of GEN Michael S. Davison.

2. These were modified armored personnel carriers with a .50-caliber heavy machine gun, two 7.62mm medium machine guns, and extra ammunition in lieu of soldiers. Lethal in their own right, ACAVs were also useful for protecting the tanks against close-in infantry attacks.

3. IIFFV OR-LL for period ending 31 July 1970, pp. 75–82; IIFFV OR-LL for period ending 30 April 1970, p. 94. Australia provided the infantry battalions, the helicopters, and the artillery (less one battery of six guns from New Zealand) for its task force. GEN Michael S. Davison, oral history, 15 March 1976 (4th session), p. 1, MHI Archives.

4. Jeffrey J. Clarke, *Advice and Support: The Final Years, 1965–1973* (Washington, DC: Center of Military History, 1988), 406.

5. Ibid., 411.

6. Ibid., 412.

7. Van Tin Nguyen, "5th Infantry Division Commander," at http://www.generalhieu .com/tulenhsd5-2.htm.

8. IIFFV PERINTREP 17-70, p. B-1-1. A rule of thumb when assessing an NVA or VC unit by 1970 was to assume its strength was that of the next smaller force. This document estimates the total strength of the three divisions as of late April 1970 at 12,130 troops (pp. B-1, B-2).

9. MACV Command History, p. C-27.

10. Tho, *Cambodian Incursion,* 6.

11. MACV Command History, p. C-27. "Enemy operations [were] characterized by extensive planning, reconnaissance, route selection and rehearsal. These activities tend[ed] to make his offensive operations inflexible and subject to allied preemptive operations." IIFFV PERINTREP 18-70, p. 23.

12. IIFFV PERINTREP 17-70, pp. 10, 22; interview, GEN John Galvin, 24 November 1992, USMA.

13. IIFFV OR-LL for period ending 30 April 1970, p. 20.

14. IIFFV OR-LL for period ending 31 July 1970, p. 100. In attacks by fire the enemy shoots at friendly forces or positions without attempting to make an infantry assault. Mortar shellings and rocket strikes are examples.

15. IIFFV PERINTREPs 17-70, p. 19; 18-70, p. 21; 19-70, p. 33.

16. IIFFV OR-LL for period ending 30 April 1970, p. 16. The last date was apparently a typographical error: Ho Chi Minh's birthday was 19 May. IIFFV PERINTREP 19-70, p. 38.

17. IIFFV PERINTREPs 17-70, pp. 4–5; 18-70, pp. 5–6.

18. IIFFV, OR-LL for period ending 30 April 1970, pp. 19–20. Judging from the quantities of materials captured, had the Cambodian incursion not occurred, Campaign X's attacks would have been far more powerful than the analysts predicted.

19. IIFFV PERINTREP 17-70, p. 13.

20. IIFFV OR-LL, 30 April 1970, p. 21.

21. GEN Michael S. Davison, oral history, 15 March 1976, p. 39, Senior Officers Debriefing Program, MHI Archives.

22. Web site of Doug Huffman, accessed 21 January 2004. http://www.users.qwest.net/

~huffpapa/700302Message.html. Unit logbook entry for First Battalion Fifth Infantry, Twenty-fifth Infantry Division for 2 March 1970. The site contains excellent personal photographs and annotated maps of the Twenty-fifth Infantry Division area of operations during late 1969 and early 1970, including the Cambodian incursion.

23. IIFFV OR-LL, 30 April 1970, pp. 21, 22.

24. Van Tin Nguyen, "Why Did Vietnamization of the Vietnam War Fail?" (paper presented at the Fourth Triennial Vietnam Symposium, Vietnam Center, Texas Tech University, Lubbock, Texas, 11–13 April 2002, http://www.vietnam.ttu.edu/vietnamcenter/events/2002_Symposium/2002Papers_files/vietnamization.htm).

25. Bunker to Nixon, telegram, eighty-fifth message, 27 March 1970, p. 18, Virtual Vietnam Archive.

26. IIFFV OR-LL, 30 April 1970, p. 22.

27. Bunker to Nixon, telegram, eighty-fifth message, 27 March 1970, p. 19, Virtual Vietnam Archive.

28. James Lawton Collins, *The Development and Training of the South Vietnamese Army, 1950–1972* (Washington, DC: Center of Military History, 1991), 97. When available, educational requirements were not high: following reforms in the late 1960s to raise standards, a ninth-grade-level diploma became a prerequisite for promotion to major (99).

29. Clarke, *Advice and Support,* 417.

30. LTG Michael S. Davison, Debriefing Report, p. 10, MHI Vietnam Collection.

31. Even so, the Airborne Division had suffered from the JGS's past tendency to parcel out its combat units into multibattalion task forces, the division staff and support units never getting the chance to operate as an entire division. Clarke, *Advice and Support,* 415.

32. Bunker to Nixon, telegram, eighty-fifth message, 27 March 1970, p. 19, Virtual Vietnam Archive.

33. Tho, *Cambodian Incursion,* 48–49.

34. MAJ Rhoss C. Lomax, IIFFV A/G-3 Plans, Memorandum for Record, "SUBJECT: After Action Report–Cambodian Border Operations 14–16 April 1970," 21 April 1970, CMH Histories Division.

35. USA Advisory Group, "SUBJECT: Combat Operations After Action Report III Corps, 24 June 1970," pp. 2, 1-3.

36. Message, LTG Davison IIFF to GEN Abrams COMUSMACV, Subject: Cambodian Border, 221258Z April 1970, Abrams Papers, CMH Histories Division.

37. Message, GEN Abrams COMUSMACV to ADM McCain CINCPAC and ADM Moorer Acting CJCS, Subject: Cambodian Operations, 231436Z April 1970, Abrams Papers, CMH Histories Division.

38. U.S. Army Advisory Group, Combat Operations AAR, 24 June 1970, p. 2; interview, LTG Dennis P. McAuliffe, 26 June 1992.

39. Ibid., p. 14-1.

40. Ibid., pp. 12-1, 12-2. BG D. P. McAuliffe, Memo for General Davison, 5 May 1970, "SUBJECT: Logistical Support Phase I and II, Operation Rock Crusher, 290001 April–042400 May 70," p. 1, CMH Histories Division. IIFFV headquarters, McAuliffe's advisory staff, and the Saigon Support Command provided the U.S. inspectors. Performing crew- and unit-level equipment maintenance was a major weakness ARVN never overcame before its collapse in 1975.

41. Interview, McAuliffe, 26 June 1992. McAuliffe laughed steadily as he recounted this story to the author.

42. MACV Command History, p. C-33.

43. Tho, *Cambodian Incursion,* 54.

44. Ibid., 55–58.

45. Ibid., 56.

46. Ibid., 59–60. There were some issues of cooperation between senior ARVN commanders, though. MG Tranh, commanding general of IV CTZ, was unhappy with Tri's giving what he felt was too little attention to the Ba Thu complex and too much to the Crow's Nest. He would have preferred to reverse the two and wanted to continue to exploit his attacks deeper into Cambodia. Message, MG McCown, CG DMAC, to GEN Abrams, 300501Z April 1970, CMH Histories Division.

47. Tho, *Cambodian Incursion,* 62.

48. Ibid., 64.

49. Ibid., 68.

50. Ibid.

51. Message, GEN Abrams COMUSMACV, to GEN Wheeler, CJCS; Info copy to ADM McCain, CINCPAC, 261135Z May 70, Subject: General Haig Visit, CMH Histories Division.

52. U.S. Army Advisory Group, Combat Operations AAR, 24 June 1970, p. 9. Fifth Special Forces Group (Airborne), First Special Forces, "Operation Report–Lessons Learned for the period ending 30 April 1970," dated 15 May 1970, p. 15, MHI Vietnam Collection. See also CHECO, figure 1; and IIFFV PERINTREPs 18-70, p. 16; 19-70, p. 25.

53. U.S. Army Advisory Group, p. 9.

54. CHECO, p. 27.

55. IIFFV G-3 Daily Journal, 14 May, item 19; 19 May, item 31; 24 June, item 38.

56. Message, Abrams to Wheeler and McCain, 261135Z May 70.

57. McAuliffe, Memorandum, p. 2. See also IIFFV G-3 Daily Journal, 2 May 70, item 57. 12 June 70, item 61, RG472, IIFFV ACoS for Operations (G-3) Daily Journal, 11 April 1970 through 31 July 1970, box 23, NA.

58. IIFFV OR-LL for the period ending 31 July 1970, dated 14 August 70, pp. 94, 153, CMH Histories Division. The U.S. guns stayed within thirty kilometers of the border, obeying Nixon's orders.

59. IIFFV G-3 Daily Journal, 23 May 70, item 34.

60. Folder 39, Operation TOAN THANG sequence of events, Inclosure 5: Sequence of Key Events, Planning Stage, March–April 1970, CMH Histories Division.

61. As ARVN's operations in Cambodia expanded and shifted north from the initial areas, III Corps relocated its headquarters to Tay Ninh East. The Fifty-third had to move the various U.S.-provided communications links to support the new site. IIFFV OR-LL for period ending 31 July 70, p. 161.

62. Folder 40, Operation TOAN THANG 42–Signal. Diagram: "US Advisory VHF Communications, TOAN THANG 42," CMH Histories Division.

63. IIFFV OR-LL for period ending 31 July 1970, p. 161.

64. Interview, Davison, 6 August 1992; GEN Davison, oral history, p. 7, and daily itinerary cards, Davison Collection, MHI Archives.

65. Telephonic interview, Earl W. Leech, 25 February 1993. Also Coleman, *Incursion,* 221–22, 227.

66. Interview, Leech; interview, Colonel John C. Witherell, 4 September 1992.

67. Interview, Leech.

68. Ibid. Leech had to talk to MACV's Cambodian liaison officer to obtain this information; the latter usually knew only where they had been when last heard from. By mid-April the NVA had killed or captured most Cambodian forces near the borders.

69. Interview, Leech.

70. Interview, Davison. There is disagreement about the role of Colonel Elmer Pendleton, the IIFFV operations officer, in planning the incursion. Volney Warner, who became the IIFFV civil-military staff officer in early June 1970, says that Pendleton developed the plan, Ewell forwarded it, and Al Haig approved it on behalf of the president. Phone interview, GEN Volney Warner, October 1992. Leech, Warner, and Davison were probably talking about three separate events.

71. Interview, Davison. This initial order apparently came in a meeting between Davison and Roberts in the former's office on 24 April from 0815 to 0900, itinerary cards, Davison Collection, MHI Archives.

72. Interview, Davison.

73. Interview, McAuliffe.

74. IIFFV OR-LL for period ending 30 April 1970, p. 6. Kenneth Osborne, interview, 24 June 1993.

75. IIFFV OR-LL for period ending 31 July 1970, p. 61.

76. IIFFV PERINTREPs 17-70, p. 8; 18-70, p. 9; 19-70, p. 13.

77. IIFFV PERINTREPs 17-70, p. 8; 18-70, p. 9; 19-70, pp. 12–13.

78. IIFFV OR-LL for period ending 31 July 1970, pp. 11, 83.

79. Interview, Davison. Many preincursion B-52 attacks were falsely reported as Arc Light missions inside III CTZ for Ewell, the targeting administered by IIFFV G-3. Letter, Colonel Charles W. Hayward, 8 October 1992. Brigadier General Douglas Kinnard, IIFFV Chief of Staff, did not know of the B-52 attacks on the sanctuaries until getting secret photographs from MACV to help plan the 1 May incursion. Kinnard, interviewed in *Vietnam: A Television History,* episode 9, "Cambodia and Laos," WGBH Boston, Central Independent Television, UK, and Antenne-2 France, 1985.

80. GEN Davison, oral history, p. 18.

81. Ibid. Then-colonel Donn Starry, commander of the 11ACR, considered SOG's reports worthless. Starry, letter, 5 July 1992.

82. Itinerary cards, Davison Collection, MHI Archives. Davison kept a close eye on the incursion, particularly in its early stages. He would often visit several units in Cambodia to see things for himself before briefing Abrams at MACV and returning to Long Binh for supper and the day's other business. As Cambodia became more routine, Davison had days in which he would not check on the units at all. GEN Davison, oral history, pp. 24–25.

On those evenings when he had not seen Abrams, Davison sent him a personal message on the day's events through the special intelligence officer, a Major Catlett. Interview, Leech.

5. TOAN THANG 43, 1 MAY TO 30 JUNE

1. See J. D. Coleman's excellent book *Incursion* for a more detailed description of the division's actions between Tet 1968 and summer 1970.

2. 1CD OR-LL for period ending 30 April 1970, MHI Vietnam Collection, p. 2. Major NVA attacks usually took place at night, trying to overrun dug-in Americans with heavy weapons and vastly superior firepower. The 19:1 kill ratio came from counting the dead

found around base perimeters after attacks. The number of enemy wounded was probably comparable to the U.S. level, about three to four times the number of dead. Interviews, MAJ Thomas H. Magness, 7 July 1992, and MG Morris Brady, 14 July 1992.

3. MG Elvy B. Roberts, Senior Officer Debriefing Report (RCS-CSFOR-74), date of report 18 April 70, inclusive 23 April 69–5 May 70, pp. 3–4.

4. Ibid., pp. 3–4. Roberts described War Zone C, not Cambodia, in this passage.

5. Ibid., pp. 4, 12. Most effective at stopping the NVA supply flow were "automatic ambushes," groups of claymore mines along trails suspected of being supply routes. Interview, COL James Anderson, 26 August 1993.

6. 1CD (Airmobile) Combat Operations After Action Report (AAR)–Cambodian Campaign, 18 July 1970, p. viii, CMH Histories Division.

7. A team from L Company, Seventh-fifth Infantry (Rangers), 101st Airborne Division was attached to the First Cavalry Division for a covert three-day patrol inside the Fishhook in late March 1970. Three other Ranger teams went in at the same time, including one from N Company, Seventh-fifth Infantry. L Company's team made no contact inside Cambodia but found signs of the NVA pulling out and abandoning camps in the Fishhook. Interview, Kenneth Osborne, 24 June 1993.

8. IIFFV PERINTREP 19-70, p. 26.

9. Interview, GEN Robert M. Shoemaker, 12 July 1992. Shoemaker does not recall if BG Francis Roberts, IIFFV chief of staff, was present or not. MG Cowles, the MACV operations chief, may have joined them at 1130, but the records are not clear on this. Elvy B. Roberts and Michael S. Davison papers, schedule cards, MHI Archives.

10. Interview, Shoemaker.

11. A task force is a temporary unit formed to accomplish a specific mission. This one's name came from Colonel William E. Burr, MACV's chief of surface operations. Pressed for a name for the operation while tired and snappish, he said, "Task Force Shoemaker." He later called that a mistake, because "some chose to believe that [Shoemaker] had named the operation as an exercise in vanity." Letter, William E. Burr II, 28 February 1993.

12. Interview, Shoemaker. He thinks he had the best of all possible worlds, commanding troops in combat while someone else handled the paperwork. An aviation officer soon joined his staff to do the necessary planning for helicopter and air units. 1CD AAR–Cambodian Campaign, p. L-1.

13. Interview, Shoemaker. TF Shoemaker Daily Journal, 30 April 1970, item 12, RG472, 1CD ACoS G-3 Daily Journal, NA.

14. Shoemaker did not learn otherwise until 2 May, when he chanced upon Davison at Katum. Davison showed him his map, which included the town of Snuol. Snuol was some twenty kilometers north of the top edge of Shoemaker's map, starting Shoemaker wondering what was going on. That evening at Quan Loi, he chanced upon a newsletter from division headquarters, which began with a summary of Nixon's 30 April statement (1 May in Vietnam) that U.S. forces would be out of Cambodia by 30 June. Shoemaker then realized there was more to his attack than he had thought. Interview, Shoemaker.

15. Interview, Shoemaker; interview, GEN Robert Kingston, 10 October 1992.

16. Task Force Shoemaker Operations Plan 01-70, Dong Tien II, dated 290700H April 1970, discussed in 1CD AAR, p. xiv.

17. Interview, Shoemaker; see also David Hackworth, *About Face* (New York: Simon and Schuster, 1989), 730–31.

18. GEN Davison, oral history, pp. 7–8.

19. Interview, Shoemaker. J. D. Coleman says that in late April, First Cavalry Division leaders saw MACV's aerial photographs of the Fishhook with bomb craters, but statements by Davison and Shoemaker disagree with this. Coleman, *Incursion,* 226.

20. A late-April meeting occurred at the First Cavalry Division's headquarters between representatives of several army intelligence units, during which the division's intelligence officer, by then LTC Michael Conrad, told them what he needed them to find out. MACV J-2 briefing paper, labeled MACD131-2-4869/72, p. 7, CMH Histories Division. However, Coleman says that division leaders saw aerial photographs from MACV during late April. Coleman, *Incursion,* 226.

21. Interview, Shoemaker.

22. 1CD AAR, pp. x–xi. This total excluded the 4,500 estimated troops of the Seventh NVA Division then known to be in the general area. Elvy B. Roberts Collection, Nomination for Presidential Unit Citation, p. 5, MHI Archives.

23. 1CD AAR, pp. xi–xii.

24. Ibid., p. xii.

25. Ibid., p. xiii.

26. Ibid., p. B-11. The logistical plans appeared in First Cavalry Division Operations Plan 73-70, dated 27 April 1970, CMH Histories Division.

27. Interview, Shoemaker.

28. Coleman, *Incursion,* 231.

29. Interview, Shoemaker.

30. Coleman, *Incursion,* 226.

31. "Operation SHOEMAKER Rules of Engagement," 1 May 1970, RG472, 11ACR Assistant Chief of Staff S-3, Operations Planning Files, Box 14, OPLAN 1-70 to OPORD 3-70, 1970–1970, NA.

32. "Operation SHOEMAKER Rules." "Reconnaissance by fire" was shooting into an area and watching to see if the fire provoked a response by any enemy forces that might have been hidden there.

33. COL Harry A. Buzzett, phone interview, 29 October 1992.

34. Roberts Collection, Nomination, p. C-1.

35. To avoid leaks, the division made the leaflets and tapes at its base camp rather than involve the experts in Saigon. Roberts Collection, Nomination, p. C-1.

36. Debriefing Report of LTG Michael S. Davison, p. 7, MHI Archives.

37. Roberts Collection, Nomination, p. E-1.

38. John D. Bergen, *Military Communications: A Test for Technology* (Washington, DC: Center of Military History, 1986), 289. See also Roberts Collection, Nomination, p. E-1.

39. Roberts Collection, Nomination, p. E-1.

40. Bergen, *Military Communications,* 290; 1CD OR-LL for period ending 31 July 1970, p. 62. Multiplexers let two or more transmitters use one antenna. An aerial radio relay began flying on the second day of the assault, linking the Quan Loi command bunker to forward elements in Cambodia. Roberts Collection, Nomination, p. E-1.

41. 1CD OR-LL for period ending 31 July 1970, p. 62.

42. Interview, Shoemaker.

43. Interview, MG Scott Smith, 6 October 1992.

44. Ibid.

45. Daily Journal, Task Force Shoemaker, 1CD, entries 3 and 4 for 1 May 1970, RG472, Assistant Chief of Staff G-3, 1CD, NA.

46. Interview, Smith.

47. Artillery raids throughout northern III CTZ lasted from daybreak to sunset. Bombs and napalm cleared an area into which helicopters would fly three to six 105mm howitzers, gun crews, ammunition, and an infantry platoon as a security force. The guns shot until suppertime, when helicopters flew everything home. MACV Command History, vol. 3, p. G-10.

48. 1CD AAR, 11 July 1970, p. 39. The cannon included thirty-six 105mm howitzers, forty-eight 155mm howitzers, four 8-inch howitzers, and six 175mm guns. These varied tremendously in range, trajectory, lethality, and shell size, adding to the planners' considerations.

49. Brady, his operations officer, Major Anthony G. Pokorny, and the artillery liaison on Shoemaker's staff were the key people in integrating artillery, rocket helicopters, and air strikes. Interviews, GEN Robert Kingston, 10 October 1992, and COL Anthony Pokorny, 19 and 21 June 1992.

50. Combat Operations AAR, HQ 1CD, 11 July 1970, p. 38, CMH Histories Division; MACV Command History, vol. 3, p. C-131. The army sources indicate 600 targets; the air force's CHECO report says 381. CHECO, p. 15.

51. Pokorny, interview, 22 June 1992. He was unsure whether this was due more to the fires driving off any would-be gunners or there being no NVA around to actually shoot at the helicopters, but he suspected a degree of both. The two task force representatives were the artillery and air force officers.

52. 1CD OR-LL, for period ending 31 July 1970, p. 57.

53. 1CD Combat Operations AAR, 18 July 1970, page not numbered.

54. Combat Operation AAR, 11 July 1970, p. 39.

55. CHECO, pp. 11–12. On 25 April the JCS had set the air priorities for Southeast Asia as being Cambodia, South Vietnam, Barrel Roll, and Steel Tiger, in that order. CHECO, p. 12.

56. MACV J-2 briefing paper, accession no. MACD1-31-2-4869/72, p. 9, CMH Histories Division. Thereafter the 1CD G-2 listeners monitored short-range NVA tactical radios using the division's "Left Bank" helicopter, a UH-1H filled with radio-monitoring gear.

57. MACV Command History, vol. 3, p. C-131.

58. CHECO, p. 16.

59. Ibid., p. 13.

60. 1CD AAR, p. 1-A, Operations Summary, Southeast Asia Collection, CMH. Standard 500- and 750-pound bombs could not flatten enough trees in dense jungle to make a helicopter landing zone. A 15,000-pound "Commando Vault" could.

61. Roberts Collection, Nomination, p. M-1. Planes also dropped cluster bombs, which scatter dozens of grenade-sized bomblets over an area the size of a football field. While hiding from the explosions, enemy troops could not shoot effectively at the helicopters and dismounting soldiers.

62. 1CD AAR, p. 1-A, Operations Summary, 1CD Combat Operations AAR, 11 July 1970, pp. 40–41, L-1. Earlier that morning the Fourth Company could not get out of the Quan Loi base camp to move to the adjacent pickup zone because the gates were locked. It took them a half hour to find the keys, but they managed to lift off on time. Assistant Chief of Staff G-3, Daily Journal, 1 May 1970, HQ, 1CD.

63. 1CD AAR, p. 1-A, Operations Summary.

64. IIFFV PERINTREP 18-70, p. 16.

65. G-3 Daily Journals, 1 May 1970.

66. John H. Claybrook, letter, dated 11 June 1992.

67. 1CD AAR, p. 1-B, Operations Summary. Though ostensibly "cavalry" units, the battalions went by the "infantry battalion" designation rather than the "cavalry squadron" nomenclature.

68. 1CD Combat Operations AAR–Cambodian Campaign, p. 1-E.

69. CHECO, pp. 14–15.

70. CHECO, figure 25.

71. MACV Command History, vol. 3, p. C-131. The 196 sorties included the 148 planned and 48 diverted to the Fishhook as emergency missions. The account claims 390 enemy dead. COSVN's forces had previously evicted most Cambodians from the border areas for security regions, so these dead were probably all NVA or VC.

72. CHECO, p. 18.

73. Daily Journal, Operation TOAN THANG 43, 2 May 1970, Assistant Chief of Staff, G-3, 1CD Daily Journals, NA.

74. CHECO, p. 22.

75. Ibid., pp. 18–19.

76. GEN Davison, Senior Officers Debriefing Program, 15 March 1976, pp. 3–4. Interview, Leech. Davison says he planned on using 11ACR from the start. Davison, interview, 6 August 1992.

77. Leech, interview; Coleman, *Incursion*, 240–41.

78. Leech, interview.

79. Coleman, *Incursion*, 245.

80. Starry, letter, 22 June 1992.

81. Interview, COL Elisha Fuller (Deputy CO, 20th Engineer BDE), 1 November 1992.

82. Davison, interview.

83. Daily Journal, TF Shoemaker, Operation TOAN THANG 43, 4 May 1970, time 1305. 1CD Assistant Chief of Staff G-3 Daily Journal, 6 March–15 June 1970, box 17, Journals (TF Shoemaker) 30 April–5 May 1970, NA. Hitting hard point targets, such as bridges, was tremendously difficult before advanced electronic guidance systems and "smart" bombs appeared in the early 1970s.

84. Daily Journal, Operation TOAN THANG 43, 4 May 1970, times 1020 through 2000.

85. Daily Journal, Operation TOAN THANG 43, 4 May 1970, time 1930.

86. Daily Journal, Operation TOAN THANG 43, 3 May 1970, log entry time 1430.

87. Interview, Anderson. 1CD Combat Operations AAR, 18 July 1970, p. A-1.

88. Interview, Anderson; Daily Journal, TF Shoemaker, 30 April 1970, item 18. Anderson did not see any cannon, but he also had never seen or heard of any enemy artillery shells before this, even as Abrams's aide. Mortars and rockets have significant drawbacks offsetting their simplicity. Mortars have limited range; rockets, although they can travel much farther, are less accurate. 75mm howitzers, though, had about twice the range of the average NVA/VC mortar and greater accuracy than the rocket. Larger-caliber guns have good accuracy and even greater range. Were the NVA to bring artillery into III CTZ, U.S. and ARVN firebases and airfields would be in grave danger.

89. General Vo Nguyen Giap, interviewed by Italian journalist Oriana Fallaci, cited in Russell Stetler, ed., *The Military Art of People's War: Selected Writings of General Vo Nguyen Giap* (New York: Monthly Review Press, 1970), 331.

90. Interview, Anderson. Roberts Collection, Nomination, pp. I-14–I-16, J-16.

6. THE FIRST CAVALRY DIVISION EXPANDS INTO CAMBODIA

1. Richard M. Nixon, *No More Vietnams* (New York: Arbor House, 1985), 120.

2. Daily Journal, Operation TOAN THANG 43, 5 May 1970, time 1430, 1CD ACoS G-3 Daily Journal, 6 March–15 June 1970, box 17, Journals (TF Shoemaker) 30 April–5 May 1970, NA; Combat Operation After Action Report, HQ 1CD, 11 July 1970, p. 42, CMH Histories Division.

3. 1CD AAR, 18 July 1970, pp. x–xi.

4. Ibid., p. A-18.

5. Coleman, *Incursion,* 250–51. Coleman, at the time the division's public affairs officer, says Casey told Roberts that if Roberts did not relieve the colonel, doing so would be his first act as commanding general.

6. Roberts had three numbered infantry brigades, the Division Artillery, the Division Support Command, and the Eleventh Aviation Group (his helicopters). Colonels commanded all six. HQ 1CD OR-LL for period ending 31 July 1970, p. 88, MHI Vietnam Collection.

7. Interview, Kingston.

8. CHECO, p. 60.

9. Interview, Smith.

10. Interview, MG Scott Smith, 6 October 1992.

11. Casey's son George, at the time an ROTC cadet at Georgetown University, was promoted to general in November 2003 and became the U.S. Army's vice chief of staff. At his promotion he noted that the four-star insignia he was wearing were his father's stars, assembled by a jeweler into the new rank. He left that assignment in June 2004 to become commander of the Multi-National Forces in Iraq. Author, present at promotion ceremony.

12. Interview, Fuller; Roberts Collection, Nomination, p. G-1. The Thirty-first Engineers also built Fire Support Bases Yen The, South I, and South II by 1 May, as well as improving Highway 246 between Tonle Cham and An Loc. The 588th built FSBs West I, II, and Beverly by 29 April. Roberts papers, Nomination, pp. G-2, G-6.

13. Interview, Smith; Roberts Collection, Nomination, p. G-7.

14. Interview, Smith.

15. Ibid.

16. 1CD AAR, 18 July 1970, p. B-11, paragraph 3-a.

17. Roberts Collection, Nomination, p. F-1.

18. These included Bu Dop on 4 May, Bu Gia Map on 9 May, and O'Rang on 21 May 1970. Roberts Collection, Nomination, p. B-15.

19. Roberts Collection, Nomination, p. B-15.

20. 1CD OR-LL for period ending 31 July 1970, p. 58.

21. 1CD AAR, 18 July 1970, p. 1-D.

22. 1CD OR-LL for period ending 31 July 1970, pp. 58–59.

23. Ibid., p. 59.

24. Interview, Shoemaker. One commander recalled blowing up "bunkers full of C-4 [plastic explosive] that were as big as this [twelve-by-fifteen-foot] room." Interview, Anderson.

25. Roberts Collection, Nomination, pp. J-12 through J-15.

26. Interview, Anderson.

27. 1CD OR-LL for period ending 31 July 1970, p. 2. USARV Daily Journal, Operation

TOAN THANG 43, 3 May 1970, log entry time 1445. RG472, 1CD Assistant Chief of Staff G-3, Daily Journal 6 March–15 June 1970, Box 17, "Daily Journals (TF Shoemaker) 30 April–5 May 1970," NA.

28. Interview, Smith.

29. Roberts Collection, Nomination, p. J-3.

30. Interview, Anderson.

31. 1CD OR-LL for period ending 31 July 1970, pp. 57–58.

32. Roberts Collection, Nomination, pp. J-2, J-3. Early May predictions for twenty to twenty-four inches of rain in May and June were apparently realized. 1CD AAR, 18 July 1970, p. vii.

33. Roberts Collection, Nomination, pp. J-2, J-3.

34. Combat Operation After Action Report, HQ 1CD, 11 July 1970, p. 43, CMH Histories Division.

35. Interview, Major Bartley W. Furey, 6 July 1992, by phone from USMA; interview, Kingston; interview, Lieutenant Colonel Thomas E. Fitzgerald, 1 November 1992, by phone from USMA; interview, Anderson.

36. Coleman, *Incursion*, 253–55.

37. Ibid., 260–61.

38. Combat Operations AAR, 11 July 1970, pp. 36–37.

39. Ibid., p. 36.

7. TOAN THANG 44: THE TWENTY-FIFTH INFANTRY DIVISION

1. Bautz normally got the support of thirty-six to seventy-two UH-1H "Hueys" from IIFFV aviation units each day to move troops and supplies. Davison loaned him medium-lift CH-47s and heavy-lift CH-54s as needed. Combat Operations After Action Report (AAR), Twenty-fifth Infantry Division (25ID), 19 July 1970, p. 2, CMH Histories Division.

2. Combat Operations AAR, 25ID, p. 2.

3. Daily Journal, 1 May, 2 May 1970, Assistant Chief of Staff G-3, 25ID, NA; Interview, Edward Bautz, 8 September 1992.

4. Interview, Bautz, 8 September 1992; Bautz, copy of three-by-five note card dated 3 May 1970, enclosed in letter dated 9 September 1992, Davison Papers, MHI Archives.

5. Interview, Bautz, 31 August 1993. This brevity was a characteristic from Bautz's (and Abrams's) days in Major General John Woods's Fourth Armored Division in France in World War II.

6. Interview, Bautz, 8 September 1992; Bautz, letter dated 9 September 1992. The additional units only partly made up for the almost total lack of detailed intelligence on what units were across the border and where. This information had to come from combat actions beginning on 6 May. Combat Operations AAR, 25ID, p. 3.

7. Bautz, three-by-five note card, enclosed with letter, 9 September 1992. This assistance included the First Cavalry Division leaving a battery in place until one from the Twenty-fifth could assume the position.

8. Interview, Bautz, 8 September 1992. The boundary change between the First Cavalry and Twenty-fifth Infantry Divisions went into effect at noon on 4 May. Bautz, three-by-five note card, with letter, 9 September 1992.

9. Interview, Bautz, 18 March 1993; interview, BG Michael Greene, 23 June 1992. The division's reliance on radio meant its messages were almost as vulnerable to NVA monitoring as COSVN's were to MACV's. Although COSVN did not have the superb codebreaking personnel and equipment available to MACV, poor U.S. efforts at radio security at battalion and below routinely gave listeners useful intelligence. To counter this, the Twenty-fifth Infantry Division emphasized radio security and coding procedures during the incursion. Combat Operations AAR, 25ID, p. 10.

10. OR-LL, 25ID, period ending 31 July 1970, pp. 101–02, MHI Vietnam Collection. Comparisons of daily task organizations. Also Daily Journal, 4 May 1970, G-3, and "After Action Report of Cambodian Operations Base Area 354," p. B-1, Headquarters Twenty-fifth Infantry Division, 17 September 1970, RG472, Assistant Chief of Staff G-3 25ID AARs 1968 through 1970, box 1, NA.

11. Headquarters Twenty-fifth Infantry Division, SUBJECT: AAR of Cambodian operations, Base Area 354, 17 September 1970, pp. D-3, D-4.

12. Letter from Corwin A. Mitchell, 15 June 1992. Example mentioned in interview, MG Ennis C. Whitehead, 21 June 1992.

13. Letter, Mitchell.

14. AAR–Base Area 354, pp. D-1 to D-3; OR-LL for period ending 31 July 1970, p. 76.

15. Daily Journal, G-3, 5 May 1970, 1815 hours.

16. Ibid.

17. Combat Operations AAR, 25ID, 19 July 1970, Inclosure 6, p. 1.

18. AAR–Base Area 354, p. D-4; Combat Operations AAR, 25ID, Inclosure 6, p. 2.

19. *Vietnam 1970: The U.S. 25th Infantry Division* (Yearbook), p. 81, personal copy of MG Edward Bautz.

20. OR-LL for the period ending 31 July 1970, p. 4. Interview, Bautz, 18 March 1993.

21. AAR–Base Area 354, p. B-3; 25ID G-3 Air Daily Log, 6 May 1970, 0845 hours.

22. *Vietnam 1970* (Yearbook), pp. 42, 64–65; OR-LL for the period ending 31 July 1970, p. 4.

23. *Vietnam 1970* (Yearbook), p. 80; interview, Bautz, 18 March 1993.

24. *Vietnam 1970* (Yearbook), p. 80.

25. Daily Journal, G-3, 6 May 1970, 1135 hours.

26. Ibid., entries at 1930 and 2020 hours; *Vietnam 1970* (Yearbook), pp. 82, 135; AAR–Base Area 354, p. B-7.

27. *Vietnam 1970* (Yearbook), pp. 80–81; 25ID Plans Summary for 6 May 1970, dated 050700Z May 1970, p. 1, NA; AAR–Base Area 354, pp. B-3, Annex II to Appendix B, E-I-1.

28. AAR–Base Area 354, pp. B-3, B-5, Annex II to Appendix B.

29. AAR–Base Area 354, pp. A-VI-1, A-VI-2, A-3, A-4. In hunting for enemy supplies, information came from many of the same types of sources used by the First Cavalry Division. These included prisoners and defectors, aerial photography, radio monitoring and direction-finding stations, RED HAZE infrared surveillance and SLAR flights, and pilots' visual spottings. MACV's radio direction-finding stations located enemy transmitters. The scale and capabilities of the U.S. electronic warfare effort were a very closely held secret, known only to a few at MACV and even fewer at field force and division headquarters. When attacks were to be based on these reports, the commanders in the field were told "Yellowjacket grid coordinates such and such." This meant U.S. Intelligence had identified some sort of headquarters there, and the units were to attack it immediately. Bautz re-

ceived several Yellowjacket missions in Base Area 354, which he gave to the mechanized battalions because of their speed and firepower. Interview, Bautz, 18 March 1993.

30. AAR–Base Area 354, p. B-4.

31. As examples, between 0800 and 1115 on 9 May, one company found two weapons caches a hundred meters apart. In less than four hours on 10 May, another company captured ninety tons of rice in three caches in an area 1,900 meters long by 700 meters wide. Combat Operations AAR, 25ID, 19 July, pp. F-3, F-4.

32. Interview, COL Harry A. Buzzett, 29 October 1992.

33. AAR–Base Area 354, p. C-5.

34. AAR–Base Area 354, pp. C-2 through C-4. By late June, Bautz's medics had treated 7,325 Cambodians in forty-two unit-sponsored "clinics." Combat Operations AAR, 25ID, Inclosure 5.

35. AAR–Base Area 354, pp. A-4, A-5, Annex V to Appendix A.

36. Interview, Bautz, 18 March 1993; Combat Operations AAR, 25ID, p. 11.

37. The rains began in earnest the second week of May. Phuoc Vinh (HQ 1CD) recorded 2.42 inches that week to Long Binh's (HQ IIFFV) 3.36 inches and Bien Hoa's 3.77 inches. IIFFV PERINTREP 19-70, p. 25.

38. AAR–Base Area 354, pp. C-1, E-1. Seven hours of airborne loudspeaker broadcasts of calls to surrender and airdrops of 1.6 million assorted leaflets helped persuade seven NVA troops to turn themselves in, a poor return for the effort made.

39. AAR–Base Area 354, p. A-7; Combat Operations AAR, 25ID, p. 6.

40. AAR–Base Area 354, p. A-VI-1-A. Some commanders hired Cambodians from nearby hamlets and villages to help evacuate captured rice. Lacking Cambodian currency to pay them, the officers "paid" for their help with troop labor in kind and with bags of rice (p. E-2).

41. AAR–Base Area 354, p. C-1.

42. Interview, Bautz, 18 March 1993; AAR–Base Area 354, pp. A-1, A-I-1.

43. Interview, Bautz, 18 March 1993; Combat Operations AAR, 25ID, Inclosure 5; AAR–Base Area 354, p. C-2.

44. Combat Operations AAR, 25ID, pp. 4, 6, A-1. "Ground Commander's Daily SITREP, 070001H to 072400H May 70," CG 25ID, dated 080100Z May 70, RG472, 25ID Daily Journals, NA. The Regional Forces were roughly akin to U.S. National Guards, generally infantry units that operated in certain provinces or CTZs. The CIDG were a local militia force, of widely varying competence.

45. Combat Operations AAR, 25ID, pp. 6–7.

46. Interview, Bautz, 18 March 1993; interview, Dominic Stimola, 9 September 1993; interview, Shoemaker, 12 July 1992; Daily Journal, 2 and 10 May 1970, Assistant Chief of Staff, G-3, 25ID, NA.

47. Interview, Bautz, 18 March 1993.

48. Bautz, personal letter, 23 February 1993.

49. Interview, Whitehead, 21 June 1992.

50. Ibid.

51. AAR–Base Area 354, p. D-2.

52. Interview, Whitehead, 21 June 1992.

53. 25ID G-3 Daily plans for 9 and 10 May 1970, RG472, NA.

54. Combat Operations AAR, 25ID, p. 7.

55. Ibid.

56. Combat Operations AAR, 25ID, pp. F-3, F-4.

57. MACV J-2 briefing papers, marked MACD131-2-4869/72, p. 10, CMH Histories Division. Maps in the Elvy B. Roberts Collection in the MHI Archives indicate COSVN as being in the Fishhook, but Bautz says it was west of Memot. "*That's* where I was told by General Davison . . . to expect it, and that's where we briefed [Abrams]." Interview, Bautz, 18 March 1993. Elements of COSVN were probably in both areas.

58. Davison, oral history, p. 19, Davison papers, MHI Archives.

59. Bautz says it was five flights of six B-52s; the division's after-action report says it was three flights of three B-52s each. Interview, Bautz, 18 March 1993; Combat Operations AAR, 25ID, p. 7. The 1970 document's numbers are more consistent with Arc light descriptions in other sources.

60. Davison, oral history, p. 20; he does not say how they knew. A defector "who had served with a COSVN office" said that this base had held about 1,000 men in twelve staff sections and two support units. "Allies Disrupt COSVN Elements in Cambodia," *Thunder!* (the quarterly publication of the Twenty-fifth Infantry Division) 3, no. 1 (Fall–Winter 1970): 17.

61. Davison credits the B-52s with fifty enemy dead. Oral history, p. 20. Bautz, however, puts the number of dead at around 250. Interviews, 8 September 1992 and 18 March 1993. "Allies Disrupt COSVN Elements," *Thunder!* 3, no. 1 (Fall–Winter 1970): 17, says the bombing killed 150. The latter is probably most accurate, since the division's after-action report, 19 July 1970, p. 8, puts the count at 241. A total of 150 bombing deaths plus ground combat would produce about this number.

62. AAR–Base Area 354, p. B-1. Also 25ID G-3 Daily Plans for 10 May 1970. Whitehead first met the commander of the latter battalion that night. Interview, Whitehead, 16 and 21 June 1992.

63. Combat Operations AAR, 25ID, p. 2.

64. Interviews, Bautz, 8 September 1992 and 18 March 1993.

65. Interview, Whitehead, 21 June 1992.

66. Combat Operations AAR, 25ID, p. 8. The haul also included some ten tons of NVA uniforms. Most important of the ammunition were the 690 82mm mortar rounds and 163 122mm rockets, which caused the most casualties and damage in enemy attacks by fire.

67. Combat Operations AAR, 25ID, Inclosure 6, p. 1.

68. Interview, Bautz, 18 March 1993.

69. Combat Operations AAR, 25ID, Inclosure 6, p. 1.

70. Ibid. The Tay Ninh ammunition supply point shipped a daily average of 200 tons of ammunition to Thien Ngon and Katum while both forward ammunition points were open.

71. G-3 orders for 14 May; 25ID daily maps (photographs), 25ID G-3 Daily Plans, 14 through 18 May 1970, RG472, NA.

72. 25ID daily maps (photographs), G-3 Daily Plans, 14 through 18 May 1970, NA.

73. Combat Operations AAR, 25ID, p. 12. LTG Davison, Senior Officer Debriefing Report, p. 8, MHI Vietnam Collection.

74. Combat Operations AAR, 25ID, p. 12.

75. SP4 William L. McGown, "Artillery Raid," *Thunder!* 3, no. 1 (Fall–Winter 1970): 39–43.

76. Ibid.

77. Interview, Bautz, 18 March 1993; interview, Buzzett, 29 October 1992.

78. Combat Operations AAR, 25ID, pp. 11–12.

79. Ibid., p. 9.

80. Bautz, Yearbook, p. 89.

81. Combat Operations AAR, 25ID, pp. F-1 through F-10. The signal school included sixty-seven AM radios, sixty-one FM radios, and a "classroom complete with charts and diagrams explaining how to maintain radio sets." "031820Z May 70 Mission," *Thunder!* 3, no. 1 (Fall–Winter 1970): 7. Without operators or repairmen, COSVN's ability to talk among its headquarters would suffer tremendously.

82. Davison, oral history, p. 19, Davison papers, MHI Archives; Combat Operations AAR, 25ID, p. 10.

83. Unmarked CMH briefing papers, p. 11. Hanoi's codes do not seem to have been sophisticated, and having the codebooks made it even easier for the U.S. National Security Agency, the world's best code makers and code breakers, to read these messages.

84. Combat Operations AAR, 25ID, p. 9. Most of the enemy casualties were inflicted by U.S. airpower. The number of NVA/VC wounded was probably around 1,500.

85. Davison, oral history, p. 26.

86. OR-LL, for the period ending 31 July 1970, p. 62.

87. Combat Operations AAR, 25ID, p. 15, and Inclosure 6, p. 5.

88. Interview, Buzzett, 29 October 1992. As the war wound down and domestic support in the United States faded, Buzzett, by then in his third war, felt his "devotion was to save the little guys' ass."

89. Davison, Senior Officer Debriefing Report, p. 9.

90. Combat Operations AAR, 25ID, Inclosure 6, p. 4.

91. Combat Operations AAR, 25ID, p. 9.

92. Ibid., p. 11.

93. Davison, Senior Officer's Debriefing Report, pp. 9–10.

94. Combat Operations AAR, 25ID, p. 10. According to the division's newsmagazine, of the 1,537 tons of captured rice, 537 tons went to feed refugees, 460 tons were destroyed, 130 tons were lost through spillage, and 90 tons were ruined by weather. SP5 Tom Bozzuto, "Rice and Refugees," *Thunder!* 3, no. 1 (Fall–Winter 1970): 28. Bozzuto does not say what happened to the 320 tons not accounted for in these figures.

95. Combat Operations AAR, 25ID, p. 13.

96. Interview, Bautz, 18 March 1993.

97. Interview, Buzzett, 29 October 1992.

98. Combat Operations AAR, 25ID, p. 15.

99. AAR–Base Area 354, p. F-2.

100. Ibid., p. F-1.

101. Combat Operations AAR, 25ID, p. 15.

102. Interview, Bautz, 18 March 1993; Bergen, *Military Communications,* 286, 289.

103. When the division occupied Cu Chi in late 1966, signalers built a 106-foot-tall antenna tower. This greatly improved the division's ability to talk with its units across the region, but the red aircraft warning light atop it became an aiming point for VC and NVA mortar crews making nighttime attacks on the camp. The light came off, the tower was lowered to get it below the aircraft flight path, and Nui Ba Den became critical to the division's ability to talk. Bergen, *Military Communications,* 195.

104. AAR–Base Area 354, pp. B-1, B-5.

105. Bergen, *Military Communications,* 287, 289; AAR–Base Area 354, p. B-5.

106. Davison, oral history, 15 March 1976, Senior Officers Debriefing Program, Davison Papers, MHI Archives.

107. AAR–Base Area 354, pp. B-3, Annex II to Appendix B.

108. Ibid., pp. B-5, B-6.

109. Combat Operations AAR, 25ID, Inclosure 6, p. 4.

110. Bautz had "never heard" of the mutual interference, but "it didn't surprise" him that there had been such a problem. Interview, 18 March 1993.

111. AAR–Base Area 354, p. B-6.

112. Ibid.

113. Ibid.

114. Interview, Bautz, 18 March 1993.

115. Combat Operations AAR, 25ID, p. 14.

116. Ibid.

117. AAR–Base Area 354, p. D-4; Combat Operations AAR, 25ID, Inclosure 6, p. 4. The Twenty-fifth Infantry Division used CH-54 Skycranes extensively for moving bulldozers and extracting eight damaged or destroyed armored personnel carriers out of Cambodia. AAR–Base Area 354, pp. D-4, D-5.

118. Combat Operations AAR, 25ID, pp. 16–17.

119. Interview, Buzzett.

120. Interview, Bautz, 18 March 1993. "I told Bautz that we'd protect ourselves. . . . I don't know anyone else that did such an operation." Interview, Buzzett.

121. Combat Operations AAR, 25ID, Inclosure 5, p. 2; Bozzuto, "Rice and Refugees," 27.

122. SP5 Stephen F. Froft, "Culture Impact," *Thunder!* 3, no. 1, (Fall–Winter 1970): 10. IIFFV helped. COL Volney Warner, Davison's civil-military staff officer from 5 June on, said his main functions during the Cambodian operation were setting up rice kitchens and "cleaning up messes" at Snuol and Memot. Interview, Warner, 1 October 1992.

123. Froft, "Culture Impact," 13.

124. Interview, Buzzett.

8. SUPPORTING OPERATIONS

1. HQ, U.S. Army Support Command, Saigon. "Operational Report–Lessons Learned, US Army Support Command, Saigon (SSC OR-LL), Period Ending 31 July 1970," p. 2, MHI Classified Archives, Secure Vault, Reel F098.

2. MACV Command History, p. C-108.

3. Ibid.

4. Taped memoir of MG Raymond C. Conroy, received 28 December 1992.

5. Ibid. Only after it was in South Vietnam en route to Tri did Conroy tell Abrams of how serious the problem had been, or its resolution.

6. SSC OR-LL, p. 2; MACV Command History, p. C-113. SSC technical assistance teams discovered in the week before the incursion that the ARVN Fifth Division's vehicle maintenance was particularly bad.

7. SSC OR-LL, p. 3. Final drives are the heavy gear assemblies on tracked vehicles between the transmission inside the vehicle's hull and the sprockets outside the hull that move the track itself. They are subject to tremendous torque and strain, particularly when moving armored vehicles cross-country rapidly across rough terrain.

8. SSC OR-LL, 31 July 70, pp. 3–4; MACV Command History, p. C-118. A more detailed listing of major repair parts was 45 tank final drives, 16 transmissions, and 25 en-

gines; 102 M113 APC engines; 32 Sheridan Armored Reconnaissance Vehicle engines and 30 transmissions; 13 heavy artillery transmissions and 10 engines; 85 2.5-ton truck engines; 160 5-ton truck engines; 25 gun recoil mechanisms; and 9 gun mounts. Each required a major investment in skilled labor and equipment to repair or rebuild.

9. MACV Command History, p. C-118.

10. Shelford Bidwell, ed., *Brassey's Artillery of the World* (New York: Bonanza Books, 1979), 46, 83, 85, 86. An 8-inch shell weighed 200 pounds; a 105mm shell, 33 pounds; a 155mm shell, 95 pounds; and a 175mm shell, 147 pounds. Powder, fuses, and packing added more weight to each complete round.

11. IIFFV G-3 Daily Journal, 30 April 1970, items 57, 58; 6 May 70, item 47; and 9 May, item 17, RG472, IIFFV Assistant Chief of Staff for Operations (G-3) Daily Journal, 11 April–31 July 1970, box 23, NA.

12. IIFFV OR-LL for period ending 30 April 1970, 14 May 1970, pp. 52, 94–95, CMH Histories Division, box labeled "IIFFV Operational Papers." In this particular case, both batteries' cannon worked through the same battalion supply officer, greatly easing the supply headaches for restocking shells.

13. IIFFV G-3 Daily Journal, 27 June, items 4, 23. The second entry contains an obvious error, listing the same totals for two operations.

14. SSC OR-LL, p. 4; MACV Command History, p. C-118.

15. SSC OR-LL, p. 4.

16. Ibid., p. 5; MACV Command History, p. C-119.

17. SSC OR-LL, p. 5.

18. Ibid.

19. Ibid.; MACV Command History, p. C-119.

20. Langgruth, *Our Vietnam,* 568.

21. Memoir, Conroy.

22. An "underground airline" was flying in weapons to Phnom Penh during April, the workers wearing civilian clothes. Interview, Conroy, 1 October 1992.

23. Memoir, Conroy.

24. MACV Command History, p. C-109; Conroy, taped memoir. The C-119 unit commander had worked in Cambodia for several years and had many friends there who helped him with the flights into Phnom Penh.

25. "Additional Information on Results of Cambodian Cross-Border Operations," Message no. PP-274/70, DTG 251359Z August 1970, MACJ232. CMH, Southeast Asia Cabinet 9, p. 2. Most of the transfer occurred during the incursion: "By 1 July, 11,688 individual weapons with 2.6 million rounds of ammunition, and 1,292 crew served weapons with 2.1 million rounds, had been turned over." CHECO, p. 11.

26. Conroy, taped memoir.

27. General Bruce Palmer argues USARV should have been the field army controlling the U.S. corps-level commands. Westmoreland, though, acted as both theater and field army commander, bypassing USARV to issue orders to the U.S. Field Forces and Marines. With no authority over tactical units, USARV became an administrative and logistic headquarters. Abrams did not change this when he took command of MACV in 1968. Palmer, *The Twenty-five Year War.*

28. MACV Command History, p. C-108.

29. CHECO, figure 53.

30. Ibid., p. 60.

31. GEN George C. Brown, 30 March 1970, quoted in MACV Command History, vol. 1, p. VI-21. Airpower consists of three missions: air superiority, air interdiction, and close air support. Air superiority is the prerequisite for the other two. Having it, the United States used its planes for air interdiction and close air support.

32. MACV Command History, vol. 1, p. VI-21.

33. CHECO, p. xiv.

34. Additional antiaircraft weapons, particularly SA-2 surface-to-air and large-caliber guns firing high-explosive shells, steadily arrived during the late 1960s from the Soviet Union to improve North Vietnam's air defense network. These less-mobile systems were more suited for defending fixed sites, such as Hanoi, Haiphong, bridges, rail yards, and airfields.

35. Kosut, *Cambodia and the Vietnam War,* 97–98.

36. MACV Command History, vol. 1, p. VI-25, Table VI-1.

37. CHECO, pp. xii, 24. In a case of RVNAF pilot error, an American adviser to the ARVN Airborne Division was nearly killed by a VNAF bomb, which it at first denied to an American FAC that it had dropped; it then claimed the bomb had hung on the rack when the pilot had earlier tried to drop it. R. Les Brownlee, interview, September 2003, Washington, DC.

38. IIFFV OR-LL for period ending 31 July 1970, p. 85. FACs generally flew OV-1B or OV-2 aircraft, small single- or two-seaters, and directed jets and larger propeller-driven ground attack planes on to targets. They were equivalent to artillery forward observers.

39. IIFFV OR-LL for period ending 31 July 1970, p. 85.

40. CHECO, p. 25.

41. There were four possible fuse settings, from instantaneous to 0.1-second delays. These made the bomb explode at different heights, the selection depending on whether the target was in the open or in triple-canopied jungle.

42. Interview, Bautz, 18 March 1993.

43. Tang, *Vietcong Memoir,* 177. After the last bomb landed less than a kilometer away, the revolutionaries were "dazed, shaking their heads in an attempt to clear their ears." See also IIFFV PERINTREP 19-70, p. 14.

44. Interview, Bautz, 18 March 1993.

45. IIFFV OR-LL for period ending 30 April 1970, p. 8.

46. LTG Davison, Debriefing Report, p. 9; IIFFV OR-LL for period ending 31 July 1970, p. 43.

47. MACV Command History, pp. C-132, C-133.

48. IIFFV OR-LL for period ending 31 July 1970, pp. 63–64.

49. MACV Command History, vol. 1, p. VI-21. Between July and September, 47 percent of all tactical air sorties were in Cambodia and Laos; by December the figure had risen to 73 percent.

50. CHECO, p. xv.

51. Kosut, *Cambodia and the Vietnam War,* 115.

52. CHECO, pp. xv–xvi.

53. Thomas J. Cutler, *Brown Water, Black Berets: Coastal and Riverine Warfare in Vietnam* (Annapolis, MD: Naval Institute Press, 1988), 354.

54. Ibid.

55. In mid-May IV Corps launched a second operation, CUU LONG II; it concerned actions on the western side of the Mekong and drove as far inland as Kampong Speu

(about ninety kilometers inside Cambodia). It evolved into CUU LONG III when the United States withdrew in late June. CHECO, pp. 10–11.

56. MACV Command History, pp. C-37 through C-42.

57. Combat Operations AAR, First Brigade, Fourth Infantry Division, dated 17 June 1970, p. 4.

58. Headquarters, Fourth Infantry Division Artillery, Combat Operations AAR, dated 9 April 1970, "Camp Radcliffe-1970,"and "USARV OPLAN ENARI," "Redeployment," Fourth Infantry Division G-3 AAR.

59. Combat Operations AAR, First Brigade, Fourth Infantry Division, dated 17 June 1970, p. 5.

60. Combat Operations AAR, First Brigade, Fourth Infantry Division, dated 17 June 1970, Inclosure 1.

61. Combat Operations AAR, Second Brigade, Fourth Infantry Division, dated 23 May 1970.

62. IIFFV OR-LL for period ending 31 July 1970, pp. 155–56.

63. IIFFV OR-LL for period ending 31 July 1970, p. 155; IIFFV G-3 Daily Log, 15 May, item 12.

64. IIFFV OR-LL for period ending 31 July 1970, p. 155.

65. IIFFV G-3 Daily Journal, 1 May 1970, item 38; 2 May 1970, item 49; IIFFV OR-LL for period ending 31 July 1970, p. 156.

66. LTG Davison, Debriefing Report, p. 8; Interview, Davison, 6 August 1992; IIFFV OR-LL for period ending 31 July 1970, p. 156.

67. IIFFV OR-LL for period ending 31 July 1970, p. 156.

68. Letter to author, COL John C. Witherell, 12 September 1992.

69. Bergen, *Military Communications,* 200.

70. Ibid., 201; IIFFV Signal Daily Journal, 4 May, item 7, 8 May, item 10; BG F. J. Roberts, Memorandum, 3 June 1970, RG472, NA.

71. IIFFV OR-LL for period ending 31 July 1970, p. 55; IIFFV Signal Office's Daily Journal, 2 May 0730, 16 May from 1300–1600, 24 May 1300, and 28 May at 1800, RG472, NA.

72. IIFFV OR-LL for period ending 31 July 1970, p. 161.

73. IIFFV Signal Daily Journal, 5 June 1970, time 1605.

74. IIFFV Signal Office, 30 April–2245 hours; 13 May–item 3.

75. IIFFV Signal Office Daily Journal, 24 April–item 6; 28 April–items 2 and 10; 4 May–items 4.

9. AFTERMATH

1. Nixon, *No More Vietnams,* 149.

2. Kosut, *Cambodia and the Vietnam War,* 155–63.

3. Mann, *Grand Delusion,* 659.

4. For an excellent assessment of the domestic political consequences of the incursion, see George Herring's *America's Longest War: The United States and Vietnam, 1950–1975,* 4th ed. (Boston: McGraw-Hill, 2002), 293–96.

5. Robert R. Thomes, *Apocalypse Then: American Intellectuals and the Vietnam War, 1954–1975* (New York: New York University Press, 1998), 219–20.

6. Kosut, *Cambodia and the Vietnam War,* 123.

7. Ibid., 129.

8. Ibid., 195–97.

9. See Fredrik Logevall's *Choosing War: The Lost Chance for Peace and the Escalation of War in Vietnam* (Berkeley: University of California Press, 1999) for a thoughtful analysis of the Johnson administration's debates in 1964–1965. Nixon inherited the consequences of Johnson's decisions, as well as many of the parameters within which Johnson and previous presidents had worked.

10. In his superb *Abandoning Vietnam,* Willbanks examines in detail both the 1972 campaign (122–98) and the 1975 campaign (199–288).

11. Kissinger, *Ending the Vietnam War,* 204.

12. In July 1970 Saigon renamed its four CTZs "Military Regions." To avoid confusion, this study has used "CTZ" throughout.

13. Unidentified soldier, quoted in "031820Z May 70 Mission," *Thunder!* 3, no. 1 (Fall–Winter 1970): 4–5, personal collection of MG Edward Bautz.

14. "A Perspective on Cambodia: An Interview with LTG Michael S. Davison," *The Hurricane,* no. 35 (September 1970), n.p.

15. Interview, Bautz, 18 March 1992.

16. An unidentified Twenty-fifth Infantry Division battalion commander, in Bautz's 25ID 1970 *Yearbook,* p. 81.

17. Joseph B. Anderson, Commander, B Company, 2-5 Cavalry, quoted in Keith Nolan, *Into Cambodia: Spring Campaign, Summer Offensive, 1970* (Novato, CA: Presidio Press, 1990), 441.

18. Kissinger, *Ending the Vietnam War,* 175.

19. MACV Combined Intelligence Center–Vietnam Report: Shadow Supply System, MR 3, 15 June 70, pp. 3–4, CMH Histories Division.

20. Davison, oral history, p. 9; "A Perspective on Cambodia," n.p. The troops asked Davison repeatedly during his visits why they had not attacked months or years earlier, and why the American public was so enraged at their actions to protect themselves and South Vietnam.

21. Davison, Debriefing Report, pp. 10–11.

22. Deac, *Road to the Killing Fields,* 83; he discusses further fighting by ARVN and FANK on pages 84–95. A VNN flotilla carried 50,000 refugees down the Mekong during the incursion; by late September 1970 about 200,000 remained in Cambodia, half the pre-coup total, p. 101.

23. Clarke, *Advice and Support,* 421.

24. Bunker telegram to Nixon, 19 June 1970, pp. 1, 4, Virtual Vietnam Archive.

25. Clarke, *Advice and Support,* 425. Clarke also noted that by the end of 1970, American advisers in the III CTZ and IV CTZ had begun to refocus on perennial ARVN shortcomings, suggesting the actions in the incursion had not been widely or permanently adopted, p. 423.

26. See Willbanks, *Abandoning Vietnam,* 87–89, for more on South Vietnamese military problems following the incursion.

27. IIFFV OR-LL for period ending 31 July 1970, p. 108. Davison also noted that "US advisors contributed significantly to increased effectiveness of ARVN tactical units." ARVN was critically dependent on the United States to integrate tanks, infantry, artillery, and airpower, as well as to maintain and repair its equipment.

28. Davison, oral history, p. 14. The RF/PF could handle internal threats but not enemy main force units. Davison, Debriefing Report, p. 10. "A Perspective on Cambodia," n.p.

29. Davison, oral history, pp. 14–15.

30. Ibid., p. 10; interview, 6 August 1992. Had the searches continued into July, "by the middle of the . . . month we would have been in a dry well situation." However, "never amongst the tons of documents we captured did we find a key to the overall NVA logistics layout." Davison, Debriefing Report, p. 6.

31. Davison, Debriefing Report, pp. 9–10; IIFFV OR-LL for period ending 31 July 1970, p. 104.

32. Davison, oral history, pp. 22–23.

33. This assessment is supported chiefly by declines in the levels of NVA and VC activity. While Tang, in *Vietcong Memoir,* 183, says the incursion "may" have set things back a year, Tho reports the JGS estimated it would take Hanoi six to nine months to reorganize its logistics system and begin to replace the lost supplies (*Cambodian Incursion,* 171–72).

34. "Additional Information on Results," p. 3. This total was by body count, not estimates. However, the Air Force CHECO report's Figure 1, plus the Twenty-fifth Infantry Division's AAR, yields 12,354 killed and 1,097 captured. In either case, the communist losses were clearly significant.

35. Davison, Debriefing Report, p. 7; "A Perspective on Cambodia," n.p.

36. "COSVN Directive on the Role and Responsibilities of the Lao Dong Party in Cambodia," dated 8 May 1970. From agent who had read notes of a VC cadre who had studied the directive, acquired at Bien Hoa, RVN, 18 May 1970, Field Number FVS-22,222, CMH Histories Division, Southeast Asia Cabinet 9, p. 6.

37. Interview, Davison, 6 August 1992.

38. Information as of 6 July 1970. "Additional Information on Results," pp. 1–2, 5; CHECO, figure 1.

39. Davison, oral history, p. 11.

40. "Additional Information on Results," p. 9.

41. Ibid.

42. Conroy, taped memoir.

43. "Additional Information on Results," p. 10.

44. Ibid.

45. MACV Assistant Chief of Staff, Intelligence, "VC/NVA Use of Laos and Cambodia after Cross Border Operations Terminate," 4 July 1970, p. 4, MHI Vietnam Collection.

46. Ibid., pp. 4–5.

47. As a Department of Defense analyst noted eighteen months later, "From the enemy point of view the most important front [in Cambodia] is the 'defensive' one north and east of Phnom Penh. Here, the emphasis has been on the reconstruction and expansion of the southern terminus of the logistic supply system from the north." Thayer, *Systems Analysis View of the Vietnam War,* 181.

48. "Additional Information on Results," pp. 6, 8.

49. "COSVN Directive," pp. 4, 6.

50. Ibid., p. 6.

51. "Additional Information on Results," pp. 5, 14.

52. *MACV,* pp. E-86, E-87.

53. "Additional Information on Results," pp. 16–17.

54. Ibid., pp. 17–18.

55. Ibid., pp. 16–21.

56. Bunker telegram to Nixon, 19 June 1970, p. 17, Virtual Vietnam Archive.

57. Clarke, *Advice and Support,* 420.

58. Ibid., 418.

59. Ibid., 478.

60. Ibid., 420. Whether the two commanders would have been so successful in the changed circumstances of Hanoi's 1972 or 1975 offensives is arguable.

61. Kissinger, *Ending the Vietnam War,* 364.

Bibliography

INTERVIEWS AND CORRESPONDENCE
(RANKS AND POSITIONS AS OF MAY 1970)

Adams, Dwight L. Colonel, Commander, Division Support Command, 4th Infantry Division.

Anderson, James. Lieutenant Colonel, Commander, 1-7 Cavalry Battalion, 1st Cavalry Division.

Bautz, Edward. Major General, Commanding General, 25th Infantry Divison.

Brady, Morris. Colonel, Commander, 1st Cavalry Division Artillery.

Brownlee, R. Les. Captain, adviser, U.S. adviser with the ARVN Airborne Division.

Burr, William E., II. Colonel, Chief, MACV J-3 Surface Operations Division.

Buzzett, Harry A. Colonel, Commander, 25th Infantry Divison Artillery.

Claybrook, John H. Lieutenant Colonel, Commander, 2-47 Infantry Battalion (Mechanized), 25th Infantry Division.

Conrad, Michael. Lieutenant Colonel, Commander, 2-8 Cavalry Battalion and G-2, 1st Cavalry Division.

Conroy, Raymond C. Major General, MACV J-4.

Davidson, Phillip. Brigadier General, MACV J-2, 1967–1969.

Davison, Michael S. Lieutenant General, Commanding General, IIFFV, and senior adviser, ARVN III Corps.

DeLeuil, Wood R. Lieutenant Colonel, Commander, 5-12 Infantry Battalion, 199th Light Infantry Brigade.

Feir, Philip R. Colonel, Commander, 1st Brigade, 4th Infantry Division.

Fitzgerald, Thomas E. Lieutenant Colonel, Commander, 2-19 Field Artillery, 1st Cavalry Division.

Fuller, Elisha. Colonel, deputy commanding officer, 20th Engineer Brigade.

Furey, Bartley W. Major, S-3, 2-19 Field Artillery, 1st Cavalry Division.

Galvin, John J. Lieutenant Colonel, G-2, 1st Cavalry Division, and commander, 1-8 Cavalry Battalion, 1st Cavalry Division.

Greene, Michael. Brigadier General, assistant division commander, 25th Infantry Division.

Hatmaker, Ray G. Captain, S-4, 1-26 Infantry, 1st Infantry Division, 1968–1969.

Hayward, Charles W. Colonel, G-3, IIFFV.

Hook, John R. Lieutenant Colonel, Deputy G-1, IIFFV, and Executive Officer, 3rd Brigade, 9th Infantry Division.

Kaufman, Daniel. First Lieutenant, executive officer, L Troop, 3rd Squadron, 11th Armored Cavalry Regiment.

Kendall, Maurice. Brigadier General, ADC, 4th Infantry Division.

Kingston, Robert. Colonel, Commander, 1st and 3rd Brigades, 1st Cavalry Division.

Kinnard, Douglas. Brigadier General, chief of staff, IIFFV.

Kovalsky, Michael. Lieutenant Colonel, Vietnam Division Plans Officer, MACV J-5.

Leech, Earl W. Major, plans officer, IIFFV G-3.

Lehan, James F., Jr. Lieutenant Colonel, Commander, 124th Signal Battalion, 4th Infantry Division.

Lenz, Robert J. Captain, Commander, B/2-8 Cavalry Battalion, 1st Cavalry Division.

Magness, Thomas H. III. Major, S-3, 2-32 Field Artillery, IIFFV Artillery.

McAuliffe, Dennis P. Brigadier General, deputy senior adviser, ARVN III Corps.

Osborne, Kenneth. Corporal, L/75th Infantry (Ranger), 101st Airborne Division.

Perkins, John III. Colonel, Field Force engineer, IIFFV.

Peters, Michael. First Lieutenant, executive officer, M Company, 3rd Squadron, 11th Armored Cavalry Regiment.

Pokorny, Anthony G. Major, S-3, 1st Cavalry Division Artillery.

Prillaman, Richard L. Lieutenant Colonel, G-3, 4th Infantry Division.

Putnam, George W., Jr. Major General, Commanding General, 1st Aviation Brigade.

Rienze, Thomas M. Major General, Commanding General, 1st Signal Brigade.

Selton, Robert W. Colonel, Commander, 199th Light Infantry Brigade.

Shoemaker, Robert M. Brigadier General, ADC, 1st Cavalry Division/commanding general, Task Force Shoemaker.

Smith, Scott B. Lieutenant Colonel, Commander, 8th Engineer Battalion, 1st Cavalry Division.

Starry, Donn. Colonel, Commander, 11th Armored Cavalry Regiment.

Stimola, Dominic. First Lieutenant, B/2-34 Armor, 25th Infantry Division.

Thurman, John R. Brigadier General, ADC, 25th Infantry Division.

Tuemler, James. Private First Class. B/2-34 Armor, 25th Infantry Division.

Walker, Glenn. Major General, Commanding General, 4th Infantry Division.

Warner, Volney. Colonel, G-5, IIFFV.

Whitehead, Ennis C. Colonel, Commander, 2nd Brigade, 25th Infantry Division.

Williams, Lewis A. Lieutenant Colonel, G-4, 4th Infantry Division.

Williams, Walworth F. Colonel, Commander, 3rd Brigade, 9th Infantry Division and 2nd Brigade, 25th Infantry Division.

Witherell, John C. Lieutenant Colonel, G-3 Plans, IIFFV.

ARCHIVAL SOURCES

National Archives and Records Administration, College Park, Maryland.

U.S. Army Center of Military History, Fort McNair, Washington, DC.

GEN Creighton Abrams Papers, CMH Histories Division.
U.S. Army Military History Institute, Carlisle Barracks, Pennsylvania.

MHI Archives

Arthur S. Collins Collection
Michael S. Davison Collection
Elvy B. Roberts Collection
Albert H. Smith Jr. Collection
Donn A. Starry Collection

MHI Classified Archives

Vietnam Collection

Other Archival Sources

Virtual Vietnam Archive, Vietnam Center, Texas Tech University, Lubbock, Texas (http://
archive.vietnam.ttu.edu)
Personal collection of MG Edward Bautz (USA, Ret.)
Personal collection of COL Bart Furey (USA, Ret.)

PUBLISHED WORKS

Ambrose, Stephen E. *Nixon.* Vol. 2, *The Triumph of a Politician, 1962–1972.* New York: Simon and Schuster, 1989.
Andradé, Dale. *Ashes to Ashes: The Phoenix Program and the Vietnam War.* New York: Lexington Books, 1990.
BDM Corporation. *A Study of Strategic Lessons Learned in Vietnam.* Vol. 1, *The Enemy.* BDM/W-78-128-TR. McLean, VA: BDM Corporation, 30 November 1979.
———. *A Study of Strategic Lessons Learned in Vietnam,* Vol. 9, *Omnibus Executive Summary.* BDM/W-78-128-TR. McLean, VA: BDM Corporation, 28 April 1980.
Bergen, John D. *Military Communications: A Test for Technology.* Washington, DC: Center of Military History, 1986.
Bergerud, Eric. *The Dynamics of Defeat.* Boulder, CO: Westview Press, 1991.
———. *Red Thunder, Tropic Lighting: The World of a Combat Division in Vietnam.* Boulder, CO: Westview Press, 1993.
Berman, Larry. *No Peace, No Honor: Nixon, Kissinger, and Betrayal in Vietnam.* New York: Free Press, 2001.
Bidwell, Shelford, ed. *Brassey's Artillery of the World.* New York: Bonanza Books, 1979.
Borer, Douglas A. *Superpowers Defeated: Vietnam and Afghanistan Compared.* London: Frank Cass, 1999.
Brower, Charles F., IV. "Strategic Reassessment in Vietnam: The Westmoreland 'Alternate Strategy' of 1967–1968." *Naval War College Review* 44, no. 2 (Spring 1991): 20–51.

Caldwell, Malcolm, and Lek Tan. *Cambodia in the Southeast Asian War.* New York: Monthly Review Press, 1973.

Carland, John M. "Winning the Vietnam War: Westmoreland's Approach in Two Documents." *Journal of Military History* 68 (April 2004): 553–74.

Clarke, Jeffrey J. *Advice and Support: The Final Years, 1965–1973.* Washington, DC: Center of Military History, 1988.

Cochran, Alexander S., Jr. "American Planning for Ground Combat in Vietnam, 1952–1965." *Parameters* 14, no. 2 (June 1986): 63–69.

Colby, William. *Lost Victory.* Chicago: Contemporary Books, 1989.

Coleman, J. D. *Incursion: From America's Chokehold on the NVA Lifelines to the Sacking of the Cambodian Sanctuaries.* New York: St. Martin's Press, 1991.

Collins, James Lawton, Jr. *The Development and Training of the South Vietnamese Army, 1950–1972.* Washington, DC: Center of Military History, 1991.

Conboy, Kenneth, and Dale Andradé. *Spies and Commandos: How America Lost the Secret War in North Vietnam.* Lawrence: University Press of Kansas, 2000.

Cook, John L. *The Advisor.* New York: Bantam Books, 1987.

Cosmas, Graham A., and Lieutenant Colonel Terrence P. Murray, USMC. *U.S. Marines in Vietnam: Vietnamization and Redeployment, 1970–1971.* Washington, DC: History and Museums Division, Headquarters, U.S. Marine Corps, 1986.

Currey, Cecil B. *Victory at Any Cost: The Genius of Viet Nam's Vo Nguyen Giap.* Washington, DC: Brassey's, 1997.

Cutler, Thomas J. *Brown Water, Black Berets: Coastal and Riverine Warfare in Vietnam.* Annapolis, MD: Naval Institute Press, 1988.

Davidson, Phillip B. *Secrets of the Vietnam War.* Novato, CA: Presidio Press, 1990.

———. *Vietnam at War.* Novato, CA: Presidio Press, 1988.

Deac, Wilfred P. *Road to the Killing Fields: The Cambodia War of 1970–1975.* College Station: Texas A&M University Press, 1997.

Diem, Bui, with David Chanoff. *In the Jaws of History.* Boston: Houghton Mifflin, 1987.

Duiker, William J. *The Communist Road to Power in Vietnam.* Boulder, CO: Westview Press, 1981.

Ellsberg, Daniel. *Secrets: A Memoir of Vietnam and the Pentagon Papers.* New York: Viking, 2002.

Giap, Vo Nguyen. *Once Again, We Will Win.* Hanoi: Foreign Languages Publishing House, 1966.

———. *People's War, People's Army.* Hanoi: Foreign Languages Publishing House, 1974.

Gilster, Herman L. *The Air War in Southeast Asia: Case Studies of Selected Campaigns.* Maxwell Air Force Base, AL: Air University Press, 1993.

Goscha, Chris. "The Maritime Ho Chi Minh Trail and the Wars for Vietnam, 1945–1975." Paper presented at the Fourth Triennial Vietnam Symposium, Vietnam Center, Texas Tech University, Lubbock, Texas, 11–13 April 2002, available on-line at http://www.vietnam.ttu.edu/vietnamcenter/events/2002_Symposium/2002Papers_files/goscha.htm.

Hackworth, David, with Julie Sherman. *About Face.* New York: Simon and Schuster, 1989.

Harrison, James Pinckney. *The Endless War: Fifty Years of Struggle in Vietnam.* New York: Free Press, 1982.

Herring, George. *America's Longest War: The United States and Vietnam, 1950–1975.* 4th ed. Burr Ridge, IL: McGraw-Hill, 2002.

——. *LBJ and Vietnam: A Different Kind of War.* Austin: University of Texas Press, 1994.

Hosmer, Stephen T., Konrad Kellen, and Brian M. Jenkins. *The Fall of South Vietnam: Statements by Vietnamese Military and Civilian Leaders.* Santa Monica, CA: RAND Corporation, 1978.

Huffman, David. Personal Web site at http://www.users.qwest.net/~huffpapa/vietnam .html. Accessed 21 January 2004.

Hunt, Richard A. *Pacification: The American Struggle for Vietnam's Hearts and Minds.* Boulder, CO: Westview Press, 1995.

Isaacs, Arnold R. *Without Honor: Defeat in Vietnam and Cambodia.* New York: Vintage Books, 1984.

Karnow, Stanley. *Vietnam: A History.* New York: Penguin Books, 1984.

Kimball, Jeffrey. *The Vietnam War Files: Uncovering the Secret History of Nixon-Era Strategy.* Lawrence: University Press of Kansas, 2004.

Kissinger, Henry. *Diplomacy.* New York: Simon and Schuster, 1994.

——. *Ending the Vietnam War: A History of America's Involvement in and Extrication from the Vietnam War.* New York: Simon and Schuster, 2003.

——. *White House Years.* Boston: Little, Brown, 1979.

Kosut, Hal, ed. *Cambodia and the Vietnam War.* New York: Facts on File, 1971.

Langgruth, A. J. *Our Vietnam: The War, 1954–1975.* New York: Simon and Schuster, 2000.

Le Gro, William E. *Vietnam from Cease-Fire to Capitulation.* Washington, DC: Center of Military History, 1985.

Lind, Michael. *Vietnam, the Necessary War: A Reinterpretation of America's Most Disastrous Military Conflict.* New York: Free Press, 1999.

Logevall, Fredrik. *Choosing War: The Lost Chance for Peace and the Escalation of War in Vietnam.* Berkeley: University of California Press, 1999.

Lomperis, Timothy J. *From People's War to People's Rule: Insurgency, Intervention, and the Lessons of Vietnam.* Chapel Hill: University of North Carolina Press, 1996.

——. "Giap's Dream, Westmoreland's Nightmare." *Parameters* 16, no. 2 (June 1988): 18–31.

MacDonald, Peter. *Giap: The Victor in Vietnam.* New York: Norton, 1993.

Malkasian, Carter. "Toward a Better Understanding of Attrition: The Korean and Vietnam Wars." *Journal of Military History* 68 (July 2004): 911–42.

Mann, Robert. *A Grand Delusion: America's Descent into Vietnam.* New York: Basic Books, 2001.

Matthews, Lloyd J., and Dale E. Brown. *Assessing the Vietnam War.* Washington, DC: Pergammon-Brassey's, 1987.

McCoy, James W. *Secrets of the Viet Cong.* New York: Hippocrene Books, 1992.

McNamara, Robert S., with Brian van deMark. *In Retrospect: The Tragedy and Lessons of Vietnam.* New York: Times Books, 1995.

Meyerson, Joel D. *Images of a Lengthy War: The U.S. Army in Vietnam.* Washington, DC: Center of Military History, 1986.

Military History Institute of Vietnam. *Victory in Vietnam: The Official History of the People's Army of Vietnam, 1954–1975.* Trans. Merle. L. Pribbenow. Lawrence: University Press of Kansas, 2002.

Morris, Stephen J. *Why Vietnam Invaded Cambodia: Political Culture and the Causes of War.* Stanford, CA: Stanford University Press, 1999.

Moss, George Donelson. *Vietnam: An American Ordeal.* Englewood Cliffs, NJ: Prentice Hall, 1990.

Newcomb, Richard F. *A Pictorial History of the Vietnam War.* Garden City, NY: Doubleday, 1987.

Nguyen, Van Tin. Web site. http://www.generalhieu.com.

——. "Why Did Vietnamization of the Vietnam War Fail?" Paper presented at the Vietnam Center's Fourth Triennial Vietnam Symposium, Lubbock, Texas, 11 April 2002. Available on-line at http://www.vietnam.ttu.edu/vietnamcenter/events/2002_Symposium /2002Papers_files/vietnamization.htm.

Nixon, Richard M. *RN: The Memoirs of Richard Nixon.* New York: Grosset and Dunlap, 1978.

——. *No More Vietnams.* New York: Arbor House, 1985.

Nolan, Keith. *Into Cambodia: Spring Campaign, Summer Offensive, 1970.* Novato, CA: Presidio Press, 1990.

Olson, James S. *The Vietnam War: Handbook of the Literature and Research.* Westport, CT: Greenwood Press, 1993.

Page, Tim. *Another Vietnam: Pictures of the War from the Other Side.* Ed. Doug Niven and Chris Riley. Washington DC: National Geographic Society, 2002.

Palmer, Bruce. *The Twenty-five Year War: America's Military Role in Vietnam.* Lexington: University Press of Kentucky, 1984.

Palmer, Dave Richard. *Summons of the Trumpet.* New York: Ballantine Books, 1978.

Pike, Douglas. "The Other Side." *Wilson Quarterly* 7 (Summer 1983): 114–24.

——. *PAVN: The People's Army of Vietnam.* Novato, CA: Presidio Press, 1986.

——. *Viet Cong: The Organization and Techniques of the National Liberation Front of South Vietnam.* Cambridge, MA: MIT Press, 1966.

Plaster, John L. *SOG: A Photo History of the Secret War.* Boulder, CO: Paladin Press, 2000.

——. *SOG: The Secret Wars of America's Commandos in Vietnam.* New York: Simon and Schuster, 1997.

Ploger, Robert R. *Vietnam Studies: U.S. Army Engineers, 1965–1970.* Washington, DC: Department of the Army, 1989.

Porter, Gareth. *Vietnam: The Definitive Documentation of Human Decisions.* Standfordville, NY: Earl M. Coleman Enterprises, 1979.

Prados, John. *The Blood Road: The Ho Chi Minh Trail and the Vietnam War.* New York: Wiley, 1999.

——. *The Hidden History of the Vietnam War.* Chicago: Ivan R. Dee, 1995.

Record, Jeffrey. *The Wrong War: Why We Lost in Vietnam.* Annapolis, MD: Naval Institute Press, 1998.

Reske, Charles F. *MAC-V-SOG Command History, Annex B: The Last Secret of the Vietnam War.* 2 vols. Sharon Center, OH: Alpha Publications, 1990.

Safire, William. *Before the Fall: An Inside View of the Pre-Watergate White House.* Garden City, NY: Doubleday, 1975.

Savage, Paul L., and Richard A. Gabriel. "Beyond Vietnam: Cohesion and Disintegration in the American Army." Washington, DC: International Studies Association, Sixteenth Annual Convention, date unknown. Copy in author's possession.

Scales, Robert H., Jr. *Firepower in Limited War.* Washington, DC: National Defense University Press, 1990.

Schlight, John. *Second Indochina War Symposium: Papers and Commentary.* Washington, DC: US Army Center of Military History, 1986.

Schultz, Richard H. *The Secret War against Hanoi: Kennedy's and Johnson's Use of Spies, Saboteurs, and Covert Warriors in North Vietnam.* New York: HarperCollins, 1999.

Shawcross, William. *Sideshow: Kissinger, Nixon, and the Destruction of Cambodia.* New York: Simon and Schuster, 1979.

Sheehan, Neil, with Hedrick Smith, E. W. Kenworthy, and Fox Butterfield for the New York Times. *The Pentagon Papers.* New York: Bantam Books, 1971.

Showalter, Dennis E., and John G. Albert, eds. *An American Dilemma: Vietnam, 1964–1973.* Chicago: Imprint Publications, 1993.

Snepp, Frank. *Decent Interval: An Insider's Account of Saigon's Indecent End.* New York: Random House, 1977.

Sorley, Lewis. *A Better War: The Unexamined Victories and Final Tragedy of America's Last Years in Vietnam.* San Diego: Harcourt, 1999.

——. *Honorable Warrior: General Harold K. Johnson and the Ethics of Command.* Lawrence: University Press of Kansas, 1998.

——. *Thunderbolt: General Creighton Abrams and the Army of His Times.* New York: Simon and Schuster, 1992.

Spector, Ronald. *After Tet: The Bloodiest Year in Vietnam.* New York: Free Press, 1993.

Starry, Donn. *Vietnam Studies: Mounted Combat in Vietnam.* Washington, DC: Department of the Army, 1989.

Stetler, Russell, ed. *The Military Art of People's War: Selected Writings of General Vo Nguyen Giap.* New York: Monthly Review Press, 1970.

Stevens, Richard L. *The Trail: A History of the Ho Chi Minh Trail and the Role of Nature in the War in Viet Nam.* New York: Garland, 1993.

Summers, Harry G., Jr. *Historical Atlas of the Vietnam War.* Boston: Houghton Mifflin, 1995.

——. *On Strategy: A Critical Analysis of the Vietnam War.* Novato, CA: Presidio Press, 1982.

Tang, Truong Nhu, with David Chanoff and Doan Van Toai. *A Vietcong Memoir.* San Diego: Harcourt Brace Jovanovich, 1985.

Thayer, Thomas C., ed. *A Systems Analysis View of the Vietnam War 1965–1972.* Vol. 1, *The Situation in Southeast Asia.* Washington, DC: Department of Defense, Office of the Assistant Secretary of Defense (Analysis and Evaluation), Asia Division, undated copy.

Thi, Lam Quang. *The Twenty-five-Year Century.* Denton: University of North Texas Press, 2001.

Tho, Tran Dinh. *The Cambodian Incursion.* Washington, DC: Army Center of Military History, 1979.

Thomes, Robert R. *Apocalypse Then: American Intellectuals and the Vietnam War, 1954–1975.* New York: New York University Press, 1998.

Tolson, John J. *Airmobility, 1961–1971.* Washington, DC: Department of the Army, 1989.

Tran, Van Tra. *Vietnam: History of the Bulwark B2 Theatre.* Vol. 5, *Concluding the 30-Years War.* Ho Chi Minh City: Van Nghe Publishing House, 1982. In Joint Publications Research Service microfiche, no. 82783. Available on-line at http://www-cgsc.army .mil/carl/resources/csi/content.asp#viet.

Turley, William S. *The Second Indochina War: A Short Political and Military History.* Boulder, CO: Westview Press, 1986.

Vietnam: A Television History. Episode 9, "Cambodia and Laos." Episode producers, Bruce Palmer and Martin Smith. Series producers, WGBH Boston, Central Independent Television/UK, and Antenne-2/France. 1985. BG Douglas Kinnard commenting on B-52 crater photos, Lon Nol, Sihanouk, and Henry Kissinger.

Vietnam Helicopter Pilots Association. *Vietnam Helicopter History (on CD).* Citrus Heights, CA: VPHA, 2000.

Walton, C. Dale. *The Myth of Inevitable U.S. Defeat in Vietnam.* London: Frank Cass, 2001.

Warner, Denis. *Certain Victory: How Hanoi Won the War.* Kansas City: Sheed Andrews and McMeel, 1978.

Webb, Willard J. *The Joint Chiefs of Staff and the War in Vietnam, 1969–1970.* Washington, DC: Office of Joint History, Office of the Chairman of the Joint Chiefs of Staff, 2002.

Whittaker, Donald P., et al. *Area Handbook of the Khmer Republic (Cambodia): DA Pamphlet 550-50.* Washington, DC: U.S. Government Printing Office, 1973.

Wiarda, Jonathan S. "The U.S. Coast Guard in Vietnam: Achieving Success in a Difficult War." *Naval War College Review* 51, no. 2 (Spring 1998): 30–45. Available on-line at http://www.nwc.navy.mil/press/review/1998/spring/art3-sp8.htm.

Willbanks, James H. *Abandoning Vietnam: How America Left and South Vietnam Lost Its War.* Lawrence: University Press of Kansas, 2004.

Index

USARV. *See* U.S. Army Vietnam
Utley, Garrick, 126

Vam Co Dong River, 52
Viet Cong (VC), 1, 2, 171n1
  assessing, 20, 179n8
  blocking, 51
  Cambodian incursion and, 132–33, 137
  casualties for, 64, 102
  dau tranh and, 5
  desertions to, 21
  logistics and, 17
  Main Force, 35, 170
  morale of, 20
  NLF and, 5
  pacification and, 15
  propaganda of, 4
  search-and-destroy operations and, 17
  supplies for, 10, 11, 159
  threat from, 11
Vietnamese Airborne Brigade, 95
Vietnamese Armored Cavalry, 95
Vietnamese Communist Party, 27
Vietnamese Navy (VNN), 145, 146
Vietnamization, 16, 39, 41, 49, 51, 105, 133, 154, 164
  Cambodian incursion and, 30, 157
  process of, 104, 159
  progress for, 22, 40, 50, 52
  prospects for, 45
  undermining, 14
VNAF. *See* South Vietnamese Air Force
VNN. *See* Vietnamese Navy

Walker, Glenn, 147
War-fighting doctrine, 3–4

Warner, Volney: on Pendleton, 182n70
War Zone C, 43, 45, 77, 108, 116, 127
  caches in, 78
War Zone D, 45
Westmoreland, William C., 35, 169, 194n27
  assessment by, 1
  attrition and, 2, 11, 36
  Cambodian incursion and, 166
  dau tranh and, 4–5
  logistics and, 7, 135
  search-and-destroy operations and, 17
  strategic defensive and, 8
  war-fighting doctrine and, 3–4
Wheeler, Earle, 33, 35, 52, 93
  Cambodian incursion and, 30, 31, 32
  intelligence and, 37
  MENU and, 32
Whitehead, Ennis, 108, 116, 121, 124, 191n62
  Base Area 707 and, 112, 117, 118
  COSVN and, 119, 120
  on Thien Ngon, 117
Williams, Lewis, 95, 97
Williams, Walworth F., 115–16, 124, 125
Withdrawal, 14, 15 (fig.), 41, 42, 59, 60, 124, 155, 164, 165, 166
  Cambodian incursion and, 104, 153, 156, 157, 161
  codebook for, 124
  pacification and, 153

Yew, Harold, 147